THE CRACK CITY STRANGLER

THE HOMICIDES OF SERIAL KILLER BENJAMIN ATKINS

MURDERS IN THE MOTOR CITY, BOOK TWO

B.R. BATES

WildBluePress.com

THE CRACK CITY STRANGLER published by:
WILDBLUE PRESS
P.O. Box 102440
Denver, Colorado 80250

Publisher Disclaimer: Any opinions, statements of fact or fiction, descriptions, dialogue, and citations found in this book were provided by the author, and are solely those of the author. The publisher makes no claim as to their veracity or accuracy, and assumes no liability for the content.

Copyright 2025 by BRBglobal, LLC

All rights reserved. No part of this book may be reproduced in any form or by any means without the prior written consent of the Publisher, excepting brief quotes used in reviews.

WILDBLUE PRESS is registered at the U.S. Patent and Trademark Offices.

ISBN 978-1-964730-22-6 Hardcover
ISBN 978-1-964730-23-3 Trade Paperback
ISBN 978-1-964730-21-9 eBook

Cover design © 2025 WildBlue Press. All rights reserved.
Interior Formatting and Book Cover Design by Elijah Toten
www.totencreative.com

THE CRACK CITY STRANGLER

Dedicated to the memory of the women who lost their lives, as well as to the memory of three officers who were kind enough to do interviews for this book but passed away during the book's production: Ron Sanders, who questioned Atkins after his arrest; Jim Dobson, the officer in charge of the case at Highland Park Public Safety; and Larry Beller, who assisted Jim at HPPS.

A portion of the profits from sales of this book support Covenant House Michigan, an organization providing homeless, runaway and at-risk youth, as well as youth who have aged out of foster care, with shelter, educational and vocational programs and seeks to remove and overcome barriers such as homelessness, unemployment, inadequate education, violence, drugs, human trafficking and gang activity that prevent young people from successfully transitioning into adulthood. Visit CovenantHouseMI.org to learn more about this organization.

CONTENTS

Prologue	11
Darlene Saunders	14
Patricia Cannon George	25
Valerie Brown Chalk	33
Vickie Ann Truelove	40
Debbie Ann Friday	45
Bertha Jean Mason	49
Juanita Hardy	54
Unknown Female No. 15	58
Vicki Marie Beasley Brown	63
Joanne O'Rourke	69
Brenda Mitchell	72
Ocinena (CC) Waymer	76
Telling Her Story at Last: Margie Osborn	79
The Hunt for a Killer	86
The First Broad Brushstrokes	90
Murder at the Monterey	106
Fast and Elusive	129
Arrest	165
'Let's Cut to the Chase'	171
Confessions	187
Timeline	189

The Path to Court	190
Legal Counsel Suits Up	198
Is This Suspect Crazy?	209
Trial	229
He Meets His End	250
Examining His Beginnings	253
Abandoned Buildings as Killing Field	272
The Case of the Missing Files	276
So Why Did He Do It?	281
Possible Triggers	283
The Mother Factor	285
The HIV/AIDS Factor	288
The Mental Health Question	293
The Rosen Report	312
The Fields Report	313
The Clark Report	315
The Abramsky Report	316
Tony	318
Killer Comparisons	326
The Racial Aspect	340
Acknowledgments	345
Selected Bibliography	348

"There was both death and undeserved disgrace. Vicki never would have gone willingly with that man."

Gloria Beasley

PROLOGUE

From the office of
Michael F. Abramsky, Ph.D., A.B.P.P.
Licensed Psychologist
Diplomate, American Board of Professional Psychology
Woodward Avenue, Birmingham, Michigan
December 27, 1993

... The bond between mother and child is the psychological foundation of personality. Much has been written of what happens when such an early primary bond is broken. Chronic depressions, hostility and gross indifference to the world often stem from a premature loss of the mother. Benjamin Atkins' mother was unavailable to him because of her own problems and then later he was taken from her. This early loss and the absence of both a mother and father at a tender age left scars and thwarted the development of Benjamin Atkins.

Prominently, there are aggressive feelings toward women. Women are seen as unreliable, objects of scorn and there are sadistic and aggressive feelings toward them. Furthermore, there are feelings of pathological envy toward other individuals who have families or could have families or have what Benjamin sees as necessary for himself.

Benjamin's aggressive feelings were nurtured by being in foster care homes where he felt second place, exposure to indifferent parenting and abuse at the home in which he was placed. Even after returning home, he was the object of ridicule of his stepfather, was often teased in school about his abandonment and felt as an outcast. Over the years and through repeated insults, strong aggressive tendencies developed. Most of the aggressive tendencies were focused on women, although there is a history of very early fighting and his brother describes Benjamin losing control when fighting and being in an almost dazed state that only his brother or mother could bring him out of. At times of aggression, he seems to have been totally engulfed by the feelings and out of control. ...

... Generally, research has found that a father figure is the main generator of conscience development. Benjamin lacked this and as a result, his conscience development remains highly immature. Essentially, Ben's conscience only developed to a point where "things are bad if you get caught." Benjamin lacks a highly internalized sense of conscience and is generally expedient in respect to moral rules. As his brother told me, "you do what you have to when you live on the streets," and thus, Benjamin's sense of right and wrong has been greatly flawed through the same developmental loss he experienced and through subsequent reinforcement by institutions where youngsters do whatever they can to survive and a street life characterized by expediency and a lack of morals. ...

... Benjamin also hears voices. In carefully examining Benjamin, the voices do not seem to be the product of a schizophrenic thought process. Others who have examined him believe this is just faking psychoses. I disagree. The voices seem to be diverse parts of his personality. ...

... Benjamin also told me that when the bodies were first discovered, he would hear about it on the radio or television and not even put it together that it was him that did the killings. It seemed unreal. ...

... When I discussed his confessions with him, he stated over a number of hours he struggled and denied and that finally they simply flowed out of him. He never denied to me that he made the confessions, but continued to remain bewildered that he had actually said these things; again, not quite grasping that the individual who talked about these deeds was really him. ...

... Benjamin is like a puzzle that does not fit ...

DARLENE SAUNDERS

She knew him as Tony. She would see him around, here and there.

They went to some of the same places to score drugs. Bumped into each other. Got high together quite a few times. And actually, she had met Tony about four years earlier, through a friend of hers named Janice, who was supposedly his sister. He, however, would later tell police that he knew Darlene only a few months, but he admitted he was confused about timeframes.

She was also a little confused about timeframes, at least as to exactly when the incident happened. The day she was almost killed. She told police in March that it had happened a couple months earlier, which would have been January. She was high when she talked to police, though. Later when her head was clearer, she said it was September or October. The more she thought about it, the more she was convinced it was October. If that fall timeframe was accurate, it would seem she was the first person he assaulted. At least on paper, in what is known in the case files. And that timeframe might make more sense because this killer didn't really know what he was doing yet. Had not yet found his rhythm. Soon he would get quicker and more efficient. And he wouldn't leave them alive.

Darlene Saunders was born in March 1956 and grew up on the east side of Detroit. She had lots of siblings. Her father was from Canada, Darlene's son Rashad explained when contacted in fall 2022 for this book, and he was still meeting aunties and uncles he hadn't known about. Just lots of family. And within Darlene's immediate family, she had the role of a matriarch, with her older siblings as well as the younger ones.

Darlene Saunders. Photo courtesy of Rashad Green.

At the time of this case, Darlene had already had all three of her kids – all of them boys. She and Rashad's father at one time owned a hardware store in Highland Park. They had a business that did plumbing and heating. They had a thirty-person work crew at one time. Darlene was incredibly smart, Rashad said. Could figure anything out. Just give it to her and she could figure it out. She did engineering work with Rashad's dad. She was a notary public who did a lot of clerical work around town. She assisted the schools with chaperoning trips and events. She was well-known. And she was a good person, her son said.

Darlene's story is similar to that of so many other females who have been drawn to the streets. It has glimpses of normalcy. Regular jobs. A regular home. Family. Interests. Aspirations. But always a pull away from that normalcy to something darker. A pull, in this case, to Woodward Avenue.

***

It followed in the footsteps of the Saginaw Trail, a path followed by the Native American tribes, connecting what would become Detroit with the areas of Pontiac, Flint and Saginaw to the north. In 1807, Augustus Brevoort Woodward, the first chief justice of the Michigan territory, platted this street along with several others in the area, working to reconstruct the emerging city of Detroit after a devastating fire in 1805. He had in mind a radial design as had been done in Washington, DC, and Paris. With this approach, wide avenues, alternatively two hundred feet and one hundred twenty feet, radiated from a large circular plaza like spokes from the hub of a wheel. Grand River Avenue jutted out toward the northwest from the heart of the city, and below it Michigan Avenue also headed west, out toward Chicago. On the other side Gratiot Avenue jutted out to the northeast. You had Jefferson Avenue heading east, toward what became known as the Pointes (the Grosse Pointes, actually). And then you had Woodward Avenue cutting right up through the center.

Some of Justice Woodward's radial plan was implemented, except for a few of the spokes on the wheel, and you can see his vision for it if you look at a map of the city's heart, with the Campus Martius and Grand Circus areas as focal points. Certainly, there sits Woodward Ave, numbered at one time as M-10, and part of U.S. Highway 10, then later known as M-1, strongly heading north and ultimately and maybe even inadvertently halving the city into an east side and west side.

Woodward Avenue was originally called Court House Avenue and other names. Justice Woodward, somewhat in jest, claimed the road's name was related to the fact that it traveled toward the wooded area to the north of the city, according to a history of the street by Vivian Baulch, longtime librarian at *The Detroit News*.

These days, Woodward Avenue is known for various things, like having the first mile of concrete paved road in the country. It is a robust mix of all kinds of stuff, from an array of elaborate historic stone churches to the more modern gas stations, fast-food joints and dollar stores. It is home to the Spirit of Detroit statue, the Joe Louis "Fist" statue, the historic Fox Theatre as well as the much-more-modern Little Caesars Arena, the Detroit Institute of Arts, the main branch of the Detroit Public Library, and the onetime site of the flagship Hudson's department store. It includes the elegant restaurant The Whitney, the former luxurious mansion of lumber baron David Whitney Jr. It is the route of America's Thanksgiving Day Parade. Further north, near the city's edge, you'll find the old state fairgrounds and the well-known Woodlawn Cemetery, where Aretha Franklin and Edsel Ford are buried. This avenue is also home to the popular Woodward Dream Cruise, a long-running, well-packed display of cars both classic and modern, though that's *another* stretch of Woodward – past the sometimes-notorious Eight Mile Road, up in the suburbs of Oakland County. At one point in the long history of *The Detroit News* spanning back to 1873, staff was said to have measured the worth of a story by, "How close is it to Woodward Avenue?"

As in any other big city, the world's oldest profession has thrived in Detroit. The Motor City's thoroughfares have provided lush breeding grounds equipped with the customary bars, strip joints, crack houses. There's the aforementioned Michigan Ave, particularly a stretch that's a few blocks out of downtown proper. There's the Cass Corridor, right downtown on Cass Ave heading through Wayne State

University's campus. Then there's Woodward Ave. Each of these pockets of prostitution has its own flavor, any beat cop will tell you. Its own atmospherics. Attitude. And many of the folks interviewed for this book, people who have traveled Woodward on both sides of the law, had a lot to say about the historic street, which is central to not only the City of Detroit but also the smaller city it completely surrounds, Highland Park.

And so it was, on that fall day, that Darlene Saunders found herself walking along Woodward Ave near the library, around Cortland and Richton streets. This part of Highland Park was all-too familiar to her. She often bought crack in the lobby of her apartment building, but she sometimes went other places for it, too. She had just come from a crack house a couple blocks north on Colorado Street this early morning, and besides that type of business, she occasionally made a sexual transaction around here, too.

It was around four-thirty a.m., give or take. Dark and still. And this was a different world back then, understand – there were no video cameras on the corners of buildings or over storefronts recording her every move like nowadays. Somebody could slip in and out of dark crevices so easily on this stretch. Unnoticed. Inconsequential. Blending into the background of this urban picture. So, like probably a bunch of times before, she dropped by the Cavalier Motel, just south of Colorado and in the block north of the library, looking for a friend of hers, Cynthia, only staying a minute. Then she stopped near the Michigan Bell telephone office across the street from the Cavalier a minute to rest.

Then she saw Tony. He saw her.

They approached each other and hugged. They even kissed, as she recalled later. Tony was not someone she ever actually dated, but they had that kind of familiarity.

Hey, how are you doing, and all that. Where's Janice, she asked him. He said he didn't know.

"Do you have a flute?" he asked her. A pipe.

"Yes," she replied.
"Can I use it?"
"Yes. I could use a hit." She had already had a little but wanted some more.

She and Tony walked over to the closed-down Howard Johnson's restaurant nearby, which sat in front of the also-abandoned Monterey Motel, a once-sought-after source of lodging now decades past its heyday. Both structures stood at the corner of Woodward and California Street and have since been torn down. The former would be consequential only to the incident with Darlene; the latter would become far more important.

Darlene and Tony took a seat at the flower bed – sometimes referred to as a flower pot in case files – on the side of the restaurant. No one else was around this early in the morning.

Darlene lit a cigarette and was about to get her pipe out of her pocket. Tony said there was too much wind out here. Let's go to the back of the building, he suggested. I know there's a table inside. So they went around the building where the door was missing; he stepped in first, she followed. Tony asked her for the pipe, and she unzipped the pocket of her jacket. Then he said he couldn't see, and he stepped behind her.

Then, to her shock, he grabbed her jacket, pulled it down around her arms and cuffed them both together. Holding onto her arms with one hand, he grabbed around her neck with the other, and then he began to rip her clothing off. She was wearing a T-shirt, sweater and jeans with the jacket. Just five-foot-three, she could not break free from him. She had more than a decade on him – he was in his early twenties and strong. She started to scream.

"What are you doing?! If you want sex, I'll give it to you, rather than hurt me like this."

"This is the way I like it," he replied.

He made her take off all of her clothes, then he forced her down on the floor, which in this mostly empty restaurant was strewn with glass and debris. The marks on her back from the glass would linger for months. As she lay flat on her back, he raped her. He then made her stand up and bend over, and he raped her again. Can I put my shoes on, she asked. No, he said.

She didn't know what else he was going to do. She didn't know why this was happening. She was crying and trying to talk to him. He wasn't listening.

He gripped her right hand with both of his hands, then he headed toward the basement stairs of this building, dragging her along. At this point she felt he was planning to kill her. Why else would he be taking her down there? She managed to push him, so he lost his footing. He went at least part of the way down the stairs, and she ran out of the building toward the parking lot.

Out into the open air again, still so eerie and dark, she was able to run ten feet at the most. He came out after her and tackled her, she later told police. From his own perspective, he told police that he grabbed her by the arm, swung her around, and they both fell to the ground.

"Rape! Help! Police!" she screamed. Tony put his hand over her mouth. Ordered her to be quiet. She bit his hand and held onto it so he couldn't do anything else with it. He tried to drag her back into the building.

That's when another voice rang out in the night air. "Where are you at????"

"In the parking lot," she yelled back. She then heard someone running toward them.

Tony took off. He later told police he panicked and ran to the Monterey, climbed through a window, headed to the other side of the motel, then found a room and went to sleep. Tony, after all, was part of the landscape of these impoverished streets – he blended in. He knew this town, knew all its nooks and crannies. So he easily disappeared right back into that landscape.

Darlene, meanwhile, had jumped up and ran toward this other person. It was someone she knew from the area. Mario. She had seen him earlier that morning, actually, as he walked by her on his way to the bus stop. Then, he went to the gas station on Glendale to get change for the bus. Now he was back, on his way to work.

He asked her what happened to her, why was she naked. She said the man had forced her to take her clothes off. She told him she was raped.

She asked him to come into the building with her so she could get her clothes. He couldn't stay long, though – his bus was due at Cortland Street just before five a.m. So he waited outside while she got her things, then Darlene headed home. Her back was all cut up. Her foot was also cut. Her shirt and jacket were torn. The zipper on her pants was damaged. She threw all of that clothing away not long after she got home.

She didn't report the attack to police at that point. She knew this guy, and she felt stupid for getting caught in this position. She was someone who normally carried razor blades around with her. Always on guard. She knew what kind of nasty stuff was out there on the streets. "I just felt like a big dummy," she later testified. "Being out in the crack cocaine world, you have to be ready for the unexpected."

That was not the last time she saw Tony, though. A few months later, after she changed her mind and did try to tell police about this incident, and they wouldn't take her seriously, she ran into him at a crack house on Burlingame. She went there to make a purchase, and Tony held the door for her as she came in.

"Tony, why did you do that to me?"

"I don't want to talk about it."

She got her crack and left. She figured she couldn't tell the police she had just seen him again; she couldn't bring the cops to that place – that would be her life. But she did tell a guy named Red at the crack house that Tony had raped her. She also told Janice what Tony did. Showed her the marks on her back.

At a later point she returned to that crack house and saw him again. This time as she left, she decided to call the police to tell them about him, that he was there. Maybe they could just grab him as he came out. But the police never came. It would take a phone call from her brother-in-law a couple months after Darlene's March police report, in May 1992, along with the help of a kind-hearted Highland Park cop named Donna who knew Darlene, to get law enforcement to take her seriously.

Darlene's son Rashad distinctly recalled the morning his mom came home crying, the fall of 1991, when he was barely a teen. It was raining that day. He and his two brothers knew something was wrong. They could tell that pretty easily by her demeanor.

"I remember my momma came home crying in the rain, but she wouldn't tell us what happened," he said. "I mean, you know, we were like her superheroes. When there were problems, we dealt with them, so you know, she didn't want us to get involved in that. I'm her baby boy, actually. I'm her youngest child.

"She always wanted to be about her baby. When something was wrong, my mother came looking for me. 'I want my baby.' That was her thing. I just came back, said, 'What's wrong? What's wrong?' She told me she was fine; she just wanted her baby. I sat right there with her 'til she went to sleep."

A long time passed before Rashad could comprehend what happened. Even sitting through a trial, a couple years later, when he was fifteen, he still didn't really understand.

"I was a kid," he said. "I mean, my main thing was I wanted to beat the guy up. I mean, I obviously didn't understand how serious it was. I was a big kid. Another funny thing about it, my momma called me Baby Huey. I was the biggest child she had."

Rashad attended every day of that trial. "I saw everything, because my momma said, 'If my baby can't go, I don't go.' I saw everything."

But then, he said, "as I got older, you know, and when we hear certain things, 'I'm the one that did that.' 'Oh! So them people? Oh!' As I'm getting older it's coming to me. But I saw everything, heard everything. You know, it was just a lot. All the way down to the news asking questions about growing up with my mother, when she was in the streets."

Rashad has dealt with a range of emotions about his mother, who died of a stroke in his arms in 2002, having an aneurysm that burst. She died in the morning, and that evening, as ironic as it was, Rashad's son was born.

"I held a grudge against my mother over what she was addicted to," Rashad said, "over what she was going through. And I never really overlooked the grudge, and it was too late to take it back."

And though he loves the city he grew up in, Highland Park, he still carries his mother's own resentment over the fact that by most accounts she should have been entitled to the reward money offered for the perp's arrest. "My mom died worrying about that," he said. Many folks would agree that Darlene was the one who was responsible for the arrest, but more on that later.

"I mean, I love my city," he said, "but they just need to do right."

These days, oddly enough, Rashad sees Mario in Highland Park all the time. He knows him as Will. He gets him something to eat when he sees him. Mario might appear to be homeless, but he does have a place to go, and he does odd jobs around town. And he's quick to remind Rashad how he helped his mother out, that one early morning on Woodward Ave.

Is it a little crazy, that they see each other all the time, more than three decades later?

"That's Highland Park for you," Rashad said.

Rashad plans to tell his grown kids more about their grandmother. That she was a part of Highland Park's history. That she was important.

PATRICIA CANNON GEORGE

The last time most—if not all—of Patricia Cannon's family saw her was around Thanksgiving. That's what her older sister Celestine later told the police, and that's what her younger brother Derrick recalled.

The family was gathering on Thanksgiving, November 28, 1991. And because there were eight siblings in Patricia's family, it was quite a big bunch of them at the house of the oldest sister, Urmerdean, about thirty to forty family members, Derrick guessed, on a call in May 2022 for this book. Patricia – they called her Pat – was invited but didn't show up that day, Celestine recalled in her statement with police. Derrick remembered her as being there then – either that, or at another big family dinner shortly before. At any rate, right around that Thanksgiving she went missing, and she would not be found until the start of the new year, at the site of a demolished house in Detroit, and she would not be identified until months after that. A long time for her family members to wonder what happened to her.

Like so many women who fall into prostitution, Pat grew up in a stable family. A mom and a dad at home who remained married through thick and thin as they raised their children. Leroy and Nezzie Cannon provided everything their kids needed, Derrick said. Leroy had a good job as a supervisor at General Motors. He worked hard. They lived in the Delray neighborhood in southwest Detroit. Pat was the fifth to be born, in May 1955, out of the eight siblings. For Derrick, this was an older sis he spent a lot of time with.

Leroy and Nezzie knew that school was important for their kids. "Go to school and do something with your life; that's all they wanted us to do," Derrick said. "My father said, 'I couldn't go to school back in the South a long time ago, so y'all just go to school and get out of here.' So we all went. I got degrees. Three of my sisters got degrees, and my brother."

School was so important to the family, that even after Nezzie passed, Derrick's two older sisters Urmerdean and Celestine took it upon themselves to make sure he stayed at Southwestern High when he ran into a bit of trouble.

"They said, you're going to go to school, no matter what. You're going to go to school. And to this day, I love them. I love them to death."

Pat attended Cary and McMillan elementary schools, then Southwestern High, but she dropped out in the eleventh grade. She met and married a man named Oscar George, and together they had three children, two boys and a girl. But at some point, she and Oscar separated, and that's when trouble started for Pat, Derrick said. That's when she became involved with drugs. Like so many other women who end up on the street.

It bothers him to this day, the fact that Pat got into drugs, since she was so smart. "Ask her anything, about money, about stocks, anything, and she would tell you anything. She was very smart. Even though she got on drugs, she used to research all kinds of stuff. And she used to tell me, 'Little brother, if you don't know, research it.' That's what she used to tell me. And I did. I miss her, too. I was raised by all women, pretty much. They used to keep their foot in my butt, too." They kept him in line, kept him off drugs, kept him in school. "She used to kick my butt anytime I did something wrong," he said of Pat.

Derrick attended Northwood University, spent some time in the Army Reserve then joined the Detroit Police, where he worked for twenty-seven years. He was with DPD at the time of this case, actually, but did not work it. "Homicide said, 'Stay out of it, Derrick,'" he recalled. He was in the narcotics division for a while, and he worked undercover. He served seventeen years as a supervisor and had the opportunity to work all kinds of other cases, though, cases that took him around the state and cases that we've seen on the news. When he retired from DPD, he worked in executive protection at Ford Motor Company's headquarters in Dearborn. He worked in the auto industry just as his dad had, the industry that has always driven the Motor City. When interviewed for this book, Derrick was recovering from a stroke, but anxious to get back to some kind of job. The influence his older sister Pat had on his young life was more than evident.

"I remember she used to take me everywhere." She was close to her little brother, but: "She was close with everybody. She used to go places. My mother would say, 'If you don't take your little brother, you can't go.' And she used to take me everywhere. I miss her. ... And then one place she took me, I didn't like. That's when the drugs started getting involved. I think I was about eight years old, but I knew it wasn't right. If my father would have found out about it, he would have gone crazy."

It's that one aspect of Pat's life that still befuddles him to this day. Still just doesn't make sense. "She was a good person, just got caught up in the circumstances. I think if she would have gone to school like she was supposed to, and listened to my mother and father, she would have been all right."

The siblings in the Cannon family have done well in their lives. Urmerdean, for instance, who was the oldest, built a brand-new house and owned her own business in the 1970s, so unheard-of for a female at the time, especially one of color, and she had connections with the mayor. Two other siblings owned successful businesses. Brother Roy, who passed in August 2022, was a well-respected pastor. Derrick always viewed their sister Geraldine as the other smartest one in the family. She graduated high school early, in fact, when she was fifteen or sixteen. "And Pat was the same way – smart as hell. She was the smartest in the family, got on drugs. I couldn't understand that," he said.

"Even though she was a drug addict, I loved the hell out of her."

***

Sometime around the family's Thanksgiving dinner, Pat was walking on a side street of Woodward Avenue in Detroit. It was the first block north of Clairmount Avenue, the east side of the street, her killer would later tell police. Right across the street from the market. Clairmount is on the west side of Woodward, and after it meets Woodward, it becomes (roughly) Owen Street on the other side. A block north of that would have been Leicester Street.

He estimated it was about eleven p.m. He didn't remember what day it was, being pretty bad with times and days.

"I was looking for a place to sleep," Benjamin Atkins said. "As I walked past this abandoned house, this woman walked up and asked me what's up."

"I'm looking for someone," he remembered telling her.

"You found me," she replied.

He remembered her as dark-skinned and about five-foot-four and a hundred and five pounds, wearing a gray jacket, possibly a turtleneck, and jeans. He figured she was around forty years old. He had two dime rocks of cocaine, and he asked her if she had something to smoke crack in. They walked around the side of the abandoned house.

"I told her I wanted to fuck, and she could smoke the cocaine rocks with me," Atkins told police. "We walked to the back of the house. It had a covered porch built into the house in the back."

They walked up onto the porch. "I asked her if she wanted to smoke first or fuck first. She said she wanted to smoke. OK. We smoked both the dime rocks up, and she tried to leave without having sex."

Atkins stopped her. "Wait a minute. I'll go buy some more," he said.

Together they went to Lawrence and Woodward, to a building on the corner that folks on the street called the old bank building. Through a door on the building, he bought a half a track of raw cocaine, about eighty dollars' worth. Then they went back to the house.

"I told her she didn't have to have sex with me, just smoke with me," Atkins recalled.

"What's the matter, I'm not a good bitch?" Atkins remembered Pat saying. "I'm too old?" She was thirty-six at the time, a tad younger than his estimate.

"I just want to smoke now," Atkins replied.

So they started smoking. "It's called chasing the dragon," Atkins explained to police. "It's a speedball, raw cocaine and rocks rocked together."

Then, he said, "she started flirting with me and taking off her clothes. She started saying, 'I'm a good bitch. I'm a good bitch.' She was smoking. I started playing with her while she was naked. I was squeezing on her tits and playing with her ass. I guess when she had smoked enough, she started to get dressed, and I told her to wait a minute 'cause she had smoked up a hundred dollars' worth of my shit. She was going to give up to me some sex. She protested by saying, 'I got to go. I got to go and check on my kids.'"

Pat started to walk out, and Atkins grabbed her arm.

"You is a good bitch, you is a good bitch," he mocked her.

He began choking her with his thumbs over the front of her throat. "I always knew that if you stop the oxygen to the brain and cut off their circulation a person will pass out," he explained to police.

After Pat passed out, Atkins took her into the house. He dragged her to the first bedroom past the kitchen. But she started to wake up. He started choking her again. She passed out again and stopped breathing. At this point she was lying face down on the floor. Atkins pulled her pants off and raped her both anally and vaginally.

"You're a good bitch," he remembered telling her lifeless body. He ejaculated. Pat's body expelled both urine and feces. Then he left. "I left her right there uncovered and everything," he said. "I didn't take anything off her but her pants. I took those down and left them there. She was naked from the waist down." He said he did not use a condom with her.

He remembered this incident as happening in fall 1991, and when he explained it to police, he said this was his first kill. The jury's still out on that one, but at the time police questioned him as if it was his first.

"I was scared because I had never killed anyone before," he said. "True enough I choked her, but I didn't know she had died until she didn't move. I shook her, but she didn't move. It scared the shit out of me. I wasn't going to tell nobody. I put her under the stairs behind this door, a closet, and left. After I closed this closet door, I left after that."

***

The demolition crew missed her when they made a sweep of the house a couple weeks later.

Then, on January 3, 1992, J&J Wrecking Co. returned to the site at 74 Kenilworth, the next street north of Leicester, in the block east of the Detroit stretch of Woodward, south of Highland Park. They began clearing rubble from this abandoned house that had been leveled the weekend before Christmas. It was typical stuff, since there are so many abandoned houses in Detroit. But it turned out to be a not-so-typical day for this crew.

It was about quarter after eight in the morning on this rainy day when Reginald, a worker on a bulldozer, saw something strange over by the chain-link fence. He had a guy on the crew, Eric, go over and check it out. They discovered the body of a female lying against the fence. She was on her back facing east. She had blood on her face. Wood, plaster and other debris, along with dirt and mud, lay all around her. She had one leg folded sideways, and both legs looked broken, possibly from the bulldozer as it was loading debris from the site.

The call came in to the Detroit Police Department at eight-twenty a.m., and the first officers arrived on the scene around eight-forty. They described her in the police report as a Black female, about twenty to thirty years old with short hair and dark complexion, thin build, wearing a black, red and white checkered sweater/coat, nothing from the waist down, but also partially covered by a white coat.

Pat had the misfortune of being logged as Unknown Female No. 1 with the Wayne County Medical Examiner. The first Jane Doe of 1992. As with the other women in this case, she wasn't exactly carrying a driver's license. These women tended to not carry identification. For one thing, a lot of them used aliases. For another, some of them had outstanding warrants.

Pat was determined to have died from ligature strangulation. She had postmortem fractures in her legs. She was noted as five-foot-one and one hundred fourteen pounds.

It took almost three months to identify Pat. Her sister Yvonne filed a missing person's report on her in February, telling police she was last seen on November 25. Celestine told police she had talked to Pat around Thanksgiving. And Urmerdean said she had not seen her since September. Finally, UF1 was ID'd as Pat, confirmed by dental records. Derrick is also on record as confirming her identity with the medical examiner.

There were several other women missing in Detroit at the time, as there likely are at any given time. Family members of those women visited the medical examiner's office in the weeks after the discovery to see if Unknown Female No. 1 was their loved one. One of those families missing someone at that point in January, a family who had been putting up fliers all over the place, was that of Valerie Chalk. Her prints were checked against the body in the morgue. But no, it wasn't her.

Because Valerie was still lying in the shower stall of a motel room about twelve blocks up Woodward.

VALERIE BROWN CHALK

"A boy's first love is his mother."

So writes André Chalk in an impact statement as part of his cognitive processing therapy in summer 2022. In the therapy workbook he has written the story of dealing with what happened to his mother. Her drug addiction. Her life on the streets. Her murder. In the decades since it all happened, he has learned that he has to sort through his thoughts and feelings. And rise above them.

"As a thirteen-year-old boy, I witnessed a lot of her behaviors and hated her for them," he wrote. When reached via phone for this book in the fall of 2022, André elaborated on that a bit. He talked about seeing his mom standing on the street corner. Her getting high. Her being gone from him and his siblings at home. "It really had a profound effect on me, and it did some damage," he said.

Valerie Brown Chalk was born in December 1956 to Buster and Jessie Brown. The family lived on Ford Street in Highland Park. Valerie attended church and sang in the church choir (she had a beautiful voice, her son said). She was the baby of the family, the youngest of five kids. Everybody knew her in this tightknit community. And though André didn't often get to see the "real" Valerie, the person his mom was at her core, unaltered by substances, he knows from glimpses here and there, and from what her family members have said, that she was a very sweet person. A big-hearted person. A funny person. A fairly naïve and innocent person, too, as the youngest.

Valerie graduated from Highland Park High School, then shortly afterward, she married André's father. They had been married only about six or seven months when things broke down. André's father dropped off Valerie and their son at her mother's house and left. It was at this point that Valerie started doing drugs. She left her baby behind as she pursued that life. "At this time," André said, "the crack era came in. And she kinda stole to the street and started doing drugs. Leaving the church."

And things just spiraled from there.

"When my brother came along four years later," André said, "that's when crack got the better of her. And then all hell broke loose. And then they had the epidemic of AIDS. And then all the drug addicts couldn't reach their highs from the crack. That's when everybody started shooting up. Getting high and all. You had crack, to heroin. And I was five years old. She used to bring her drugs, was shooting up in the house. I'd always be telling my grandma, 'Grandma, she's still in it; she's doing it.' I saw everything. I was the oldest. I would see her standing on the corner, I would see her high."

Valerie had two more children, each one also taken in by her mother, Jessie Brown Butler, being loved on by not only her but Valerie's sister, as well. The kids would still see their mother from time to time.

"She would periodically come over to my grandma's house for food and you know, some money," André said. "But she would float in and out. She would float in and out of the house."

Valerie would keep the details to a minimum, Jessie later told the media, knowing her mother did not approve of her lifestyle. But Valerie did care about her children, Jessie said, and she did try treatment a couple times. Meanwhile, Jessie and her other daughter were determined to keep the four children together and give them a decent life. To set a better example for them.

"She was always welcoming to her daughter," André said of his grandmother. "That was her baby. So that was my first experience of unconditional love. Seeing how my grandmother would constantly let her daughter come back. No matter what she did, no matter what she stole from her, she would always let her baby come back home."

The last time Jessie saw her youngest daughter was in early November 1991.

***

Benjamin Atkins was sleeping in rooms at the Monterey Motel off and on in later 1991, a few weeks after he had fled the scene there with Darlene Saunders. Now, on this particular morning – early, about three a.m. – he had been smoking crack and decided to take a walk.

He headed a couple blocks south to Woodward and Tennyson and saw a woman strolling along in the snow. He walked up to her, said what's up. She told him her name, but he didn't remember it later. He said he was Tony. Asked her if she had something to smoke crack out of. She said she did. He remembered her as five-foot-four, maybe a hundred and fifteen pounds. Thin.

"I told *[her]* that we would have to go to my sister's house to smoke," Atkins later told police, "but we would have to sneak through the back door."

That's a confusing bit, because evidently, they did not go there at all. They headed around the east side of the Monterey.

"I had no intentions really of smoking crack with her," Atkins admitted. "I pushed her inside this bathroom window that was on the ground level of the motel. I jumped in the window after her. I picked her up and put one hand over her mouth, and I had her around her waist, locking both her arms like on the side of her. I walked her south across the motel courtyard to the apartment I was sleeping in. It was on the second floor, upper level, two doors east of the stairs. I threw her on the bed that I had been sleeping in that had been left over from the motel."

Then, "I proceeded to choke her around her neck until she passed out. I choked her while she was lying face up. I had my thumbs, both of them, on her Adam's apple with my fingers interlocked behind her neck. I choked her until there was no fight in her."

He then removed all of her clothes. "I took her bra and tied her hands behind her back crisscross with the bra. I took one sweat sock off her foot and put it in her mouth." That was to keep her from screaming, he said, because he knew that the Highland Park police sometimes checked inside the motel.

"I took some curtain rod string and tied it on her mouth and the sock. I think I tied the knot with a square knot. I'm not sure." Or maybe just a regular loop knot, he said.

He started to choke her again, and he raped her. He used a condom – a yellow one, he said.

"I kept choking her until she was lifeless." And while he was doing this, "I kept calling her bitches and hoes. You bitch, you hoe." He continued until Valerie was dead, ejaculating at some point.

He felt her pulse. He felt her heart. He pressed against her stomach to see if all the air was gone. He had read a book about the respiratory system. "I guess you can say this n—-er knew what he was doing," he told police.

Once assured that she was dead, he dragged her into the bathroom and put her in the shower stall.

"I found some asbestos, it was white with tinfoil or silver stuff on it, on the floor of the room where I had the sex with her. I put the asbestos on top of her and left and closed the door. I closed the bathroom door. I put enough of the stuff on her so that no one could see her."

Then he headed down to Burlingame Street, a few blocks south. He left Valerie's clothing there in the room, figuring anyone would surmise it was just left behind by someone in the motel. Police asked what he was wearing that morning, and he remembered it as burgundy corduroys, a black turtleneck and a long goose-down jacket. But that clothing would be gone now, he told them, as he was also sometimes staying with his brother and his brother's girlfriend at the time, and at one point they got rid of his stuff.

He did not go back to that room of the motel, he said.

***

Valerie would lie there, hidden, for two or three months. Her family, meanwhile, knew that something was wrong, knew that her assistance checks were piling up at her mother's house. They filed a missing person's report and posted fliers all over both Highland Park and Detroit. André Chalk remembers that pretty well; he still has one of those fliers somewhere. His whole family banded together to try to find his mother, he said, and he specifically remembers hanging up the fliers with his uncle. Slender, five-foot-six, with brown eyes, the flier described Valerie, and it included her photo.

In February 1992, three bodies were discovered on the same day in three different rooms of the Monterey, after a scrapper alerted police to one of them. Jessie Butler heard the news, and her heart sank. She would later tell the media that she had felt right away one of those females had to be Valerie. It took a couple weeks, but indeed, one of the women, logged as Unknown Female No. 14, was ID'd as her daughter by dental records and a rather unorthodox fingerprinting method (more on that later). Valerie had been discovered face up in the shower stall of Room 68, lying with one foot up against the side of the stall, gagged, with insulation material stuffed into her mouth. André remembered when the detectives came and told his grandmother the news. At last, his mother had been found, amid all this talk in the neighborhood of a serial killer being on the loose.

In her late sixties at the time and using a walker after enduring many operations for a damaged knee, Jessie was weary and felt she was grieving alone. She shared a special bond with her baby, a bond of faith in the Lord. She wondered about the families of the other victims. Could she maybe talk to them? When the perp was arrested months later, she told *The Detroit News* she was struggling to find a way to forgive him. She would later attend his trial.

André was interviewed by well-known local news personality Amyre Makupson for WKBD Channel 50 at the time of the case. He, his three siblings and their grandmother were photographed in *The Detroit News*, a clipping he still has framed on the wall.

These days, when not at his job for the railroad or working through his therapy, André executes another mission. A very important one.

"I go around to schools and just talk with African-American boys about, even though you go through different situations in your life, you can rise above whatever things you go through. You can rise above them. You can rise above whatever adversity you have. There's no stuff you can't use. You can be successful in life. That's my big thing. I try to do a lot with young boys in schools."

He is envisioning his therapy workbook eventually becoming a published book, another avenue to encourage boys of color, whatever situation they are in, whatever life throws at them. Even if they're not dealing with a mom on the streets or the crimes of a serial killer.

"The truth is," he writes in his workbook, "everybody is addicted to something, whether it's shopping, food, sex, and yes, drugs and alcohol. We don't choose to be addicted. What we choose to do is deny our pain!!

"The good news is that every choice you make supersedes and overrides every other choice you make.

"So today you can choose to be in peace instead of in pieces!!"

André keeps learning. He keeps researching. He was watching a recent Netflix series on convicted Milwaukee serial killer Jeffrey Dahmer, even though friends said he shouldn't watch stuff like that. He has researched Benjamin Atkins' life, too. Learned about Atkins' childhood, about Atkins' own mother. Learned more about the genetics of addiction, how a parent can pass it along to a child. None of the circumstances around this killer's life justify the crimes, André asserts, but the research helps for understanding. And for healing. For closure, he says. So he wants to know those things as he continues to write the story of his own life.

"This wound from my mother – it can heal," he said. "And I can cope with it and go on and have a successful life, and it won't affect me in the way that it has. With my relationships with women and things of that nature."

He writes in his workbook: "Let your story, whether it's less of pain or greater of pain, be a story of triumph, overcoming, and a vessel of tools that can inspire to help someone overcome their adversities and valley experiences in life."

VICKIE ANN TRUELOVE

Six months before she was killed, Vickie Truelove was crouching her tiny, five-foot-one, one-hundred-ten-pound frame inside the kitchen closet of a basement apartment on Detroit's east side, hiding with the door barely cracked as she watched her friend Reggie get shot and killed on the couch by a couple drug thugs looking for their money. Big silver guns, they had. She didn't know the name or variety. But she did know the shooters, at least by their street names. Shannon and Bobby Dee, aka B.J., aka L.A. They had taken the iron gate off the apartment door to get in here. Both of them fired shots at Reggie as she watched, afraid to make a sound, as the blood ran out of Reggie's body.

Reggie's girlfriend, whose name she didn't remember, and another girl that was there named Pam must have just scattered somewhere; she didn't hear or see them from where she was. When the two guys stopped shooting, Bobby Dee kicked Reggie in the side of his torso. A moan came out of his body. Then they left. Vickie stayed in the closet a couple minutes, then saw Reggie's girlfriend and Pam run out the front door. After a little more time – she didn't know how long she stayed in that closet – she climbed out the kitchen window and ran around the front of the building, over to a field, where she lay down in the brush. She stayed there a while, then ran down an alley, went over to Chalmers Street and ducked inside a vacant house. After her fear had subsided a bit more, she came out of the house and called police from a pay phone on Jefferson Avenue. There, of all things, she spotted Shannon and Bobby Dee, parked at Newport and Jefferson in a '91 Ford Escort. Four-door, blue, with a sunroof. It was after five a.m. The two men didn't see her. She ran off, and then the police came and picked her up.

At six-fifteen a.m. on June 19, 1991, she was giving a statement to Sergeant Knight in Detroit Police's Homicide Section.

Vickie, born in May 1952 and now on the far side of her thirties, had a record with police, having been arrested in the 1980s for possession of narcotics and other charges. And even in April 1991, she had filed a police report against a man who she said took her home because she was homeless, then would not let her leave and forced her to have sex with thirty other men. She had escaped by climbing down from a second-story window.

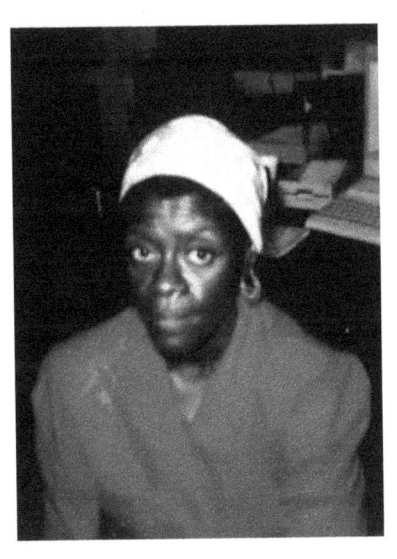

Vickie Truelove when she was interviewed by police in 1991. Photo from DPD files.

Now, though, Vickie was witness to a murder, maybe even involved in it for all they knew, and therefore even more on DPD radar. So when they lost track of her at the end of November 1991, police looked for her. They left messages with her boyfriend, Joe, who had been living with her on Henry Street. They dropped by places where they knew she visited or stayed. Various hotels and whatnot. No luck. Some of the addresses they were given didn't exist. Folks at one place on Erskine in Detroit, a place so affectionately called the House of Love, said she had stayed there all night on November 26 but had not been back. DPD even checked the Wayne County jail. Vickie wasn't there, either.

When they connected with Joe, he was looking for her at that point, too. The last time he saw her, in the first week of December, she was walking with a trick up toward Woodward. He had heard she was staying off and on with some other guy named Joe – a white guy – either at the Huntington Hotel on Alexandrine Street or the Billinghurst Hotel a block up, on Willis. She also went to the Charlotte Bar a lot, he said. Somebody else said they saw her on December 5 at Columbia and Park. Vickie's daughters, Nina, age nineteen, and Sheree, age twenty-three, said they last saw their mother in early December.

***

When making his statements to police upon his arrest, Benjamin Atkins remembered Vickie as the second of his three Detroit murders, following the one at the house that was torn down. He was thinking it was fall of '91 but admitted, again, that he couldn't remember dates. It was nighttime, and he thought it was a Saturday. Probably between eleven p.m. and midnight, he said.

In addition to his confessions to police, Atkins described the crimes to a psychiatrist during multiple examinations leading up to his trial. When discussing this particular encounter, he noted that he had just "indulged with a male," and that these incidents tended to start out that same way, with a male encounter in which he was paid, then smoking some crack, then a walk to calm his mind, as was the case this time.

So he was walking down Woodward Ave when a woman approached him and asked what's up. He told her he was looking for someone to smoke crack with. She said he could smoke with her.

"See, I didn't have any crack," he told police, "and it never was my intentions to smoke crack with her. That was my little way to get her to go with me."

She suggested an abandoned nursing home off Woodward near the supermarket, three blocks north of Clairmount Ave. They entered the building through a broken window on the north side.

"After we got in there, I just grabbed her around her mouth and threw her down and started choking her. She was face up. I placed both thumbs on her Adam's apple and locked my fingers behind her neck and I choked her until she passed out."

This was on the first floor of the nursing home, and when she passed out, he took her up to the second floor, where there was a mattress lying on the floor. He placed her on the mattress and undressed her while she was still unconscious. He used her bra to tie her hands behind her back.

"I started calling her bitches and hoes while I was choking her," he said.

Her body went limp. He took out a condom he had with him and raped her. After he ejaculated, he checked to see if she was dead. He felt her pulse and her heart, and he pushed on her stomach to make sure any remaining air was gone. He covered up her body with the mattress.

He remembered her as around five-foot, maybe a hundred and five pounds, dark-skinned and thin. Small build. She had short hair. About age thirty-five. She had been wearing a blue jean jacket and two pairs of pants, along with white Nike gym shoes. He said had never seen her before this encounter.

***

Vickie was found on January 25, 1992, on the second floor of the former Longfellow Nursing Center, 9520 Woodward near Westminster Street in Detroit. She was lying face down with her hands bound behind her back, bound with her own clothing, it appeared. She was on the floor next to a mattress. She had a sock in her mouth and a sweater tied around her face. She was frozen but showed early signs of decomposition. The medical examiner said she was killed anywhere from a few days to more than month earlier.

She was Unknown Female No. 10 before her boyfriend Joe ID'd her body at the morgue, and her sister Joyce and her daughter Sheree also made an ID a couple days later. Joyce had not seen Vickie in a year. Vickie's parents, Milton Favors and Emma Hands, were deceased at the time. Vickie left behind four kids, as well as an estranged husband, Willie.

DEBBIE ANN FRIDAY

At one point she was thought to be his first victim. Maybe that was because she was the first one found. And when she was found in December, there was no inkling yet that a serial killer was haunting the main street of the Motor City.

Debbie Ann Friday was born in December 1960 to Charles Friday and Sadie Williams. She had three children. Not much else is known about her, and no one could be reached to speak for her in this book. A few tidbits can be scraped together from the case files: Back in 1985 or '86, Debbie was thrown out of a third-story window over some drug deal, her Uncle Herb recalled. Her mother last saw her on December 4, 1991. Herb last saw her a few days later, on the afternoon of the seventh, when he picked her up and drove her somewhere, then gave her a ride back again "while it was still light," he later told police. Debbie would sometimes stay at a crack house for a few days. Then, an aunt last saw her on December 8, when Debbie cooked her dinner before departing the west-side house. Steak, macaroni and cheese, and vegetables, the *Detroit Free Press* would later report.

"Who's the guy this time?" her aunt recalled asking Debbie after her niece had done the dishes and was headed out the door.

"He's a guy I know in Highland Park," Debbie said. "I have to meet him over there." Then she was gone.

Debbie had a boyfriend her same age named Calvin, who stayed over in the Linwood and Davison area; they worked at the same place. Calvin last saw her a few days later than everyone else: near Clements Street at around three-thirty p.m. on Friday the 13th.

***

It was pretty cold that night, twenty-five to thirty degrees. There would be some intermittent rain and snow in the air the next day. Atkins was on the porch where he was staying with his brother and his brother's girlfriend on Elmhurst in Highland Park, within a block of Woodward, when he saw this girl standing in front of a crack house three doors down. She was in her late twenties or early thirties, he later recalled, five-foot-two, kinda wide, maybe a hundred thirty-five to a hundred forty pounds, with dark-brown skin, short hair. There was something about the way she looked that interested him, so he walked over and asked her what's up.

She said she was looking for something to smoke, and he said he was a dealer and had something for her.

"Good," she replied, "because I wouldn't mind getting busy."

He asked her if she had a place to go, because they couldn't go to his sister's house. (When he later told a psychiatrist about this incident, he said they actually went back to his home so he could drop off some groceries.) She suggested a place down the street, an abandoned four-story brick apartment building.

On the walk over to the building, the woman noticed some crack lying on the ground and picked it up, he later told police. It seems a tad ludicrous, but perhaps it happens. They then entered the building. It was partially boarded up, but you could get in through the rear door. Just inside, there was an entrance to the basement, but at this time it only had one step. Someone had placed a green cloth chair there so you could step on it to get down to the lower level.

Once in the basement, they first smoked the rock she had found on the ground, then he said they should move away from this basement window. So they walked to the other side of the basement.

"She sat down," he told police, "and I grabbed her around the neck with my thumbs on her Adam's apple, and I started choking her, and she passed out."

He took her jacket and top off, but then she started to wake up.

"I started choking her again, and we struggled for about ten minutes, and then she passed out. I took her belt off and then her pants off and then her socks and shoes off. At first, I put her sock in her mouth, and I tied her jacket around her face."

Then her dragged her between two poles in the basement and ripped in half the blue jeans he had taken off her. He tied one of her legs to one pole with half of the jeans, and the other leg to the other pole with the other half. This left her face down and spread-eagle. "I took either her bra or a piece of her shirt and tied her hands behind her back. Then she started to wake up."

The sock was coming out of her mouth. He choked her again. She passed out again, and he raped her vaginally and anally, repeatedly. She began to wake up once again. This continued on for a while, until she appeared to be dead, at which point he felt for a pulse, felt for a heartbeat, and pushed on her back to see if the air was out of her body. He told the psychiatrist he also spanked her thirty or forty times, "just as he had been spanked with cords," the report said.

He then went home and took a bath.

Debbie Ann Friday was found in the basement of an abandoned apartment building at 170 Elmhurst in Highland Park on December 14, 1991. Because of the trauma to her head, police at first thought she may had been shot. They recognized her as a prostitute they had seen working the area. She was labeled as Unknown Female No. 48 for a minute, five-foot-five and one hundred and fifty-three pounds.

Sadie Williams ID'd her daughter's body. A couple years later, when called to the witness stand at the killer's trial, Sadie squeezed her eyes tight in pain, the newspaper said, as she recounted that day. "I came right after they called me ... Oh, Jesus, oh, Jesus ..."

When done testifying, she walked past Benjamin Atkins in the courtroom.

"You took my baby," she said.

Then she was led into an adjoining witness room, from which her pained cries could be heard for several minutes.

BERTHA JEAN MASON

Bertha Jean Mason had been living with her boyfriend William for several years. He considered her his "common law wife," as the term used to go. That's what he told the police, his common law wife. Of course, it's so common now that the term has fallen out of fashion.

Bertha was born in July 1965 to Robert Truelove and Rosemarie Williams, whose maiden name Bertha used as her own. Rosemarie, along with Bertha's brother Larry and her aunt Bernice, would later attend the trial of Bertha's killer. And there were other family members of Bertha who were quoted or pictured in the news at the time of this case: her great-aunt Nettie, cousin Curtis, grandmother Graty, sister-in-law Patricia, nephew Larry Jr. All representing her. That included William, who testified at the trial.

William was twenty-five years older than Bertha. When she was out, he would stay at their home on Josephine Street in Detroit with their four small kids – three boys and a girl who were age one to four at the time of this story. He knew she was smoking crack, but he didn't know for sure about any prostitution. Bertha wouldn't tell him. She knew he would go looking for her if she told him where she was or whom she was with. "She would just say that she would talk people out of their crack cocaine," he later told police, "and sometimes run for them to get it. She would say she worked people. She said she never had any sex with them." Still, William had his suspicions.

The last time he saw Bertha was at home on Saturday, December 14, 1991, around six p.m. He was upstairs and she was downstairs. The kids came upstairs crying, telling him that their mom was gone again. He went downstairs, checked the front door, which was locked. He checked the side door, and it was cracked. He saw her footprints leading out the driveway in the snow. He tried to follow the tracks for a while before they faded. They went toward Holbrook Avenue, which was one block south, on the east side of Woodward. She was wearing jogging pants that night, he recalled, along with a white shirt with multicolored stripes and some white "British Nikes." She had a black coat that she would also be wearing.

William had grown accustomed to Bertha slipping out like that while he was busy doing something else. It seemed to happen a couple times a month. One time was even while they were staying with Bertha's mother. She would usually be gone for a day or two, sometimes up to five days. There was one time when she was gone for longer than a week, but she called that time, unlike this time. And she would always return when her check came in the mail. He would always try to be with her when she went out to cash her check because one time when he wasn't with her, she was gone again for days.

On December 19, though, her check came, and she wasn't there.

***

Bertha's killer remembered it as a Sunday morning. Early. Around ten a.m. That was early for him, anyway. He thought it was fall, but he was a little off on that.

He was walking toward Holbrook when he saw this girl. He remembered her as "kinda big," about five-foot-six and maybe a hundred sixty-five pounds. His recollection was pretty accurate on that part. She was light-skinned, he said, and it looked like she had run a straightening comb through her neck-length hair. She was wearing jogging pants (red, he thought) and a Hawaiian-type shirt. Gym shoes, sweat socks. Maybe a skull cap, too. She was standing at the Shell gas station at Holbrook and Woodward.

She asked him what's up, and he said he was looking for someone to smoke with. She said they could go to her place. He didn't want to go there. Anyplace else?

She took him to an abandoned building a couple blocks south, behind a check-cashing place on the east side of Woodward. They walked to the back of the building, the kitchen, and he grabbed her feet. ("See these big hands I got?" he told police.)

Bertha fell to the floor, and he sat on top of her and choked her until she passed out.

"I choked her the same way," he said. "It's always the same way. Both thumbs over the Adam's apple and the fingers interlocked behind her neck."

When recounting this incident later during his psychiatric examinations, Atkins remembered Bertha cussing at him, calling him a bitch. He felt an intense anger toward her and said he didn't even know why. He hit her in the face many times.

When she passed out, he took her top and bra off. He put one of her socks in her mouth to keep her from screaming, then tied her bra over her mouth. He took a nearby wire hanger and tried to tie her hands behind her back with it, but it didn't hold. As he was pulling her pants off, Bertha started to wake up and try to get loose. Then he used something else to tie her hands; he didn't remember what. And he choked her again.

She passed out again, and he raped her anally. She started to wake up again. "I guess you would, too, with some shit like that," he told police.

He continued choking and raping her, calling her "bitches and hoes."

When Bertha appeared to be dead, he checked her pulse and her heart, pushed her stomach for any remaining air. He then dragged her to the hallway and threw her down some basement stairs. He remembered her body falling "kinda awkward," and he remembered seeing a light coming up from the basement. He closed the basement door.

He had wanted to place her body in the old refrigerator that was sitting there in the kitchen, but that didn't work, so he just left her clothing in the fridge.

He had not known this woman, he told police, and he didn't use a condom with her because he didn't have any condoms on him. He did return to the building within the next few days to see if she was still there, and she wasn't. "I thought she had walked off or some shit."

***

Between December 18 and 20, William went walking up Woodward Avenue looking for Bertha. He ran into a girl they knew named Mary, who said the last time she saw Bertha was that Monday before. It would have been the sixteenth. Bertha had stopped by Mary's place briefly and had told her she'd be back.

The day after Christmas, Bertha's mother filed a missing person's report. William followed with his own report a few days later. "Everybody got worried because she had never missed a holiday," he told police. They called around to hospitals looking for a Jane Doe.

On December 30, police responded to a call at 8642 Woodward in Detroit, south of Highland Park, at Alger

Street east of Woodward, behind a check-cashing place. They were directed to 12 Alger, where someone had spotted a body. It was a vacant three-story brick building, and the owner had just returned from vacation to check the place.

The padlocked front door had been forced open. Some of the windows were broken out, some boarded up. Bertha was found lying on her back on the stairs leading to the basement. She was nude except for a white sock on her left foot, its stripes in red, yellow and blue. The other sock was in her mouth, and her hands were tied behind her. Police would discover, scattered here and there, some of her other clothing items – pieces of them, at least – that William recalled from that night. William's memory would prove the most accurate of anyone who had last seen the victims of our case.

"It's difficult to say at this time," a responding officer noted in his report, "whether or not she was forced into that house, but it's a definite that force was used on her."

Bertha was assigned body #10741-91 by the Wayne County Medical Examiner, Unknown Female No. 52 for 1991, pegged at five-foot-seven and one hundred and sixty-nine pounds. William ID'd her body on New Year's Eve.

Police spoke with other prostitutes who worked that area and had seen Bertha around. One, named Brenda, had gone with a john into that same building. She described this recent "date" to police – it stood out to her because she had been particularly scared and ran out of there right after their transaction concluded: "Once we finish, you never know what's on their minds."

Another girl said she heard a female screaming the night before Bertha's body was found. It sounded like it came from behind the check-cashing place. She heard a man tell her "Shut up! Shut up!" then the screaming stopped.

Bertha was twenty-one weeks pregnant when she was killed. The medical examiner noted on the autopsy report that it was a girl.

JUANITA HARDY

Born in June 1968, Juanita Hardy grew up in Detroit and went to Mumford High School on the west side in the 1980s. She was adopted as a youngster, but both of her adoptive parents passed away when she was still a kid. She had a guardian, maybe you could call her a foster mom, named Carrie. She also had a brother named Grant. She was sometimes known as Joann Denise Hardy – at least that's how her fingerprints ID'd her. So perhaps that was her name on the street. Juanita was her real name.

Only a little more info can be culled together from the case files about Juanita, as attempts to contact people who knew her came up empty. At the time of this case, Juanita lived on Collingwood Street in Detroit, west of Woodward and east of the John C. Lodge Freeway. She reportedly had a bad crack problem. There's even a note in the files that she apparently had a Detroit cop friend who would come over and smoke with her. She told her friend Lisa that her pimp hit her; he was largely unknown except that he drove an older Thunderbird or Cadillac. Juanita also may have worked at a topless bar on Livernois. She had a couple kids, a close friend named Tammy and another friend named Gwen who lived on Elmhurst. She had a baby daddy named Marvin, whom she took to court in 1988 for child support, though her kids at one point went to foster care.

Carrie said she last saw Juanita in fall 1991; she disappeared a month or two later.

***

He thought it might have been February. There was snow on the ground. But it was "before the big snow," he said, which might have referred to a big snowstorm in mid-January that year. It's likely it was early January or late December, as he indicated this incident was the second of three at the Monterey. One news report after his arrest said this one occurred shortly after Christmas, though it doesn't say that in his confession. Could have been from a different statement, could have been said out loud but not noted in the official written statement, could have just been a mistake. It's easy to get so many incidents and so many confessions confused. Because yeah, this is a lot.

At any rate, he saw this girl walking along Woodward. Five-foot-four or so, maybe a hundred twenty pounds, though he described that as a "hefty" build. He didn't remember her clothing, but he thought she had a skull cap on. He mentioned a skull cap in several of his statements on the victims.

So he saw her, he asked her if she had anything to smoke out of, and she said yes. He suggested they go to his "sister's" house, though they would have to sneak in through the back door.

"So we walked down the alley between the Monterey Motel and the houses," he told police, "and when we got halfway down the alley, I grabbed her from behind with my hand over her mouth."

He dragged her further down the alley to a little opening in the gate, then dragged her inside the gate. He threw her on the ground right there by the gate. He started to choke her with both hands, again with his thumbs over the front of her neck.

"Why me?" she asked him during the struggle.

"Because you're that bitch."

When she passed out, he dragged her along the north side of the Monterey, about four rooms down, then took her inside one of the rooms. She started to come to, so he choked her again. He took off her shirt and her bra, using her bra to tie her hands. He removed her pants, shoes and socks.

She started to wake up again. He grabbed a rope or tie from a nearby curtain and put it around her neck to choke her. She passed out again, and he raped her vaginally, as she lay on the ground face up. He called her the same names as with the other victims, "bitches" and "hoes." Once again, Juanita started to awaken, and he tightened the curtain tie around her neck to continue choking her. This time when she passed out, she had no pulse and no heartbeat. He pushed on her stomach, as with the others, to relieve it of any remaining air and assure she was gone. He raped her again and ejaculated. And even then, he choked her again, just to make absolutely sure.

He dragged her into the bathroom of this motel room and threw her in the shower stall, then placed her clothing on top of her. He also put some "asbestos," he said, on top of her, as he had with Valerie Chalk. The stuff you put in the ceiling, he explained when police inquired further. The stuff that has foil on one side.

Juanita had her hands tied behind her, still, and he remembered putting socks in her mouth, and maybe even using the curtain tie to secure the socks in place. When pressed further, he admitted he did not recall exactly what he used to try to cover her body. He never returned to that room of the motel.

***

Juanita Hardy was found at the Monterey Motel, Room 35, on February 17, 1992, along with two other females discovered that day. She was found in the same position as Valerie Chalk, and she had some "insulation material" stuffed in her mouth, one report said. She had that same material on her torso. Her body was partially frozen. Five-foot-five, one hundred fifteen pounds. She had a pierced earring in her right ear, gold in color with some kind of Egyptian motif, the medical examiner noted.

She was tagged as Unknown Female No. 16 until her fingerprints identified her as Joann/Juanita after Carrie had contacted police about her being missing. Her brother Grant was notified. Authorities had to determine what would happen to her two minor children. Carrie was told she would have to go through probate since she never legally adopted her. Juanita's body was released to the James Cole Funeral Home on March 13.

UNKNOWN FEMALE NO. 15

We still don't know her name.

We don't really know what she looked like. There's an artist's conception based on her decomposing body. But who knows how accurate that is.

We don't know how long she was lying there, in a shower stall at the Monterey Motel. We don't know when she disappeared, or even who missed her.

Her fingerprints were run in the system with no match. So evidently, she didn't have a record. Maybe she wasn't on the street very long.

There were some names that were considered and eliminated for her, based on those off-the-grid fingerprints. Jesseenia. Teresa. Dora. Antoinette Renee. Kim. Marguirite. Diane. Marlo. Barbara Ann. Shavara. Cheryl. Rosalyn. Jacqueline. Laura. Deborah. Veronica. Sylvia. Mona. Leslie. All missing, but none of them appeared to be her, though for a couple of the women, police were unable to make a positive ID from the prints, so the possibility remained that one of them could be her. Still, the process of elimination did not seem to move her any closer to identification.

She is known in the case files as Unknown Female No. 15, so we'll just call her Fifteen. Kinda like Eleven on *Stranger Things*, or Seven of Nine on *Star Trek: Voyager*. But not really.

Fifteen is the most unsettling aspect of the case for this author. The victim who stands out. Is it possible that her family knows she is this Jane Doe but just never came forward? Is it *more* possible her family just never knew what happened to her? Figured she disappeared into the street and never came back out again? So many questions.

So in an effort to wring out every last drop of liquid in the barely damp sponge of her case files, here is what we know:

- She was a Black female.
- She was five-foot-nine and one hundred twenty-five pounds on the autopsy report.
- She had black hair about an inch and a half long.
- She was estimated to be a teenager in one report, though the medical examiner put her age at twenty to thirty.
- She had no appendix.
- Her other organs – gallbladder, kidneys, liver, etc. – showed as normal.
- She showed no pre-mortem scarring or tattoos.
- She was said to be wearing gold-metal pierced earrings, one in each ear, and silver-metal rings, one on the ring finger of each hand. The jewelry could have been gold and sterling silver, or costume jewelry – the reports don't get any more specific. (These rings are not seen on Fifteen in the video of the crime scene, however, so this detail in the reports may be a mistake or may have been confused with one of the other Monterey victims, such as Valerie Chalk, said to have worn a ring on each hand.)
- Her uterus was described by the medical examiner as "non-gravid," or not pregnant.
- Her toxicology screens were positive for alcohol, cocaine and volatiles/ethanol, benzoylecgonine (the compound tested for in most cocaine drug urinalyses,

formed by the liver when cocaine is processed in the body), negative for barbiturates and morphine.
- Evidence appeared to show she and the others at the Monterey were killed before mid-January's snowstorm. Fifteen likely disappeared in early January, possibly late December.

There are very few possibilities at the DoeNetwork.org and NamUs.gov sites of females who went missing in 1991: Mattie Lenore Jones (whose name comes up in the case files – her dental records were pulled when Fifteen was found) went missing a little too early – April 1991 – and was too short, only five-foot-two. And she's older, age thirty-two. Those same three characteristics apply for Caprice Cade, who went missing that June, though she was in her twenties so was a little closer in age. Faye Elizabeth Wright disappeared closer to the timeframe, in October 1991, but with a height of five-foot-two and age thirty-seven. Patricia Lynn Pouncy was slightly taller, five-foot-four, and disappeared in January 1991 and was thirty-three. Then Charlita Sonya Harris disappeared in November, but was way shorter than Fifteen, only four-foot-eleven. Her age of only twenty-five could fit, however. She had brown medium-length hair.

Perhaps the missing female who fits best is Gerri Nicole Anderson, age twenty-four, five-foot-eight to five-foot-ten, one hundred twenty to one hundred fifty pounds, with short black hair. She had pierced ears, too. Gerri disappeared in October 1990, which makes it possible – she could have been on the street a year before encountering Atkins. Gerri had a brown jacket, and you'll see in a minute how Atkins described Fifteen's clothing. Gerri was said to have signed over the title of her car, a burgundy or maroon 1987 Ford Merkur, to a known drug dealer, then was never heard from again. One self-described "Internet sleuth" says she met Gerri in Detroit in June 1990 and years later was so struck by her story she actually wrote a short Kindle book on the theory that Gerri was the Jane Doe from the Atkins case.

None of the women listed as missing in 1992 fit. And Fifteen was not even included in the "Unidentified" section of DoeNetwork.org until July 2022, when this author sent them the info. After the site added the listing for her, it was amplified in a news article on the ClickonDetroit/WDIV-TV Channel 4 website in February 2023. Then later in 2023, a cold-case investigative group based on the West Coast announced that they identified this Jane Doe via forensic genetic genealogy, working with a detective in Michigan, but said the family did not want her name to be released. It was verified for this book with phone calls to local law enforcement.

For now, publicly, she remains a mystery, and we are left with the above bullet points, and what Atkins himself said about Fifteen, which may or may not be true …

***

It was around eleven p.m. that night, and it was cold and snowy. She was the third female he took to the Monterey Motel.

He saw her at Woodward and Richton, which is just north of Monterey Street. She had on a brown jacket and skull cap and corduroys, he recalled, and shoes or boots. He remembered her as being about five-foot-four and maybe one hundred thirty-five pounds.

This girl asked him what was up. He told her he was looking for someone to smoke with.

"I told her we could go over to my sister's house," he later told police, "but we had to sneak through the back door."

And in another similarity to the Juanita Hardy encounter, Atkins and Fifteen walked down the alley between the

Monterey and the homes on that nearby street. About halfway down the alley, he grabbed Fifteen and put his hand over her mouth. He shoved her through an open window of one of the motel rooms, then climbed in after her. He started choking her with his hands. He held his thumbs over the front of her throat.

After she passed out, he carried her to the south side of the building, into a room on the first floor. She was coming to, so he started to choke her again with his hands, again with his thumbs over the front of her throat. When she passed out again, he dragged her over to a mattress lying in the room and started to take her clothes off.

"I remember tying her hands with some piece of clothing," he said. She was lying face down, and he raped her both vaginally and anally. He did not use a condom with her, he told police.

"I kept calling her a dirty rotten bitch. She started to come through *[sic]* again, and I proceeded to choke her some more. Then she wasn't breathing any more. I continued to have sex with her until I got off. Then I made sure she was dead by checking her pulse on her neck and her heart. She was dead. Then I dragged her to the bathtub and threw her in the shower, and there was some wall paneling on the floor and I slid it between the shower and the toilet so nobody could see her behind it. Then after I thought she was well-hid, I left."

He did not return to the Monterey again. About a month to a month and a half later he heard on the news that the three women were found there.

During their struggle, Fifteen had desperately asked him, "Why me?"

"Because you bitches deserve it," he replied.

VICKI MARIE BEASLEY BROWN

A high school classmate of a young Vicki Beasley might have looked at her across the room during second-period geometry and thought, "That pretty girl's got the world by the tail." And he might have been right. However, like many of the females in our story, substance abuse derailed a bright future for Vicki, along with encountering a cold-blooded killer. But let's step back a bit.

Vicki Marie Beasley was born at Hutzel Women's Hospital in Detroit in July 1948, the child of Clarence and Gloria Beasley. She had four siblings—two brothers and two sisters. When Vicki was around eleven years old, the family moved to New York for a while, residing in the Manhattan area. Later, they returned to Detroit, where their extended family, including Vicki's grandmother and great-grandmother, lived.

Vicki attended Detroit's Northwestern High School and graduated in 1966. She received accolades in high school that included titles like "Miss Congeniality" and "Prettiest Face."

After graduating, Vicki worked at Stouffer's Restaurant, a national chain with a couple of Detroit locations, long before it became known for its frozen food. However, Vicki's life took a different turn soon afterward. This marked the beginning of a decades-long cycle of addiction.

She became involved with a man in Detroit who introduced her to the world of drugs, and together they had a daughter named Renée in 1967. It wasn't until six or seven years later that she met another man with whom she had a son named Eddie, and this period seemed to be a turning point for Vicki.

Vicki Beasley, on the left, with her family.
Photo courtesy of Renèe M. Beavers.

Hers was a life marked by struggles, resilience, and moments of hope, as explained by Renée when contacted for this book. Vicki's journey was intertwined with challenges arising from substance abuse but also with determination and creativity that shone through in various aspects of her life.

Vicki's creative spirit was evident in her ability to transform everyday items into works of art. Long before the popularity of home improvement shows like those on HGTV, Vicki was turning discarded materials into treasures. She had a knack for repurposing items like plastic rings from beer cans, giving them new life with a coat of spray paint, and arranging them as decor on her walls. She was a singer, a painter, and a woman of many talents, making her presence felt in various creative endeavors.

Renée admired her mother's tenacious work ethic. Vicki demonstrated her commitment to providing for her family through various jobs, including roles at an auto painting plant and a mattress factory. Renée fondly recalled the beauty Vicki brought into their home, making it a welcoming and creative space long before interior design became a popular trend. "She always made our home really beautiful," her daughter said.

Amid the challenges Vicki faced due to addiction, she found moments of stability. Her relationship with Eddie's father, Willie, offered a period of respite. During this time, Vicki's determination to overcome her addiction allowed her to experience a period of relative normalcy. It was a time of progress and a break from unhealthy relationships.

However, Vicki's journey was still marred by the cyclical nature of addiction. Despite her best efforts, she fell back into substance abuse patterns. Her daughter Renée recounted the moments of hope and disappointment as Vicki's struggles with addiction continued to affect her life. "It was just that she was still functioning," Vicki's daughter said. "She could still manage her life and the kids."

Vicki had two more daughters, Carmen and Monique. She eventually married Jerome Brown in 1989, but their relationship also faced difficulties. The cycle of addiction continued to affect her life.

As time passed, Vicki's relationships and circumstances shifted. While not all of her relationships were healthy, they each contributed to her story in their own way. Renée herself demonstrated remarkable resilience and emerged as a beacon of strength amid the challenges. Her journey to build a healthier and more fulfilling life took her across continents and led to her founding, with her husband, a business dedicated to fostering positive relationships called the Rich Relationships Refuge. Renée and her husband have authored books, produced a podcast and a YouTube channel, and taught online courses. Renée's journey led her to advocate for those impacted by addiction, particularly the children who suffer the consequences.

"The kids don't have a choice," she said. "And so, for me, I had to grow up really fast. And I had to be very responsible. ... One of the things that really helped me was understanding that you can't control who your parents are, but you can control the choices you make."

***

As we turn to March 25, 1992, the presumed date of Vicki's death, Vicki's son was sixteen years old, and her oldest daughter, Renée, was twenty-three and living in Germany with her husband. Vicki had her two younger children with her as she was living with friends of the family on Trowbridge Street in Detroit. She had been separated from Jerome for about a year. On that day, Vicki reportedly mentioned that she was going to the store to buy food for school lunches and cigarettes.

The man who confessed to killing Vicki remembered it as "still snowing out" at the time. He was walking down Cortland between Woodward and Second Street. As he got to the intersection at Second, that's when he saw her.

Vicki wore a wig from time to time, and he remembered the wig that night. It was red. He described her as in her late thirties or early forties, dark-skinned, about five-foot-four or so, slim build – "skinny, in fact." He didn't recall what kind of clothing she was wearing.

"What are you getting into?" she asked.
"What do you have planned?" he replied.
"We could have a little fun."
The two walked down Second near Highland Street.
"What do you want to do, smoke some crack?"

"Yeah," she said.

Atkins bought two ten-dollar rocks of cocaine at a house on Cortland and Second. In the basement.

He told her he stayed at 111 Highland. He said that because he had planned to take her next door to that building to smoke and have sex with her, he told police. He also lied to her that he worked at 111 Highland, and for whatever logic he was trying to apply to the situation, he said he didn't want his boss to see him with a girl and smoking dope.

They got to the building next door to 111 Highland, at 121, and went around the back. There was furniture blocking the back door, and she didn't want to climb over all the furniture to get into the building. He remembered this as being around midnight or one a.m.

"So I just started choking her face forward using my thumbs on her Adam's apple," he told police, "and my fingers locked behind her neck."

Vicki passed out, and he lifted her over the furniture to take her inside. He carried her to the west side of the first floor, to the first apartment there. Once he dragged her into that apartment, he started choking her again. Evidently, she had started to wake up. But then she passed out again. He took her pants off and raped her both vaginally and anally. He told police he did not use a condom. Once he had ejaculated, he choked her again.

"I made sure she was dead. I checked her pulse in her neck, and I felt her heartbeat," he said. "I pushed the remaining air out of her body."

He dragged Vicki's body to a closet near the den of the apartment. He covered the lower part of her body with some clothing, he believed with the pants he had taken off of her. There was a jacket lying nearby, so he used that to cover her up, as well. He then smoked his drugs and left.

***

Two days later, Vicki's mother, Gloria, received a call from the landlady informing her that Vicki was missing. Gloria Beasley filed a missing person's report with the Detroit police on April 2, 1992. She listed the landlady as the last person to see her daughter.

"We knew my mom was missing for about fifteen days," Renée remembered. "April 1 is my little sister's birthday, and she would have never missed her birthday. So we knew for a while that she was missing before they found her. My husband and I were in Germany when we received the news of her murder."

Vicki's body was found by a man who was searching for furniture inside a vacant apartment building at 121 Highland in Highland Park on April 15, 1992. Gloria identified her at the morgue on April 16. Vicki was forty-three years old.

"There was both death and undeserved disgrace," her mother said when Atkins' verdicts were announced. "Vicki never would have gone willingly with that man."

Despite the darkness that emerged in her final days, Vicki's memory lives on through her daughter Renée's determination to create positive change. Renée's journey to empower individuals and couples in relationships is a testament to the strength that can emerge from adversity. Vicki's story reminds her children and grandchildren that even in the face of addiction and hardship, there are moments of creativity, resilience, and healing potential.

JOANNE O'ROURKE

She was known as Joanne (or Joann) O'Rourke and Joanne Mae Ollie. Which was her real name? Were either of them her real name?

Very little is known about her, similar to Fifteen, whose fate as a Jane Doe she almost shared. Ironically, her "Unknown Female" tag was the reverse of Fifteen's – 51. And it was 51 for a couple weeks.

We know she was born in August 1951. We know she had a sister named Katie in Muskegon Heights, on the west side of the state. We know she had a husband named James, who died before she did. She had an address on Ford Street near Woodward in Highland Park, a couple blocks north of the Davison Highway. That's about it, however, because as with several other victims, no one could be reached to speak for her for this book. So let's get right into it from the killer's perspective.

He remembered it as the night of the last big snowfall they had that year, in 1992. Likely it was March. Maybe April. Maybe even February. She was too decomposed to tell. But the building was last checked on February 20, so it had to be after that.

He was sitting at the bus stop at Woodward and Cortland Street, a few blocks south of the Davison. A woman walked past. Five-foot-three and about a hundred fifteen pounds, he guessed. Maybe forty years old. He remembered blue boots, a blue skirt and a brown jacket. His memory was a little faultier than usual with this incident.

"How are you doing?" he asked her.

"Alright. What are you getting into?"

"You. I've got something to smoke. Can we smoke it together?"

"Do you have a place?"

"We can go right next door to the church," he said. The building he was referring to was a three-unit storefront structure on the west side of Woodward between Cortland and Richton streets. Of the three units, the one on the north side of the building was occupied by a soup kitchen, called "SPIN," which stood for Serving People in Need. It had been a bank at one time. The center unit, which had once been a restaurant and a politician's headquarters, and the unit on the south side of the building were both vacant. There were items in the center unit indicating a "Refreshing Spring Tabernacle" had once occupied the space, as well. In his psychiatric exams, Atkins remembered telling the woman that he worked in the building, and he remembered smelling that there was construction going on there at the time of this incident.

So they went to the front door. It had a lock, but you could just pull the screens right out and open the front door, he explained to police. They stepped inside the building, into the center unit, and he closed the door behind them. She stood against the wall, and he grabbed her feet out from under her. He sat on her chest and started to choke her. She passed out pretty quickly, and he started to undress her. She was not wearing underwear, he said. But he said she wasn't wearing socks either, and he was incorrect about that.

They must have been near the windows just north of the entrance, because he then dragged her over to where there was some debris in another part of the room "so no one could see me."

"You don't have to do this," she pleaded when she came to. "You don't have to do this."

"Shut up, bitch."

He said she didn't put up much of a fight after that. He raped her.

"Stop it, son," he remembered her repeatedly saying. "Stop it, son." She tried to pry his hands from her neck but passed out again.

He continued to rape her vaginally, then anally. Once he ejaculated, he started choking her again. She then appeared to be dead. He tied a plastic bag over her head (in his psych exam he remembered using multiple bags). Once he had tied the bag(s) tight, he continued choking her. "Die, bitch," he said as he watched her.

When he was sure she was dead, he placed her body near some garbage and debris and piled some of it on top of her, then left.

It was months before Joanne was found at 12223 Woodward in Highland Park. It was June 15, 1992, a warm day, upper seventies. Neighbors had been noticing a smell coming out of the building.

Only the dark velvet high-heeled boots Joanne was still wearing could be seen sticking out from under a pile of cardboard boxes in the northeast corner of the front room of the building's center unit. She was lying on a pile of garbage. She had two plastic bags tied over her head and around her neck, a white one with a black one over it. She had panties around her left ankle and her hands were tied behind her back with a bra.

Lying on her body was a blue sweatshirt that said, "Don't worry, be happy."

BRENDA MITCHELL

"Woman found dead of drug overdose," the small headline read when Brenda Mitchell was found in April 1992. Actually, we called that a "header" in the news biz, not even a headline, and the whole bit was merely a news brief on the right rail of page 3C, local news section. For cause, one of her initial death certificates read "Pending – acute cocaine and alcohol abuse." Maybe it was the fact that she wasn't bound and gagged like the other victims, and she was partially clothed. Maybe it was just a mistake. But her mother took exception to that, as she made clear to the press a couple years later at the trial. No, it was not a drug overdose. It was murder.

Brenda was born in May 1953 (though one of her death certificates says 1951) to Booker and Maggie Mitchell. She had an older brother, Fred, and an older sister, Dianne, as well as a younger brother, Frankie. They grew up on the east side, on Dean Avenue between Outer Drive and Eight Mile Road. Brenda graduated from Central High School. She seemed headed in the right direction, completing training to become a nurses' aide. But soon after she moved out of the house at age nineteen, she got into drugs. When she had her first baby, she brought him to her mom to raise. That boy would be age sixteen at time of her death and would be quoted in the media as her killer's trial was under way. Brenda also had another child.

Brenda's heroin and cocaine problem found her living at the Hotel Granwood, a four-story, eighty-unit, brick residential hotel that once sat at Woodward and West Grand Street, north of the Davison Highway. She had a tough time with rent, though, and reportedly had just moved back to her mom's place on Dean. Her family members estimated they last saw her on April 7 or 8, 1992, though one report says she had been gone a couple days longer.

***

Maggie Mitchell said this man knew her daughter, that they had smoked crack together at the "motel on Woodward." She was likely referring to the Granwood, but it's unclear if she was remembering Atkins correctly, because in his statement for the crime, he seemed to indicate he was meeting Brenda for the first time.

He remembered it as the spring, just getting warm. It was nighttime, and he was walking north on Woodward. He was looking to score some drugs, and at Pasadena Street, a block north of West Grand, a woman approached him and asked what he was doing tonight. He described her as in her middle forties, about five foot tall, and very slim. She was wearing beige pants and a beige jacket. She was looking for something to smoke and volunteered her services to him.

"Let's see what happens," he told her.

She took them to a house on Pasadena where they got twenty dollars' worth of crack. She told him she lived at the Granwood. They cut through the alley between the hotel and an abandoned house on West Grand. That's when he grabbed her from behind, his hand over her mouth, and dragged her to the back of the empty house, taking her up the steps and in through the kitchen. He then took her into the living room, where there was a box spring lying on the floor. He threw her down and started to choke her.

But this was not going to be a choke-and-repeat scenario as with his other victims. "She went out easily and died right then and there," he told police.

He partially undressed her, leaving her blouse on, and raped her vaginally and anally. He ejaculated. He checked to make sure she was dead, put the box spring on top of her, and left. When describing this incident during his psychiatric exams, he said he then went to the crack house where he was staying, smoked and went to sleep.

Did this woman say anything to you, police asked.

"No, she didn't have a chance."

Brenda Mitchell was found on April 9, 1992, inside an abandoned house at 26 West Grand in Highland Park. She was lying face down, with blood coming out of her nose, with a mattress and box spring on top of her (though the police reports varied, and Atkins only recalled a box spring). She was wearing a yellow sweater, a cream-colored blouse that was open, and no pants or underwear. She did have on white ankle-length socks. On her left pinky finger she wore a gold-colored ring with an "M" on it. There were fecal smears on her legs, as the medical examiner would note. Red toenail polish. She was five-foot-four and one hundred fifteen pounds, small like so many of the other women in this case.

She was Unknown Female No. 28 until her fingerprints determined her identity, though word was getting around at this scene, and one of the two women who alerted police to the body thought this looked like the sister of someone they knew, Dianne Mitchell. Dianne, Frankie and Fred all came to the scene that night.

The officer at the scene could see no clear cause of death, but police knew this spot as a place for drugs and prostitution. One did note that she appeared to be beaten about the face.

They had no idea, though, as they were at the house that night, that this woman's killer was right across the street.

Watching. He had walked by the house that morning, around six or seven a.m., when no one was there. It was likely the day after he killed her, based on the statement of the woman who found her. So now here he was again, so close by as they processed the scene.

Frankie ID'd Brenda's body at the morgue. She was buried at Lincoln Memorial Park in the eastern suburb of Mt. Clemens. After her killer was arrested to much media fanfare four months later, Maggie Mitchell called Highland Park police and learned that he had confessed to killing Brenda.

"I had to call them to find that out," she told *The Detroit News* for the August 26, 1992, edition. "They never called me, and they haven't officially changed the cause of death. … She was found with blood on her nose, nude from the waist down, with a mattress over her face, and they called that an 'overdose.'"

On August 28, the medical examiner's office issued a new report listing her manner of death as homicide, with the cause as asphyxia by strangulation.

OCINENA (CC) WAYMER

For all they knew, she could have been lying there as long as three months. May 1992 was when her grandmother, Ruby, last saw her, and that was at Ruby's apartment on Manchester Parkway. Ruby filed a missing person's report on her in June. And police did not know where she was until her killer revealed it.

Ocinena Waymer, nicknamed CC or CeCe, was born in October 1969. She lived at Ford Street and Second Avenue in Highland Park, west of Woodward, in the same block as her grandmother's apartment, just a block or so from Joanne O'Rourke's address of record and just a few blocks from where Valerie Chalk grew up in the other direction. She was single, apparently with no kids. She had a sister named Charee. When Ruby last saw CC, whom she knew had an issue with crack, CC had called a man named Wayne on the phone, then left, saying she had to go get her sweater.

***

He said they called her CC, or Cecilia. Or even Ceilia. He had known her for about four or five months. Had seen her around. She hung out at Grand and Woodward in Highland Park, he said. He described her quite accurately as five-foot-six and one hundred twenty or one hundred thirty pounds, with a medium build, dark skin and short hair. About thirty years old, he said — he was on the high side for that.

He said it was late June, though later court testimony would put the incident at the beginning of June. He was walking north on Woodward at about three or four a.m. when he saw her at Grand. He remembered her wearing a white skirt and blouse "hooked together." She asked him if he had a lighter, and he said yes. She led him to a garage behind the Popeye's Chicken. She stayed with her boyfriend, she explained, so that's why they couldn't go to her place.

When they entered the garage, which had an open large sliding door on the east side, he gave her the lighter. She started smoking the crack and gave him some.

"What are you doing out here, CC?"

"I'm that bitch," she replied.

"Right. You that bitch."

She started to flirt with him, he said. She pulled up her skirt and showed him a bare bottom without any underwear. She kept repeating, "I'm that bitch."

Then he grabbed her from behind, put his hand over her mouth and grabbed her arms with his other hand. He threw her on the ground.

"You're right – you're that bitch," he told her as he started to choke her. She was face up, and he put his thumbs over the front of her neck as with the other women, interlocking his fingers behind her neck.

When she passed out, he took her belt, which he remembered as black plastic, and tied her hands behind her back, "criss-crossed." He would have used her bra, but she wasn't wearing one, he said. He ripped her blouse in the back while they were struggling.

Her hands then came loose and she woke up, so he choked her again, face down this time, continuing to tell her, "you're that bitch." After that, he dragged her to the steps that led to the garage's basement.

"That's when I found this box with a cord inside," he told police. He used the cord to choke her this time, and she passed out again. Then he tied her hands again with the belt.

"I went into this little pouch I had on," he said. "I pulled out this rubber, latex kind. She was still gasping for air, she lying on her stomach."

He raped her. After he ejaculated, he continued to choke her with the electric cord. When she appeared to be dead, he did his customary checks – pulse, heartbeat, stomach. He threw her down the stairs to the basement, then threw a cardboard box over her.

As he was leaving the garage, he felt blood running down his right leg. He went to Detroit Receiving Hospital and was treated in the emergency room with five stitches in his leg. He didn't realize he got injured in their struggle.

When he was arrested in August, he gave police the tipoff during his questioning that there was a female they did not yet know about. CC was then found at the bottom of the basement stairs of a vacant, brown-brick, auto-repair garage at 20 West Grand near Pasadena Street in Highland Park on August 21, 1992. The building was behind a Popeye's on Woodward at the time; nowadays there's something else there. It was about two blocks south of where CC lived, as well as next to where Brenda Mitchell was found.

CC was skeletonized. "No internal organs," the medical examiner noted. There was a cloth gag on her, and around her neck was the electric cord of a can opener – with the can opener still attached. Her wrists were bound. A white sandal was still on her left foot. Listed on record as five-foot-five, her one-hundred-twenty-five-pound frame was down to just sixty-four pounds at that point. She became Unknown Female No. 63.

TELLING HER STORY AT LAST: MARGIE OSBORN

She loves Barbie dolls, Marilyn Manson and her pet rats, one of them affectionately named Sushigirl. She has kids, and she has been with the same loving man for more than three decades. For her birthday, she asked in Facebook for donations to the Missing Murdered Indigenous Women Coalition of North Carolina. She lives a normal life, with a diverse set of interests. Her family is diverse, too – a blend of color.

For Margie Osborn, this is all quite amazing, because she might not be here at all, if things had gone differently during one particular incident in her younger years. At only age fifteen, she survived an encounter that she later realized could have made her the very first victim of the Highland Park Strangler. Most people who are closest to her still don't know this about her. She has kept this dark, ugly secret from almost everyone for many years.

Born in the mid-1970s, Margie was only a teenager when she got into drugs and would wander Woodward Ave looking for some action. She was from the area of Six and Seven Mile roads, and it was a pretty rough place. "If a person was from there, it was the norm to see drugs and violence," Margie said when contacted in 2022 for this book.

"At that time I dropped out and ran away from home, because at that time I was living in Ferndale," she said. "And I ran to my hometown, which is Highland Park. Well, people consider Seven Mile a part of Highland Park, because they share the same zip code."

She started doing drugs at the age of fourteen. "So when I went to the Woodward area, I started to prostitute myself, not by choice; I was sold into it when I ran from home. But that was the period of time when I met that monster."

"This was me, around the time of my encounter with Atkins," Margie says of this yearbook photo, courtesy of Margie Osborn.

Margie's incident with Benjamin Atkins occurred before any of his other known attacks, which, as in the case of Darlene Saunders, could have worked in her favor, as he had not yet polished his technique. Also as with Darlene, he was not a stranger to her; she had seen him around Woodward Ave. Knew the place where he occasionally worked. Other places where he hung out.

"It was late December of 1990," Margie said. "I remember he asked me if I wanted to get high with him, and I said sure, I have nothing else to do. So we go to this abandoned house right off of Woodward." The side street, Margie does not recall.

It wasn't long before things went wrong. "Soon as he took a hit of crack, his whole demeanor turned evil. It was like he was the devil himself. Next thing I know, he hit me in the face, saying to me, 'I'm gonna kill you, bitch.' I was shocked and scared.

"So he tried to grab me by the throat. But my street smarts kicked in. I was thinking about any way to get away from him, so the one thing that saved me was my gift to gab. I'm lying to him about me having a baby, my family was looking for me, and the only thing that saved me was when I told him, 'Look, take my money.' When I said that, it was like he came back into sanity. But after I gave him whatever money I had, he socked me in the jaw and left."

This young girl was still very scared. "I waited to make sure he was gone. I never went back to the pizza place he worked at, and I kept this to myself for years."

She didn't go to the police. She felt too much shame – another similarity with Darlene's experience. She didn't tell her family, even the mother who later, as bodies would turn up and he would become known as the Woodward Corridor Killer and the Highland Park Strangler, actually worried that her daughter could become the next victim. Her mother knew full well that she was out there living that life.

"I remember my mother saying that she used to look for me in the morgue, when the killings happened. But I never told her that I actually survived Atkins."

Margie saw Atkins one more time after the attack, though he didn't see her.

"The cops really don't know how far he went on Woodward," Margie said. "I had seen him by the Seven Mile area more than once, buying dope. I even spoke to him a few times, because I also was on drugs at that time, and I even ate pizza from where he used to work at. At first, I didn't feel any bad vibes off of him."

She remembered the pizza place Atkins worked at as being on Woodward and Glendale Avenue. An orange building with the inside trimmed in black. It was torn down years ago, she said, after he was arrested. A few other places Atkins frequented were still standing when Margie spoke for this book. "Not many places but a few," she said.

"Back then people would go up and down Woodward for drugs," she said. "I even saw people from the Cass Corridor come to the neighborhood for drugs. Prostitution was bad during that time, and I saw so many things go on in that neighborhood.

"I know those places because I used to go to some of the same places he used to score his drugs from. One I can remember was Ferris and Woodward area, and by Cortland and Woodward right by where the old Monterey hotel was. That's what we called it back then. And by the old Cavalier Motel. That place was right by the hotel he killed his victims. A lot of those places are gone but I remember where they used to be. I even remember the place where he almost got me; it's torn down, though.

"A lot of people used to get creeped out when he got high, because he would get mad, saying all women were hoes, all kinds of horrible things."

Besides the attack, there was another particular time, just a few weeks earlier, when Atkins gave her the chills.

"I was walking down Woodward trying to catch a trick, and this was late at night. I was with a friend of mine. As we were walking, he was following us, down toward where the old Sears building used to be. We ended up going to this gas station close by, because it was creepy how he was following us. It was like a lion stalking its prey. He was just creepy; he gave off those vibes."

There was no questioning the fact that neither Margie nor her friend would bother reporting this other incident – or any creepy one – to police. It's the same old story, and every female out there on the streets knows it. It has happened to prostitutes for a long, long time. "That's sad how law enforcement doesn't take a street person seriously," Margie said.

No nonchalance from law enforcement or anyone else can make it less painful. "When a person goes through that kind of traumatic issue," Margie said, "it always lingers. Although it was decades, I still find myself thinking about that time, and why he didn't kill me. Every time I passed by the Howard Johnson site, I always would instantly look at it and a cold chill would run over me. I would always think that it could've been me that would've ended up there."

Still, she stuffed the secret, and kept moving forward, somehow. "I was too ashamed to talk about it. My children don't know the details but heard through my family that I encountered Atkins."

Margie left the lifestyle, but it took a while. This encounter with Atkins did not quite cure it for her.

"I stayed in the streets until I was about thirty-three. Had another terrifying incident that I survived, and that's when I left the streets, because I felt my luck was going to run out."

It was 2009 when she had another incident with a monster.

"The last incident, the guy grabbed at my throat, but he only got me by my jacket collar, and he forgot to lock the car door. So I opened the door, and he only had me by the jacket. I left my shoes, and I ran and hid between abandoned houses that were around, and when I was hiding, I could see him circling around looking for me, so I stayed hidden for what seemed like eternity. And when I knew he was gone, I walked a mile home barefoot and scared. This guy, he put me in the mind of Atkins, his M.O., because when he got me somewhere dark, he started to act crazy, called me all kinds of names."

Margie has seen what's been reported about Atkins over the years, what was said about him by her fellow survivor, Darlene Saunders. What was understood, or not understood, about this fast-moving serial killer with national notoriety.

She has her own perspective, informed by talking to him on the street before any of the other stuff happened. Observing him, like a normal Joe, part of the dark landscape of that drug-infested culture. She begs to differ on a few of the things she has seen and heard.

"He wasn't gay," she said. "He used that lie to deflect his crimes. I didn't get any impression on his sexual orientation. He did it as an act; he wasn't gay. I'd seen him more so interact with women, but the only time I saw him acting strange was when I got high with him."

But, she said, "Everything else was true; he also had a bad childhood."

Margie knew him by the name Tony, though she got that from others on the street; he never directly told her his name. And he never said anything about his family directly to her, she said.

"He was a very bad person," she said. "He changed, soon as he got high. His facial expression was very chilling and cold. I still got a small scar on my arm from when he grabbed my left arm. I am surprised that I made it through the ordeal."

As Margie looks back at that time when she was a teenager, it carries some ironies you could scarcely believe.

"Do you remember the serial killer they just busted in 2019? DeAngelo Martin?" she asked this author. "I was friends with one of his victims as a teen, and she introduced me to crack."

Arrested after police were notified to a decomposing body found inside a vacant Detroit home on June 5, 2019, DeAngelo Martin pled guilty to the murders of four women and the rape and sexual assault of ten others in September 2022. He's now serving out his sentences. Margie's friend was named Yvonne Cobern, suspected to be Martin's final victim and found rolled up in carpet in an abandoned house on the east side of the city that same month as his arrest.

It's almost unfathomable, knowing that two close friends each encountered a different notorious serial killer, and unfortunately only one lived to tell about it. But the irony doesn't end there. One of Martin's known victims was actually Margie's cousin, Annetta Nelson.

In the decades that have passed since Atkins attacked her, and in the years since her departure from the street, life for Margie has settled quite a lot. She has stability. So she doesn't look back all that often. But she is glad to get something like this off her chest.

"Now I have a great support system, I have my dad, my husband, and great friends," she said. "It is a tragic thing I saw over the years. God was by my side during my darkest hour."

THE HUNT FOR A KILLER

You might recall that aforementioned Justice Augustus Woodward, who in the early 1800s first platted what would become known as Woodward Avenue. Well, this same judge also attempted to start a town at what is now Woodward Ave and Highland Street, a few miles north of the spokes-in-a-wheel design he envisioned in Detroit. He bought a large ridge in a farming community in 1818, called it Woodwardville in 1825. But the town withered on the vine. Then another Detroit judge tried to develop the same spot as a community in 1836, calling it Cassandra. No-go on that, as well. Rather ironic, then, that the village of Highland Park that finally emerged there in 1889 is not exactly flourishing these days, either.

The enclave – nestled within the City of Detroit just like another nearby small city, Hamtramck – was intended to flourish, of course. Henry Ford plopped a big ole automotive plant there in 1909 – you'd have to expect prosperity with that, right? The population surged, and the village became a city in 1918, reportedly to protect it financially from the expanding Detroit around it. The Chrysler Corporation was founded in Highland Park in 1925, bringing more health. But darkness followed for the burgeoning city. A KKK-related vigilante group moved in, drawing membership from high places and weaving murders and conspiracies into the city's history. With a changing economy Ford started closing down some of its operations. Detroit's 1967 riots caused white flight from Highland Park just as it did from Detroit, and the two cities have shared a Black majority demographic since then. Then Chrysler moved its headquarters out of Highland Park in the 1990s. Even Dutch elm disease changed the landscape of what was nicknamed "The City of Trees." In 1991, there were more than twenty thousand residents; in 2020 that number was less than ten thousand.

The small city's dire financial straits prompted the State of Michigan to appoint an emergency manager for it in the first decade of the 2000s. City workers were laid off. Buildings such as the landmark McGregor Public Library were closed. Streetlights came down due to unpaid electric bills. And crime didn't mind a bit.

Back when the city was growing in the 1910s and 1920s, municipal buildings were constructed on Gerald Street off Woodward. The Highland Park Police Department was headquartered at 25 Gerald Street in 1917 and remained there for years. In the 1980s, the city merged its police and fire departments into a public safety department. So it was one crew that managed the emergencies for this small city, just three square miles in size, with Woodward Ave at its center and the Davison Freeway cutting through the other way, east and west.

John Mattox was the director of Highland Park's Public Safety Department at the time of the Benjamin Atkins case. As such, he was quoted a lot in the media. Mattox worked in the Highland Park force "thirty years, two months, and one day," as he promptly put it when reached via phone for this book in 2022, now settled into retirement. He started out as a patrolman in HP and spent his whole career serving this community in which he was raised. He graduated from the original Highland Park High School, before the newer one was built on Woodward Ave. He attended various other schooling, including University of Detroit Mercy (where he had classes with Benny Napoleon, who would go on to become Detroit's police chief) and a couple months at the well-known FBI academy where so many other officers got useful cred for their careers. He saw lots of changes in his city over the years. The politics were the worst of what he saw, he said, and we'll get into that later. But he did explain a bit more about the configuration of the Public Safety Department. How that worked, in contrast to a standard city police department.

"You had some divisions there," Mattox said. "Basically, the veteran officers had an opportunity to choose what side. The firemen basically wanted to stay firemen. The policemen wanted to stay policemen. The younger officers in the patrol division and the firefighting division didn't have that option. They were assigned to each side. From time to time would have to go out and do patrol work, or if they were doing patrol work, respond to a fire, also, which means you carried your gear with you. And if they had a fire, as needed you would respond with it. It's something that a lot of newer agencies have gone to because of cost and manpower. And it works well in a newer community, a brand-new community, but not in an older community. Because you have a combination of homes, apartments, factories and all this throughout the city, where if you go to a newer community, it's mostly residential and the factories are in a given area. One section is residential and in the next block is a factory. And everything would be new, which means that more than likely it was up to code and had less of an opportunity to have some of the old problems that you have in older communities. Older homes may not have some of the same features that they have now in these newer homes."

Larry Beller, who was tapped to work the Atkins case when he was a patrol sergeant for HP Public Safety, was born and raised in Detroit. He worked at his uncle's gas station in Highland Park after school when he was thirteen, then he bought and operated his own gas stations as an adult. He also owned a bar up north for a time. But he felt a pull to law enforcement. He applied to departments around Detroit and Dearborn, but one told him he had a bad eye and another said he was too tall (because the more-than-six-foot Beller could not sit in a police car wearing a hat, believe it or not; "the chief was about five-eight, so maybe that had something to do with it," Beller adds with a laugh). He finally got onto the HP force when he was thirty and spent his police career there. He worked in the building on Gerald Street. "They closed that, and we moved into the city hall," he said, "and they moved the city hall down on Woodward Avenue, on the south end there." That move was years after the Atkins case, however.

Beller made lieutenant in 1994, and he was in charge of the detective division. He remembered the public safety configuration with a bit of a head shake, as we discussed it over lunch in 2022: "The thing is, as a detective you wore a shirt and tie, and a suit or a sport coat. You'd go fight a fire, and you're wringing wet with sweat and smoke. So you'd come out, your white shirt is gray. You've got to wear it the rest of the day if you don't have a spare there."

At that same lunch was Beller's colleague Jim Dobson, officer in charge of the Atkins case. Like Mattox, he was quoted in the news a lot during the case. Also like Mattox, Dobson was a local boy, born and raised in Highland Park. Mattox, Dobson and Beller did note that at the time of the case Highland Park still had a detective staff that did not respond to fire. But for the most part, it was an ordeal at times, to juggle responsibilities. Dobson shared his own take on the public safety thing:

"That worked fine in some places where you don't have a high incidence of crime and a high incidence of fire. But in Highland Park, you had both. There were times where you'd go down, get your prisoner, bring him up, start talking to him, and the alarm would go off, you'd have to say, 'Aw!' You'd put him back in the cage, go fight the fire, and you'd come back and you'd be like this!" He threw up his hands in a wearied, frustrated gesture. "You'd have to continue on. ... You're not worth a nickel. You'd fight a fire for two hours or whatever."

Still, the department had a reputation for being pretty tough. "They told us at the Eleventh Precinct, do not cross Six Mile," one retired Detroit police officer said. The joke for the Eleventh and Twelfth Precincts: Chase 'em to Highland Park and let them take care of it.

HPPS had only about a hundred officers in 1991. Then they laid off eight officers to make that ninety-two, Mattox remembered. And that staff of ninety-two, serving a population of about twenty thousand, had no idea they were about to be thrust into the investigation of a fast-moving serial killer, one that would take the air out of their lungs at times – much like he did with his victims – and even put them in the national spotlight.

They also had no idea they had just arrested this killer, on October 11, 1991, for trespassing on and vandalizing city property at 12100 Woodward. Atkins and a thirty-nine-year-old Highland Park man named Diosdado were seen breaking into and taking a sledgehammer to the building and were then found hiding in the building having in their possession screwdrivers (sometimes called "burglar bars," as a cop in Georgia once told this author). Atkins had no address on record at the time and had a prior charge of littering in 1989. For the trespassing charge, he failed to appear at his arraignment on November 4 and a warrant was issued with a bond of a hundred and fifty dollars.

And 12100 Woodward, by the way, was the Monterey Motel.

THE FIRST BROAD BRUSHSTROKES

You can see in our studies of the thirteen women known to have been assaulted by Benjamin Thomas Atkins, aka Tony, for the majority who did not survive, he made some good attempts to conceal their bodies. So good that many of them lay dead for months. It was mid-December 1991 before one would be found. Three others were likely dead at that point but undiscovered.

At seven a.m. on Saturday, December 14, 1991, Detective Sergeant Jim Dobson got the call at home. Report to an apparent homicide scene at 170 Elmhurst, near Third Avenue, a couple blocks west of Woodward. Body of an unknown female found.

Dobson arrived on the scene at eight-twenty a.m. with Detective William McLean, and other officers followed. They entered the vacant apartment building through a rear door that was wide open, then descended to the basement via a green cloth chair that had been placed there for the missing stairs. The building was cold and dark. No heat, no lights.

The woman was nude, lying on her back on the concrete floor, head pointed northeast, with her mouth gagged and her hands tied behind her back with a bra and part of a shirt. She had a scrape mark on the left side of her face and on her left shoulder. Blood had pooled and dried around her head, where she had a one-inch gash. It looked, from the dust patterns on the floor, like she may have been dragged a few feet. Lying nearby were fake fingernails and a gold-colored perfume bottle. There was also some clothing lying west of the body, and it looked like it was ripped: A red coat, some jeans (maybe bib overalls?). A couple dimes lay there. A lighter. A couple clothing buttons. And two high-top black shoes, one of them missing its laces. Partial footprints showed in the dust of the floor, south of the body.

There were several pieces of plywood lying on the floor of the southeast part of this basement room. Dobson thought there may be a drop of blood near the boards. He sketched the scene in his report, and he and the other officers went about surveying some folks in the neighborhood. One heard three women and two men fighting a couple days before. She also saw a mysterious male in a thick, blue, three-quarter-length coat ("Triple Fat Goose," the description in the police report read) lurking around a couple times recently. He had a bushy moustache and a goatee, she told police. About thirty-six years old, five-foot-six and maybe one hundred thirty pounds. She saw him in the first week of December and asked him what he was doing, and he said he was just taking a shortcut through the yard between her house and the vacant building. She told him not to do that. She felt he was lying. A few days later, she saw him at Woodward and West Grand. (There is such a thing as a "Triple F.A.T. Goose" brand jacket, by the way, existing to this day, a sort of puffy down jacket.)

An evidence tech arrived at eight-forty-five a.m. to process and sketch the scene, logging and bagging several items: torn pieces of Lee blue jean overalls and three metal buttons marked Lee found separately, a torn Bassett-Walker sweatshirt size XL, blue Hang Ten underwear size 32/34, a torn white T-shirt, a pair of black "North Coast Footage" shoes/boots size 7.5, three red fake fingernails, a bottle of nail glue, a bottle of Avon "Candid" cologne, a pair of gold-colored pierced earrings, a white tube sock, a yellow cigarette lighter, a yellow five-inch comb, a dime, and blood samples. The tricky thing about collecting evidence from a crime scene at an abandoned building like this, as former Public Safety Director John Mattox said, is that you have no way of knowing what might pertain to the crime and what might have been there a while, just left behind by somebody else. It's particularly true in a building known to be used by prostitutes and/or transients. Normally at a crime scene, you have to look for what's different. What's out of place. Here, there's all kinds of stuff out of place. You could be gathering a bunch of miscellaneous trash having nothing to do with your crime. But gather it, you must.

The bindings from the woman's hands, as well as the gag from her mouth, were processed as evidence, along with nail clippings and hair samples. Three rolls of film were shot of the scene.

She was given Case No. 10197-91 and was the 48th unknown female found dead in Wayne County in 1991. She was identified later that day or the next day as Debbie Ann Friday. Dobson and his crew reached out to her family members, as well as her boyfriend, Calvin. They learned when she was last seen, which was only the day before she was found, and that she had a drug problem. They already knew her, though, as a prostitute working the area.

On December 18, the medical examiner determined that Debbie was killed by strangulation. She also showed contusions on her neck, scalp, lip and right elbow. She had postmortem abrasions on her face, right breast and right shoulder. Her tox screens were positive for cocaine but negative for alcohol, barbiturates, morphine, benzodiazepines.

"Body found in building" read the small brief on the right rail of page 3C, the local/city news, of the Sunday, December 15 edition of *The Detroit News*.

Highland Park, considered a small town by so many who have lived there, would see only about twenty homicides a year around that time. The FBI's crime stats show twenty-one homicides reported in HP in 1990, twenty-two in 1991, then nineteen in 1992. So when Debbie Friday was found, HPPS wanted to know what kind of animal would do this. Later that same month, though, unbeknownst to the Highland Park officers, the case would hop a jurisdictional line into the behemoth of a neighbor that surrounded them. While HP officers were putting their time and energy into the type of case that didn't happen all that often for them, Detroit Police were about to log yet another dead prostitute. She would be one of the six hundred and fifteen homicides reported in Detroit in 1991.

It was December 30, a cold and cloudy day. The owner of the building at 12 Alger, located at Woodward about a mile or so south of Highland Park, had just gotten back from vacation and wanted to check on his buildings. First name Sam, he lived up in Southfield, north of Detroit, and worked for Ford Motor Co. in the western suburb of Dearborn. He owned this building and the one next door. He had last been there earlier in the month, on December 19, to make sure everything was OK. It was then. It wasn't now.

Sam and the man who was with him that day, Willie, hightailed it to the check-cashing place next door on Woodward and had them call 911. Dead woman found inside a building. They had no idea who this woman was, had never seen her before. It was about eleven-thirty a.m.

Officers Benjamin Koyton and Danny Marshall of DPD's Thirteen Precinct arrived and went inside the building, then radioed it in. Sergeants Thomas Wilk and James Bivens of the Homicide Section arrived. An evidence tech, Paul Kulesa, followed.

It was a three-story brick building with a wooden front door on the north side bearing a padlock that had been forced open. The apartment was marked as No. 2. Once police stepped inside the foyer, with no lights on and just daylight filtering in, they saw fresh human feces on the floor to their left. In front of that was what looked at first like a table leg propped up against the wall. There was a red substance near the bottom of the table leg, but police didn't think it looked like blood. The leg turned out to be a spindle from the handrail in the stairwell going up to the apartment's second floor. From the foyer, police followed the small hallway to a door leading to the basement. That's when they saw her.

Inside the building was twenty-eight degrees, the reports say, and the woman's body was frozen. She was lying on the steps to the basement, on her back, with her upper torso on the steps and the rest of her on the landing where the stairs made a right turn and continued downward. She was nude except for a sock on her left foot. The matching sock was in her mouth. Her hands were bound behind her back with a dirty white shoestring. There were several cardboard boxes near her feet on the landing. Also lying next to her, a McDonald's foam container. She had bruises on her face and neck and "some type of damage to vagina and/or anus," Bivens noted on his report. There was blood on her privates.

A torn shirt, white with multicolored stripes, was lying on the first step leading from the landing. Other pieces of the shirt were found behind the door of the kitchen that was further down the hall. Another piece was found in the foyer. A black waist-length coat and red pants were found in the kitchen. The coat had a cigarette butt on it. A dirty white gym shoe was found in the kitchen, too, with the shoelace tied, and it looked just like the shoelace binding the victim. The stove in the kitchen was overturned. On the floor of the foyer police also found a yellow envelope with a phone number and "$10,000" written on it. In a room on the other side of the kitchen, a spent nine-mm shell casing lay on the floor. It looked old, but police had the evidence tech take it anyway.

They kept Sam and Willie at the scene, talked with them further, determined they had nothing to do with this. After officers left the building, they checked with some of the prostitutes who were out on Woodward. A couple of them had seen the woman in the area but didn't know her name or where she lived. One recognized her from working "the stroll" on Woodward near Burlingame. Police went there and could find just one prostitute to show the woman's photo to; nope, she didn't know her.

The evidence tech collected the wood spindle that came from the stairwell, the McDonald's foam container, a cardboard box, several pieces of clothing including the black jacket and a warmup suit, a gray clothing button found at the top of the stairs, the cigarette butt, the envelope, the shell casing. The fast-food container and the envelope in particular would be checked for prints in DPD's crime lab in the second week of February with no results. Blood and hair samples and swabs, as well as fingernail clippings, from the victim were sent to the lab. She had type A blood. No trace evidence was found under the fingernails. A seminal fluid stain was discovered on the black coat – it was the only noteworthy finding from the several items taken from the scene, though the sock from her mouth was bloodstained. The substance on the stairwell spindle turned out to not be blood.

Asphyxia from strangulation, the medical examiner found. There were abrasions and contusions around her neck from a ligature, along with multiple contusions on her head and chest from being beaten. "The manner of death was a homicide," Dr. Laning Davidson said. Like Debbie Friday, this woman showed only cocaine on her tox screens.

By the time police spoke with a woman named Marlene on the afternoon of January 2, Unknown Female No. 52 had become Bertha Jean Mason, identified by her boyfriend, William. Marlene said Bertha had stopped by her place in the first week of December at around dawn, stayed about a half-hour, then left to get some money from her "old man." She never saw Bertha again, but she did see her "old man" out looking for her (Marlene is likely the woman William mentioned as Mary, as she fits the description to a T). She said Bertha worked the area of Holbrook Avenue, two blocks north of Alger, and Philadelphia, two blocks south. Bertha's grandmother Graty said the last time she saw her was the first week of December.

Police also talked with a prostitute named Brenda, who said she last saw Bertha just before Christmas, noting glibly to her at the time that they only had a couple shopping days left. Bertha was new to the area, she said; she had only seen her around a couple times. That last time, she remembered Bertha wearing a dark short jacket. Brenda herself had gone with a john into 12 Alger on December 23. It was a creepy incident that caused her to run out right after their business was conducted. This guy was a "regular walker," she told police; she had seen him about five times before, but for whatever reason this time she was scared. Partly because, she told police, you just don't know what these johns are going to do. She remembered the front door of the apartment being wide open, its padlock just hanging there. They went up to the second floor, where there was a mattress. She described him as a Black male with medium brown skin, thirty-seven or thirty-eight, five-foot-nine, kind of a muscular build, maybe one hundred seventy to one hundred eighty pounds. He had a moustache and short nappy hair with a receding hairline. He had a gap in his teeth. He told Brenda he lived in an "AFC home on Taylor between Second and Woodward." He always seemed to wear the same clothing, she said, plaid or checkered pants, a three-quarter-length brown jacket, and one of those "Russian-looking" hats.

This guy told her one time that he hated prostitutes. He said his mother had been a prostitute. He seemed sad when he said it. "I tried to talk to him about it, but he just cut it off," she said.

DPD watched the area of Taylor Street for a man fitting the description of the one Brenda described. They talked to another prostitute named Kenyetta in early January, and she described a creepy dude that seemed to be the same guy. This guy wanted to take Kenyetta into the building on Alger, too. Police then spotted someone matching the description on Taylor, and detained and questioned him, but came up empty. He wasn't their guy.

When DPD interviewed Bertha's boyfriend William on January 2, after he had identified her at the morgue and as he relayed the details of that last night he saw her at the house, seeing her footprints leading away from the house, what he knew and didn't know, giving quite a bit of insight into their lives together, police asked him what restaurants Bertha might go to if she was out.

"She loved McDonald's," he replied.

***

Everett Monroe remembered it was raining that morning.

"I was at Homicide at the time," the retired Detroit cop said via phone in 2022. "And I remember I was working days, and Sergeant Kenny, Joanne Kenny, got a scene, which means that we have to respond to a homicide or whatever. I was working with Joanne that particular day. We responded to the scene, and we did our preliminary review of the scene."

But it was a messy affair for him and his partner.

"There was a lot of debris," he said. "And Joanne and I went and did like a survey, immediate area survey, and it was raining. I remember Joanne's stockings were all torn up from climbing through the building. And we ended up going and stopping by a store so she could go and get another pair of stockings. This was like early in the morning when we responded. The wall was there. A portion of the building was still – the outer structure was still intact. But you could see on the other end, they were tearing it down, and so forth. It was just a lot of debris, and she was laying on this pile of debris."

It was eight-twenty a.m. on January 3, 1992, when J&J Wrecking Co. had put in the call after seeing something strange in the rubble they were clearing of an abandoned house being torn down on Kenilworth. The house had been mostly demolished on December 17 or 18, as the crew recalled, and J&J had already hauled away one load. Now they were back to keep clearing the site. Amid the wood, plaster, concrete, dirt and mud, a woman lay on her back, partially clothed, with blood around her nose. She was lying against a chain-link fence in the backyard of the property. Monroe remembered he and his partner had to crawl through a window on a partially intact wall to get to her. She was described in one police report as wearing a plaid shirt in red, white and black or blue, along with a white coat, but no underwear or pants. Her body was pointed east, with one leg folded sideways and "scraped up." She had a thin build and dark complexion. The bulldozer driver told police he had checked the lot before beginning work that morning, so she had evidently been covered up at that point, then unearthed by the dozer.

A glimpse of the Kenilworth scene that day, with the body redacted. Photo from DPD files.

This site used to be a crack house, Detroit Police knew. One of the other DPD officers on the scene surmised in his report that she had been dumped there just a few days prior.

He figured she wouldn't have been there before December 18 when the wrecking crew, per its usual practice, checked the site before beginning demolition. (Atkins said he hid her body in a closet under the stairs, however.) On this January morning, the bulldozer driver said he checked the lot from the front and from the alley and didn't see her, so she was likely uncovered after they started working. The reporting officer speculated that her leg and nose injuries were due to the bulldozer, then went on to make an interesting note: "There were no signs of strangulation that I could see."

But it would turn out to be ligature strangulation, as the medical examiner found. The M.E. also found sperm in her vagina. Tox screens turned up negative for alcohol, barbiturates, cocaine, opiates and amphetamines.

Neighbors on Leicester Street couldn't tell police a thing, and the body remained a Jane Doe for a few months. Family members of missing girls around the area came to police to see if their girl was the one. A thirty-seven-year-old Detroit woman named Shirley, for instance, really felt like the photo of Unknown Female No. 1 looked like her cousin Deborah, who was missing since September and had been working the streets of Highland Park and along Cass in Detroit. Police ran fingerprints against several missing females.

On January 14, the Wayne County Medical Examiner's office faxed the information on this unknown female to Detective Sergeant Larry Beller of Highland Park Public Safety, to check against a missing person HPPS had. Four holes pierced in her right ear, one hole pierced in her left ear, and red-purple fingernail polish, the description sheet included, along with the vitals such as medium-length, straight, dark-brown hair and such. The M.E. had clarified that she was wearing a "100 percent acrylic 'wool' shirt, size 34, plaid, dark blue, red, light brown"; a "Ricki" brand sweater, size small, with red and blue stripes and a white collar; and a light gray nylon jacket with white fur around the hood. She was not HPPS' missing person, of course, and there was still no inkling the two municipalities were sharing a case.

Monroe, who spent more than twenty-five years with DPD, would go on a few years later to work the case of another big Detroit serial killer, John Eric Armstrong, as a member of the interagency Violent Crime Task Force. He was one of a handful of officers who interrogated Armstrong. His career in law enforcement later took him to Georgia to serve as a police chief, and his son, Everett Monroe II, has followed his footsteps into law enforcement – serving, ironically, with Highland Park as of this writing. But for the elder Monroe, the Atkins case, with that rainy day in 1992, still stands out.

"About a couple of days later, myself, Joanne, and Sergeant *[Kenneth]* Day, we were sitting down talking about this particular scene. And he made mention that he had a scene very similar where the lady had been strangled and there was a sock found in her mouth. And so, we were like, well, you know, it looked like this was going to be strangulation, as well."

DPD was starting to wonder if they had a serial on their hands. It was an uneasy feeling among the troops, but it was not necessarily shared by those higher-up at the department. At least not that they were willing to admit.

"Now, to backtrack," Monroe said, "there was a missing person report on our victim. And, you know, she was an average person, worked every day. And so forth and so on. And her husband made a report regarding her missing. And so that, we were able to tie the connection of the missing person and the body that we found, so it did not fit your typical street girl profile where a lot of people go, 'well, you know, this is a street girl,' and so forth and so on. So by me not really being assigned to a squad, I was bouncing around from squad to squad. So there was a period where the case was being worked, but I do remember that Sergeant

Day was very adamant that we got a serial killer going on out here. The Homicide detectives kind of talked together and started comparing notes, saying, this has got to be the same guy. He's got the signature mark of taking the socks off. Got strangulation. We've got crack involved in it. Street walkers. And everybody was like – well, not everybody, but I'll say the management of Homicide was like, 'oh, nah, it's too early to tell; yeah, we got a couple similarities in a couple cases, but, you know, we don't want to alarm the people.' Leadership was kind of saying, 'well, let's wait and see; it could be a copycat.' I mean, just the usual politics. But I think the investigators knew that we were looking for the same guy."

Reinforcement for their theory came later in January, when a thirty-seven-year-old Detroit man named Maurice was walking by the former Longfellow Nursing Center on the east side of Woodward, a block north of Kenilworth, and only a few blocks from his home. He noticed one of the plywood boards had been pulled up from this vacant building. He went home and got his tools, then returned to the building and went inside, thinking he could score some scrap metal. "I was in there a little while," he told police later that afternoon at headquarters at 1300 Beaubien. "At first, I seen a bulkiness in the corner of the room. I turned my flashlight on and seen that it was a body. I didn't touch nothing and left. I went outside to see if I seen a police car. I stood there about fifteen minutes. When none came by, I walked to the store and had them call police."

DPD arrived at three-o-five p.m. on January 25 and entered the brick building though a first-floor window on the south side (though another report says they forced a door to gain entry). They went up to the second floor, second room on the south side of the building. The room had three windows facing south, plywood covering them. There in the room was the nude, frozen body of a woman lying face down near the east wall of a bedroom, her head toward the south. The room temperature was recorded as twenty degrees on this snowy day. Her hands were tied behind her back with a yellow T-shirt, and she had a sweater wrapped around her face and neck. When the sweater was removed, a sock was discovered stuffed in her mouth. Litter was strewn everywhere. A mattress lay nearby. There was a bundle of clothing lying next to her head. Dirt and debris were on the backs of her legs and on her back. It looked to police like she had been rolled over postmortem. In the doorway, a small steak knife lay on the floor. "I doubt the knife has anything to do with this," Sergeant Danny Maynard noted in his report.

The evidence tech shot two rolls of film and collected several items from the scene, including the steak knife, a brown coat, a dark blue or black coat, a torn pair of blue jeans with a broken zipper, the yellow T-shirt, the stained multicolored sweater wrapped around her along with a white bra used as a binding, a white sock, a pair of white tennis shoes size 7, and a gold tone earring.

It was death by strangulation and suffocation, the M.E. determined for Unknown Female No. 10 of 1992. She joined four gunshot victims, someone who died in a house fire, and a handful of others on the medical examiner's daily case ledger for January 26.

People were going in and out of the building all the time, police heard as they surveyed residents of the cross street, Westminster. People who looked like they were homeless, one lady said. They were getting high there or engaging in prostitution. Another resident described one of the girls using that building as a slim, short, dark-complected female around age thirty, with big breasts and a couple missing teeth, nicknamed "Holler, Holler." She wasn't the victim, though – the resident had just seen her earlier that day. No one reported noticing anything unusual at the building recently.

The woman was quickly identified through her fingerprints as Vickie Truelove, a local prostitute police had been keeping tabs on as the witness to a drug murder. On January 27, her boyfriend Joe came to the station and told police the last time he saw her was the first week of December, when she was walking with a trick near Woodward. It was a guy in his late thirties with a medium complexion and a receding hair line, who bought crack from where Joe and Vickie were living on Henry Street. The guy had told Joe he was living off Woodward with his mother.

Vickie's tox screens came up negative for alcohol, barbiturates and morphine, positive for cocaine. On February 4, her nail clippings and hair samples, along with her binding clothing, were sent to the lab for processing. Nothing of any note was found. The other clothing found at the scene was sent to the lab on February 19 to check for any trace evidence.

So now DPD had three females – all of whom they knew or suspected were prostitutes – found strangled in less than a month's time. The public was still unaware there was a possible serial killer roaming the streets, but the evidence was undeniable for Sergeant Kenneth Day – officer in charge of the Truelove case – and others in the department. Ironically, *The Detroit News* had reported on New Year's Day 1992 that homicides in Detroit had surged in 1991. The story said the city logged at least six hundred ten homicides at that point, up five percent from 1990. In a "bloody December" alone, seventy-two people were slain. "We had a bad month," Homicide Inspector Gerald Stewart was quoted. It was small consolation that Washington, D.C., had just taken away Detroit's distinction of murder capital of the U.S.

Just three days after Vickie Truelove was found, on January 28, her killer again came on police radar. DPD officers were checking abandoned buildings in the area in their follow-up to this latest discovery. Several blocks south of their scene, at 20 E. Euclid, a vacant apartment building they knew prostitutes often used, they found what appeared to be a homeless man sleeping on a couch in a room on the second floor. It was around ten a.m. They woke him up, asked him his name. Calvin Atkins, he said. He said he had no money and had been sleeping in vacant buildings since his wife put him out just before Christmas after a "violent fight." He of course did not have the owner's permission to be there. Police found a crack pipe and soiled men's underwear in the pockets of his long gray and white jacket described as "Triple-Goose," no doubt the puffy, down style of jacket mentioned earlier. (Whether or not this indicates he was the suspicious man mentioned by the area resident interviewed at the Debbie Friday scene is unclear – this of course could have simply been a popular jacket style at the time, and the colors varied in the reports.)

Police contacted the woman at his Elmhurst address, who clarified that she was not his wife or girlfriend – she was the girlfriend of his brother. She had seen him off and on since Christmas and last saw him on January 19. He had been living at their apartment periodically, staying for a couple weeks then disappearing for a while. He never says where he goes, she told the officer, adding that he's a little "off."

Benjamin Atkins as he was questioned by police in January 1992, from DPD files.

They then took him to the station. Benjamin Thomas Atkins. Age twenty-three. They would detain him on a misdemeanor charge. At two-fifteen p.m., Sergeant Kenneth Day took his statement, for which the only relative or friend Atkins would list was his mother's boyfriend of years earlier, Ernest.

His brother put him out last month, he said.

"What other vacant buildings have you been staying in?" Day asked.

"The Monterey Motel in Highland Park, and this vacant house right off Woodward near the Sears in Highland Park."

"Do you ever stay at any other places," Day pressed.

"Yes. Sometimes I spent the night with some of the gay johns I pick up at the Continental Bar and the Shopper's Lounge downtown."

"Have you heard about any prostitutes being murdered in the Woodward corridor area?"

"The only thing I heard was last night," Atkins said. "This prostitute named Kim. She asked me if I had heard about two girls that had been killed. She told me that they had been killed in vacant houses. That's all she told me. She told me she was going to be out there, and if I saw her to keep an eye on her."

MURDER AT THE MONTEREY

Bush Sr. was in office. Then-candidate Bill Clinton and his indiscretions with Gennifer Flowers were factoring heavily in the news headlines. Ross Perot was running for office, as well – remember him? Coleman Young had been mayor in Detroit a long time, but Dennis Archer would soon gear up to win himself the hotseat. Michigan-based store chain Meijer was doubling coupons like so many other retailers. HIV/AIDS was in the news a lot, much more than it is nowadays, as people still had a lot of fear of it back then. In fact, if you look at the headlines of those early '90s newspapers, you will see AIDS was what COVID-19 was in 2020-2022. Much on people's minds. It was of particular interest when an arrest was made at this time in Detroit in an unrelated case of a serial rapist with HIV.

And as all that stuff was spinning around them, John Mattox, Jim Dobson and the crew at Highland Park Public Safety still toiled away on that Debbie Friday murder, oblivious to the fact that three more of their perp's bodies had shown up in Detroit. On January 8, they sent the evidence collected at the Friday scene to the Michigan State Police lab in the northeastern suburb of Sterling Heights. The lab returned a report a few days later that they had detected human blood on the sweatshirt and sock, and they collected hairs from the various items. They would complete their analysis on March 5, finding no identifiable latent fingerprints on the items.

Before that final report rolled in, though, the HPPS officers would get kicked in the teeth again. Hard.

Everett Monroe remembered how things looked, 'round about February 1992, from his perspective over in Detroit. "As time went on, I ended up being assigned to Violent Crime," he said. "So I kind of lost the intimacy of the case. Being assigned to Violent Crime, we were dealing with other stuff, so you know, I kind of lost connection with the case. Later on we were asked to assist in patrolling – well, not patrolling; we were asked to do some surveillance on Woodward, because they were feeling, well, yeah, maybe we might have a serial killer. So we were asked to go out there and kind of be in the shadows and kind of see what was going on. And talk to some of the street girls and find out their opinion. And pretty much they were telling us, 'yeah, this particular person is missing,' and 'this particular person is missing,' and so it kind of snowballed into being a serial killer.

"We just patrolled Woodward for a while and watched the activity. If there was a guy looking kind of, 'maybe this might be the guy, it may not, we don't know,' we would follow him and see their activity and stuff like that. Because during that time, we were really like looking for a needle in a haystack. We really didn't know which way to go.

"And then later on in the case, that's when a guy's once again going into a vacant hotel, right there at California and Woodward. They went into the building looking for copper and stuff like that, and they found a group of bodies that Benjamin Atkins had stored there, and so forth."

***

Back in its day, the Monterey Motel was quite the place, sitting at the corner of California and Woodward in Highland Park, catering to a blossoming era of this small Detroit enclave. The Monterey was a million-dollar motel in the 1950s, with two levels of rooms in two buildings angled toward each other and separated by a parking lot. The southernmost building held the reception area, restaurant/lounge and swimming pool, along with rooms lined up in rows east to west. The pool was state-of-the-art, and the lounge, called the Sunken Ship, boasted windows looking right into the side of the pool. The motel and its adjacent Howard Johnson's restaurant were owned by a businessman who also owned local car dealerships in the '40s and '50s.

"That was once a beautiful place, when it was built," Larry Beller recalled of the Monterey. "It was built mostly for Chrysler Corporation, because Chrysler was still in Highland Park, and all their executives would come in from out of town. They stayed there." Beller used to go to the restaurant from time to time, remembered it as a first-rate place. He chuckled at the memory of the observation window in the lounge, which he said was where the bar was, running along one wall. "You could see people swimming in the pool. And it was kinda funny, because people that were swimming in the pool didn't know somebody was watching them. You'd get a little playing around once in a while."

But the motel operations shut down, and from 1984 to 1990, it was a homeless shelter – nicknamed a hometel by the man who ran it. Then in June 1990 the Monterey was shuttered altogether, and it went to the city of Highland Park for back taxes and water bills. In the first few months after it was closed, the building was watched twenty-four hours a day, but after that there were time and budget constraints. Transients started to call it home. Vandals and looters descended. The doors to the rooms disappeared, as did the windows and the fixtures in many rooms. Some windows got boarded up, and even that plywood was broken away in spots. Sinks, toilets and pipes went missing. Police made frequent runs to the Monterey and began to call it a "hooker haven." When it was first closed, the city council rejected a plan to raze the motel and put fast-food eateries on the site. "We felt you would have undesirables hanging out in a twenty-four-hour operation," the mayor rather ironically told the media.

The Monterey very much reflected the sad state of affairs of that region of Woodward Ave. Right across Woodward from where the motel once sat is the street also named Monterey, running many blocks to the west. Author Alan Bradley, in his own perspective on the Atkins case, spent time there as a kid and said folks there not-so-lovingly called it "Murder-Ray" for the large amount of homicides before and after Atkins ever wandered by.

Now we arrive at Monday, February 17, 1992. A cold and foggy day. There was some snow on the ground. And it was indeed a scrapper happening upon a body, once again. Specifically a local man named Larry who lived on Monterey Street, looking for plumbing parts in that sprawling structure once quite grand and nice, once so well-regarded, now sitting abandoned and easily disregarded, in the day-to-day life of Highland Park. Larry needed to fix his mother's toilet.

It was early afternoon. As he wandered around one particular dark room, No. 18 on the lower level of the south building, roaming in and out of nooks and crannies and having to clear some stuff out of the way to navigate the place, he thought he saw a couple legs. It struck him as perhaps a mannequin. He lit a match to get a better look. Then he ran on out of there.

He was able to flag down a passing patrol car. Officers Sheila Herring and Bobby Ward checked the scene.

She was lying in a shower stall, face down, her head turned to the right, with her buttocks and legs up against the side of the stall. She was nude. Her left leg was grotesquely folded behind her, her bare foot hovering in the air above. She was gagged and her hands had been bound at her back. There was evidence of rodent damage on her left arm. Her right arm had what the medical examiner on the scene called "skin slippage." There were what appeared to be strangulation marks on her neck. There was mold on her body. A mattress was leaning on its side against the shower stall and in the doorway, in an attempt to block sight of the body. The mattress had a section of woodgrain paneling leaning against it.

Jim Dobson was on the scene that day, along with Larry Beller, after the initial responding officers had called it in. To this day, Dobson credits Beller for finding the other two women. Let's have a look around, Beller was thinking. Let's check the rest of the motel.

"Jimmy and Walt Chapman were on call that night," Beller recalled. "I think it was like at three o'clock in the afternoon or something. We were still at the station. And they got a call that they found a body down there. ... I wasn't doing anything, and I said, 'I'll go down right with you guys.' So I went down there, and we went in, and we were investigating in that room where the body was. And I started going through some other rooms there. Because they were all like fifty rooms or something like that."

As they began to take a look inside every other room at the motel with Officers Herring and Ward, it was Room 35 that next presented a horrifying scene. Upper level of the south building. Like the first woman, she was also lying in a shower stall, nude, her feet bare. Her legs were pointed upward, resting against the light-colored tiles, her right knee bent at ninety degrees. Her head rested on the opposite edge of the stall, facing up. She had been bound and gagged and had markings on her neck. Her gag of yellow material had fallen loose, and there was insulation material stuffed in her mouth. There were insulation pieces on her body, too, concealing most of her before police lifted them away. There was mold. She had a gold-colored earring in her right ear, and skin slippage on her left ear. Her right arm was twisted away from her body, most of it sticking out of the stall past her head. Beller noted in his report that her right shoulder appeared to be broken.

Room 68, on the lower level of the north building, yielded the third and final shocking discovery of the day. She was also in the shower stall. Her body was mostly concealed under a mattress, but her right leg was resting up on the tiled wall, her socked foot barely peeking out. The rest of her was crouched against the opposite side of the stall, her left knee drawn up near her head. She was lying on all kinds of debris, whatever it was, pieces of this and that, there in the shower. She was gagged with black material but not bound. She wore a wedding ring on her right hand as well as a ring on her other hand, and pierced earrings of a yellow metal. She had insulation material stuffed in her mouth. It looked to police like she had the bites of a rat or other animal on her arms.

Three bodies, right under their noses for who knows how long. No indication when they were left there. The same guy who killed Debbie Friday? It had to be, right? Similar scene and M.O. It was a devastating blow for the public safety officers. They called in some bigger guns: A four-person team from the Sterling Heights lab of the Michigan State Police reported to the scene.

"We called in the state police because we realized after we had three bodies that we had to get extra help," Beller said. "We had our own evidence techs, but they weren't that good. So we called in the state police. And they sent their evidence techs out. I mean, a crew, out. And they made a videotape of the scene."

The MSP lab techs arrived at five-fifteen p.m. – by this time pretty dark for the Michigan winter – and began processing, staying until two-thirty a.m. One technician carefully stepped around with the video camera, providing some minimal narration room by room, first in Room 35, as the portable lights revealed the gruesome scene and the generator on the MSP truck outside rumbled in the background. Some of the floors in the motel were reported to be wet that day, and a dripping sound can be heard in Room 68 in the video. Room 18 still had a wall of light-brown paneling intact. Looks like Room 35 did, too. But everywhere, in every room, just about every square inch it seemed, debris: food wrappers, broken glass, pipe insulation/asbestos, drug paraphernalia, construction material. A black cigarette lighter in Room 35 lying next to a wire clothing hanger, zoomed in on the camera. A pill bottle in Room 68. A liquor bottle. Urban decay. And sadly, another camera zoom on what appeared to be chipped red polish on the toenails of the victim's left foot in Room 18. That would be Fifteen.

The scene was also photographed per standard procedure, and the three bodies were taken to the Wayne County Medical Examiner's office around eight p.m. The mayor and a couple of his officials also showed up to the scene that day.

From the first victim, the bindings and other materials were taken for analysis, including a white bra of size 38C, and a torn white thermal underwear shirt of Gitano brand, size 37-39. The paneling lying against the mattress was processed for prints; none found. Techs also collected for analysis from Room 18 a blue piece of tissue, a cigarette butt, a Mogen David wine bottle and a Hawaiian Punch can.

A still shot from the Monterey crime scene video, showing the clothing and other rubble on the floor of Room 68.

For the second victim, they found a very important palm print on the shower stall of Room 35, one that would show up later in court. It was on the tile wall on the left side, five feet above the floor. Among the items they collected from the room were a gag made from a torn black knit sweater, amber drape material that was tied around her head, a couple cigarette butts, three cigarette lighters, a Mohawk Vodka bottle, an earring, a condom and a Trojan condom wrapper, white boxer shorts size XL depicting a black Bart Simpson with the words "Stop killing black youth," blood from the pushed-in Plexiglass window, and a blood sample from the floor of the bathroom.

For the third victim, a couple more important items found: A yellow condom and a piece of tissue that would test positive for semen. Though this killer had tried to hide the bodies, meticulous he was not. Also taken for processing from Room 68 were white nylon panties with knife marks in the crotch, white cotton panties size 5 by Fruit of the Loom, the pill bottle, a mascara tube, and several other clothing items like white boxer shorts, a dark gray T-shirt with "Chicago" on it, and yellow sweatpants and a matching torn yellow sweatshirt, size large, the latter of which appeared to have blood on it. Lab reports noted that a pair of brown socks with plant material on them was also collected from the scene.

Blood and hair samples and vaginal swabs were taken from all three women, as well as fingernail clippings.

John Mattox didn't go to the first Highland Park crime scene, but he went to the Monterey scene, and every scene after that. He elaborated further on the challenges of combing for evidence in an abandoned building:

"It was what you might call a clusterfuck. And what I mean by that is it was an abandoned structure. You had people who have gone in there and stayed in there, homeless people, for a period of time. And each time, they were very destructive. They were taking anything of value. So when you responded to a scene there at the motel, the detectives that were dispatched to the scene to investigate a homicide where a body was, you were trying to determine what could be evidence and what is trash. What is debris, what is the abandoned building structure? You know how everything is just thrown about, and you don't know what is what. So you're investigating a scene that is not pristine. It's absolutely the worst conditions that you could possibly have, to investigate a homicide, because you're looking for things that are out of place, and you're looking for things that the culprit left in the way of evidence."

The time of year his crew were investigating these crimes didn't help, either. "Because you had snow on the ground, and like really, if it snowed you couldn't tell if it was prior to the snow or after the snow. So you had all these factors working against you."

Despite these challenges, there were key pieces of evidence collected at the Monterey that would prove to be clinchers for the case.

"Now, DNA was just coming in to be then," Mattox said, "and I can remember this one female evidence officer from the state. She was the one that picked up on this. You've got to remember that you had drug addicts, and there were people that were frequenting this place. So you had needles and stuff like that, that were thrown about and so forth like that. But she noticed a condom. And she collected it. And eventually, there was a match at some point. And we argued about that, because at that time in order to get the DNA done, it cost six grand. Nobody wanted to pay for it. And it was all new. Everybody was kind of skeptical because DNA had just come in to be. It had just started. And at that time you could only get a one-shot deal. If you used DNA, you couldn't break it down and duplicate it like they can now. You got one shot; that was it. And they weren't able to test it for various things." The technology has advanced so much since then, he said. "They can just take a speck now. Then, you had to have a certain quantity. It's remarkable what they're doing with that now."

Mattox's public safety crew held a news conference at three p.m. on February 18. Right afterward, Dobson and Chapman manned a hotline for tips.

"Bodies found in shut motel," read the headline on the right-rail story on page 3A of the *Detroit Free Press*, February 18. Its compatriot *The Detroit News* wasn't messing around, though. Front page, above the fold, extremely large headline: "Did serial killer slay 3 women in motel, 3 others?" The *Freep* was the morning paper and *The News* the afternoon paper in their joint operating agreement, so *The News* could afford to advance the story just a bit. It was always a good idea, since these two newsrooms were still fierce competitors, though their business operations such as circulation and advertising had recently been merged.

Police were refusing to say this was a serial killer, *The News'* story said, though one Highland Park officer admitted it was a possibility they were considering. Dobson was also quoted, equally (and safely) noncommittal. The media didn't know that at that moment, the officers were looking at a suspect from a set of serial killings that had occurred along Detroit's Cass Corridor in the 1970s. This man had been investigated for those killings but dismissed, and that perp, nicknamed the Bigfoot Killer for his reportedly large hands and feet, has never been found. This dismissed suspect's case file was pulled, plus there were a couple other names being bandied about from tips here and there. Prints were compared with the palm print found at the Monterey. An officer from the Troy P.D. to the north thought he had a suspect and faxed over the info for him, too.

Valerie Chalk's photo accompanied the story on *The News'* front page, which noted her mother was anxiously waiting to hear if Valerie was one of the three at the Monterey. Then, on the inside, was the sidebar André Chalk still has framed on his wall, which included a photo of himself, his siblings and his grandmother.

"We used to walk, and we'd sing church songs," Jessie Butler told *The News*. "But things didn't work out so well with her. She started telling me, 'Mama, please get me out of Highland Park. My friends are doing things I don't want to do.' Now I don't know if she's out there dead or alive."

Nearby residents were interviewed for both papers' stories, with complaints ringing forth about what they would see going in and out of the Monterey, and their feelings that the place should be torn down. They would eventually get their wish.

For its second-day coverage on February 19, *The News* looked at the fear that accompanies prostitutes in one story, then in another pointed out similarities between the three victims and other women recently found, reiterating that police didn't want to go on record with that serial killer thing. The *Freep*'s coverage noted that police were looking into a connection with unsolved slayings dating from the latter 1980s in Inkster and other nearby cities to the west.

The deaths of Debbie Friday, Bertha Mason, Patricia George and Vickie Truelove had barely been a blip on the radar, but alas this killer's work had come out of obscurity.

The Wayne County Medical Examiner found asphyxia by suffocation and strangulation as the cause of death for all three Monterey victims. There was no way for the M.E. to determine just when each of these three females died. The closest estimate was at least a few days but possibly much longer due to the fact that the bodies were partially frozen for the middle of winter. Laning Davidson, M.D., performed the autopsy for all three much like a broken record. "The manner of death was a homicide," each report somberly read. Toxicology screens showed the first victim positive for alcohol, volatiles/ethanol, benzoylecgonine and cocaine, negative for barbiturates and morphine. The second victim negative for alcohol, barbiturates and morphine, and positive for cocaine and benzoylecgonine. The third victim was positive for alcohol and cocaine, negative for barbiturates and morphine.

The Monterey discovery prompted, once again, area residents to contact police to see if their missing family members were among the women found. Where fingerprints were concerned for ID'ing these girls, police faced a big challenge. The bodies were greatly decomposed. Evidence appeared to show that all three of these women were killed before mid-January's snowstorm, though police could only surmise they were killed at different times.

"We had a tough time identifying them," Beller remembered. "There was one that they couldn't get any prints. But the state police, we talked to them out at the lab, and they said if they bring the hands out, we've got something that they put the hands in to cook them or peel them or something. So we had the medical examiner cut both hands off at the wrists, and we took them out to the state police, and they identified her."

Dobson also recalled that method with the same kind of general impression and not too many details: "They did a process. They peeled skin. They did a bunch of different things. And they were able to come up with the identity."

It was a gruesome but effective process. Within a couple weeks police had usable fingerprints for all three girls and they had the identities of two of the three. A local dentist, Dr. Allan Warnick, also assisted, comparing dental records to confirm identities. A graduate of University of Detroit Mercy, Warnick became involved in forensic dentistry while serving in the Dental Corps of the U.S. Air Force after earning his D.D.S., helping identify flight crews in airplane crashes, according to a bio from the UDM site. He authored the "Forensic Dental Identification Team Manual" for the Michigan Dental Association in 1989. Dr. Warnick practiced in the western Detroit suburb of Livonia but spent at least one day a week assisting morgues in several different counties.

Though police were unable to know exactly when each of these three females was killed, at least two of them now had names: Juanita Hardy and the particularly long-lost and hard-sought Valerie Chalk. Beller, Chapman and Dobson performed the unenviable task of notifying their family members. But how do you go about finding someone to notify, since these girls were living on the street? Off the grid before the phrase even became popular? It was a dilemma they would address throughout the investigation of this case.

"It was difficult," Beller admitted. "It was difficult." Though they were not carrying driver's licenses, "most of them had records, arrest records," he said. "Most of the time they would fill out an information sheet when they were arrested and include like the next of kin."

But did they fabricate this info some of the time, too? "Oh, yeah, yeah. It was mostly – I think most of them had kids, and it was always the *[woman's]* mother who was taking care of the kids."

Beller and Dobson had a particular friend who worked in the welfare office, so he had contact information on the females who were receiving checks. They relied heavily on this intel, though the friend would surely have lost his job at the time if this practice was known. "Back in those days, you had to have a subpoena to get an address and a phone number. You had to serve a subpoena to Michigan Bell. And you had to have someone who worked there. My son-in-law worked there," Beller said.

"If you ever get a chance, befriend somebody in the welfare department," Dobson said, not so much in jest, "because that's where the best records are. ... This guy did miracles for us, serving subpoenas on numerous, numerous cases."

And the next part made that look easy. "It was difficult going over," Beller said, "because we had to break the news. But they had – most of them, I think by the time we got there, and it was in the papers and everything, they kinda knew already."

In the days that followed the discovery at the Monterey, and all the types of reporting that had to ensue, especially on the law enforcement end, there is naturally confusion in the files as to which of the three females was which – which was found first, which was in which room. Between the records of the police and the medical examiner and the news media, contradictions abound, carried through in subsequent years by the occasional podcasts on the case. Here is the snapshot based on an aggregate of reports in the files:

- Room 18: Fifteen, found first by police, aka Unknown Female No. 15
- Room 35: Juanita, found second, aka Unknown Female No. 16
- Room 68: Valerie, found third, aka Unknown Female No. 14

Since the "Unknown Female" numbering comes from the county medical examiner, it's not necessarily going to match the order in which police found the women. In this case, the women are numbered in the order the MSP lab techs analyzed their scenes. In the MSP's crime scene video, however, the rooms are shown in the order 35, 18, 68.

Tips were coming in from other females who had been approached on the street in suspicious incidents. And at last, Highland Park police and Detroit police were going to meet and compare notes.

"That's when we went to Detroit," Jim Dobson recalled, "and we said, 'Hey, we've got a problem, but we think it's also your problem.' And they kinda just went, 'ha, ha, ha.' They didn't want the bad publicity. They didn't want people to panic, and everything else. We tried. We tried to share, and it didn't quite work out."

On Friday, February 21, Dobson, Beller and Chapman from Highland Park met with four men from DPD – an officer, two lieutenants and the head of the Homicide Section. They had four dead in Highland Park, three in Detroit. All known or suspected prostitutes. All known or suspected crack addicts. All females of color. All strangled. All nude or partially nude. All found at abandoned buildings. Most or all raped and sodomized. There were the bindings they wanted to take a closer look at. What kind of knots where those? There was the weird thing with the socks – sometimes just one on, sometimes one stuffed in the mouth. The cops shared about similar incidents over the years. They talked about a suspicious character or two around town, like a guy named Carl who sometimes slept at the Monterey, another guy named Donald who was the one living at the AFC home on Taylor, mentioned by prostitute Brenda. A third guy named Johnny. But the man who had been arrested for being in buildings he shouldn't have been, in both of their jurisdictions – including at the Monterey – did not seem to come up in conversation. Of course, in all fairness, they no doubt encountered lots of homeless people on the beat, only some of which were taken into the station.

During the meeting, it was the head of DPD's Homicide who put the damper on things, as Beller recalled. "He denied that there was a serial killer. After we had the meeting, I come back, and there was a Detroit detective, I can't remember his name now, but he was in the meeting, and he had worked on some of the Detroit cases. And he called me. I knew him, and he called me after I got back. And he says, 'He's lying to you. This is a serial killer. These are all related.'"

At that point, the two jurisdictions still did not work together on the case, though HPPS did get DPD's help with a cadaver dog to search vacant buildings on February 20. It would take the involvement of another party to more effectively bring things together in this investigation. That's around the time that the Detroit office of the FBI came aboard, and their agent, Paul Lindsay, got additional officers from the Michigan State Police involved, as well. More on that later.

In the week that followed the Monterey discovery, Dobson and Chapman worked the streets, talking to people, trying to get any lead they could. On February 26, officers met with an artist from WDIV-TV Channel 4 to have drawings made of the three Monterey victims. Channel 4 had the exclusive on the drawings before they were released to the *Free Press*, along with heights, weights, ages. The next day, the MSP had ID'd Valerie Chalk.

Beller and Chapman knocked on the door of Jessie Butler at one-thirty p.m. on February 27 to let her know her daughter was one of the Monterey women. Several of Valerie's family members then came in to the station to speak with police. Valerie's boyfriend John also spoke with police, saying he had heard from a family member that Valerie was dead before the missing person's report was filed. He wasn't the only one – police heard that a man named Butch also knew it early on and even stopped by Valerie's family's home to tell them. Valerie's friend Betty had heard it from someone else a day before Christmas. No wonder the family had such a feeling of dread when the news hit about the discovery at the Monterey.

Juanita Hardy's foster mom Carrie visited the police station the next day, and Juanita's prints were tested against Unknown No. 16 with positive results. Police talked to Juanita's brother Grant on March 2 and her friend Lisa, who had attended Mumford High with her, two days later.

John Mattox recalled why Dobson and Beller ended up playing such a large role in the investigation:

"Me and my deputy and another officer, we were trying to find out who we wanted to assign to this case, because these bodies were popping up. We wanted one investigator to handle the whole thing, not five or six investigators doing the same thing and doing duplication. So we had talked about this, and we all agreed on Larry Beller. Why we picked Larry, because Larry was an individual that when he got involved in something he didn't have an axe to grind, whether it was white or black, male or female, young or old. He didn't bring any biases to the table. And this is why we all agreed on Beller. Three officers. And we said, well, who works well with Beller? And we started throwing out names and so forth like that. And we eventually came up with Dobson."

Mattox also recalled how he first became familiar with the term serial killer, a term borne of the '70s and '80s heyday of such crimes but one he had not had personal experience with until this case came along. He had been talking with one of the reporters covering the investigation, Corey Williams of *The Detroit News*.

"I had never even heard of the term in law enforcement like that, a serial killer," Mattox said. "He was the first one I heard use that term. And I didn't have a clue what he was talking about, but I didn't let him know that," he added. "Hey, I'm supposed to be the chief of police. And matter of fact, he brought in a book on the Green River murders. He brought this book and said, 'Read about it when you get a chance.' I read it that night."

Mattox found the case of the Green River murders similar, though one big difference between that case and the case in Highland Park was the speed of the murders. The Green Rivers murders went on for years, while the Highland Park Strangler seemed much quicker. Still, as the thoughts around this unknown perp were gelling in the minds of Mattox and others on his force, the concept of a serial killer introduced by this reporter struck a chord, no matter what DPD was willing to say about it.

"I remember he came up to my office, and he's running it to me, and I'm like, that's the first I heard of that. I wasn't aware of *[the homicides in]* Detroit. And I'm sure that they had more than that, because the area that they were tearing down homes was the first one that they discovered this body. And if in fact there was one, this individual, when I say he more than likely knew that area, if in fact he killed somebody, it would be in that same area, because they were always a walking distance from Woodward Avenue, except that one. It was walking distance, but it was a block and a half. Well, two blocks really, and if you're going to kill somebody and you're walking with them, that's a little bit remote. You have to have the cooperation with the person, because he's walking through a residential area. They had all these apartments. And these apartments were full with people. So any disturbance or any like struggling with somebody would be noticed very quickly."

As the case went on, Mattox and crew could only speculate just how far these homicides – and this killer – were stretching.

"We were always wondering if there was anything in Hamtramck," Mattox said. "We never heard from 'em, but if it was, I never heard of anything, you know. But we knew that there was stuff occurring on the Woodward corridor. And that was all the way to Eight Mile Road. But I say Woodward corridor, because it had to be some location where you had public transportation. After that, the transportation was not public. What I mean by that is they had transportation there, but it wasn't as active as the system in the city of Detroit and Highland Park. So you kind of narrowed your area down. It didn't go any further than Six or Seven Mile Road."

Mattox recalled the news media crawling all over the investigators while they were working this case. Some of the reporters used to sit on his car as it was parked outside the station. They were feeling if it was cold, which meant he had been in the building, or if it was hot, maybe he just got back from some hot story. Reporters monitored the police radio and responded to the calls that sounded like they could become stories. Sometimes they would beat the police there.

The aggressiveness of the media once the Monterey blew up the case also stood out in Jim Dobson's mind all these years later. "The news media spared no mercy," he said. One from their ranks, WXYZ-TV Channel 7 reporter Cheryl Chodun, was a friend of his. Someone he was on good terms with. She would try to follow him home to get info, he said. He would ask her about the media's approach to a story like this, how merciless they seemed and how they would go for sensationalism, from his perspective. Even how during interviews they would ask how a person "feels" after something so tragic happens. It left him befuddled.

Whatever the media was or was not doing, it wasn't the greatest of their worries, from Mattox's view.

"This case was not supposed to be solved," he said. "And I'll tell you why. Because number one, we had no cooperation with the city of Detroit Police Department. None in the beginning. Absolutely none. And they weren't speaking to the state police nor the FBI. So we were in the middle. ... Eventually I did get a chance to speak with the governor *[John Engler]*, now, and the governor told me this. He said, 'You are from a Democratic community. I'm a Republican. I can't say that I'm going to reach out and assist you with X amount of men, but what I'll do is this.' They had no love for our mayor. None."

Mattox said the word that was out about the Highland Park mayor at the time is that he had an issue with drugs, and the mayor himself later admitted to that. "Our mayor couldn't be trusted," he said. "He had a very poor reputation. Detroit didn't want no part of that. They didn't want any leaks. And we were having leaks. We finally found out that. I was sharing information with the mayor, and he would turn around and call the news media, and like, well, that was the leak."

In the midst of the manhunt, as negative publicity intensified, the mayor claimed in the media that the killer couldn't possibly be from Highland Park – he was only dumping bodies there. But a profiler, MSP Detective Sergeant David Minzey, contradicted that, surmising the killer lived along the Woodward corridor.

Mattox said, "You had these jurisdictional lines between cooperation with the state police and the FBI, and that was the political part of it. So that's where we were. We were in a bind. Now, we were from a poor community that didn't have resources to conduct a serial killing. It drains your department, absolutely drains manpower, equipment and money. Now I called *[William]* Sessions, who was the FBI director, and I called him because of James Harrington. James Harrington is a name that you will probably never hear in this investigation, but he was the one to kind of put it together. James Harrington was the training officer for the FBI. I had met James Harrington at church. I met him at through Father Cunningham. And this is even before the incident started taking place. He said any time you need any help let me know. We tried to get Detroit to admit that they had some bodies. They flatly refused. Flatly refused. Said no. I called the chief, who was *[Stanley]* Knox at that time. He was acting chief. And you know, he blew me off. So we knew that there was homicides that were occurring on Woodward Avenue, more than the two that they admitted to. And they flatly refused to give us anything. They were ordered that. They were ordered not to exchange any information."

DPD's homicide chief who had been less than helpful in the meeting with HPPS was an associate of Mattox, someone he knew outside of the case, so it was even more disappointing for him than it was for his officers.

"He denied everything," Mattox said. "And then we were going to get together. I remember one time I called him and set up an appointment and we were going to have dinner down in Greektown. And he calls me back and said he couldn't meet with me. And I said, 'Why? We're just meeting together.' He said, 'I've been ordered not to meet with you.' And I don't know how they found out about it. We didn't put it on the PA system, or we didn't send a teletype to any departments, you know. It was just, he and I were going to meet. But I remember that very well. And I saw him maybe twice since then and he avoided me – I guess he got extremely busy going in an opposite direction, would be probably a better term."

And so Harrington was instrumental in connecting Mattox with some FBI contacts, and he also helped him connect with the governor. Another office that Mattox remembers getting full cooperation from was the Wayne County Prosecutor's Office.

"We had some good cooperation from the prosecuting staff," he said. *"[John]* O'Hair was the prosecutor at the time for Wayne County. And I remember going down to his office, and I laid the whole thing out to him. And he said, 'We will assign a prosecutor to your unit, and we will cooperate with anything that you need.' Now, this was the first appointee that said, hey, we will go to bat on this, and you can reach us at any time of day or night. That was O'Hair."

Over at DPD, Everett Monroe saw the tide begin to slowly turn at that time, among those in leadership, regarding the serial killer question. "It was later on when leadership said, 'Well, we've got to stop and listen to the troops, because they're out there every day. They're seeing this every day.' So we've got to kind of set ourselves to look for one person."

But that didn't mean they were going to buddy up with HP. Monroe saw the situation from a different angle than Mattox.

"We didn't work too much with Highland Park," Monroe said. "Highland Park was having some serious problems, and we only intermingled with them when we had to. And fortunately, we didn't ever team up with Highland Park. Because you've got to remember, we had other cases going on, as well, and some of them were in Highland Park. And so we were handling those cases, and if we ran into some information that seemed to be vital to the serial killer case, then we would pass that on to Homicide. But we didn't really work with Highland Park too much. Now, Homicide may have been a little different."

On March 12 and 13, the MSP lab completed its analysis of the items collected from the Monterey. Semen was found on the condom and tissue paper that was in Room 68, the Valerie Chalk scene. Blood was also detected on the outside of the condom, but in an insufficient sample size. No semen was found in the other items tested, such as the panties, sweatpants and the other condom found. Saliva was found on three cigarette butts tested, with an indication of blood type O. Human blood was found in Room 35, the Juanita Hardy scene, "A, B, O analysis was inconclusive," the report noted. "Further testing is possible." The vaginal, rectal and oral swabs from all three victims came up negative for semen. Their fingernail clippings produced nothing of value. No trace evidence came up on the bindings. And though the palm print on the shower wall would prove valuable, the other items tested did not produce any usable prints.

Also on March 13, Dobson, Beller and Chapman again met with a few of the Detroit officers, minus one Homicide chief, to formulate what they believed was a profile of their perp. They figured that with the prolonged method of killing this guy was using, homicide was the purpose and not sexual gratification. He was undressing his victims to degrade them. But he wasn't going to these scenes prepared; he wasn't taking anything with him to really assist in the homicides, they noted. He might be taking clothing from the victim to give to someone, they theorized. And they believed he had these traits:

- Very strong – dumb
- May have military history
- Calm, not a hothead, in control
- Strange acting – introvert
- Not talkative – loner
- May be on medication for mental illness
- Low opinion of women
- Same social class as victims
- Lives in area – familiar with area
- If he does have a vehicle, it will be old – junk

FAST AND ELUSIVE

She knew this was Tony. She could feel it.

Three girls found at the Monterey, basically the same place where he had attacked her. It was splashed across the newspaper and television. Everybody was talking about it, especially those she saw on Woodward Ave. But they were talking about a nameless, faceless man out there somewhere. She was thinking about Tony. She knew it in her heart. "Because of the way that they were done and the way I was done," she later testified.

She even knew Valerie – their kids knew each other, too, went to school together. It was all just awful.

So in March 1992, Darlene Saunders took herself to the police station. Told them her story. Told them about Tony, how he raped her, how she barely got away. How she wouldn't have gotten away if Mario hadn't been there. She made the report to Officer Lindsey Pace of DPD on Friday, March 6 at eleven-fifty a.m. She described Tony as five-foot-five to five-foot-six, one hundred seventy to one hundred eighty pounds, dark complexion and muscular. He's a drug dealer who takes women into vacant buildings, she said.

She was brushed off. "What they told her was go home," her son Rashad recalled. "Because we're well-known over here. They told her to go home. You've got a home to go to, Darlene. Go home."

And the investigation charged on. On March 20, Detroit Police Officer S. Myles was giving a witness from a different homicide case a lift home from court. The witness' name was Robyn, and she started talking to Myles about the women who were killed in Highland Park. Myles took a statement from her. She knew Valerie Brown, and she said another one of the women killed might have been named Pat. She was missing, too. Her friend Lonnie had told her that he knew who killed them. It was a guy Lonnie had gotten high with a few times. "He said the guy told him that he approached the girl about sex in exchange for crack cocaine," Robyn told Myles. "He did not say if he approached them in a car or walked up on them, but wherever they went, when he got them there, he would get them naked. Lonnie said the guy told him that he got Valerie naked and then he strangled her until she was unconscious, then he had sex with her, and while he was having sex with her, he started beating her. After he had sex with her, he suffocated her, tried her up [sic] and dumped her in the Monterey Motel. He told me the room number, but I can't remember. He said the guy picked Valerie up on Woodward between Glendale and Cortland."

Robyn was hearing all of this from Lonnie over the phone on a day in early February, and when Lonnie mentioned Pat, too, their phone conversation got cut short before he could elaborate, only saying that Pat was "with Valerie," that she was dead like Valerie. Robyn knew both Valerie and Pat for four or five years, she told Myles, but she knew Valerie on a more personal level. Pat, she had only seen around on the streets. Valerie worked from Glendale to Davison, and Pat tended to work Hamilton. Robyn had worked the same area as Valerie the previous June, but the last time she saw Pat was in September. Pat had family living on Glendale between Hamilton and Lincoln.

Robyn said Lonnie would not tell her who this man was, worried that if he found out Lonnie told, he would try to kill her. "Where can I find Lonnie?" Myles asked her. Robyn gave his description and said Highland Park had a file on him.

"Did he tell you why the guy killed them?" Myles asked.

"No, he did not tell me, but Lonnie said he thinks the guy gets his rocks off by doing this."

Myles' fellow officer Randy Hutnik learned of all of this. Hutnik had been working the Detroit side of the case and had been in the meeting the week before to profile the killer. He also was in the meeting with HPPS on February 21. Hutnik reached out to Walt Chapman in HPPS. Do you have any women missing named Pat, or any recent prostitution arrests of a Pat? No. Hutnik then called DPD's Vice and got a list of all women named Pat arrested for prostitution since June 1991. He got eight names. (Detroit saw 2,439 prostitution arrests – termed A&S, for accosting and soliciting – in 1991 and 1,611 in 1992, while Highland Park reported 5 in 1991 and 30 in 1992.) Hutnik took a look at the reports of missing women and found one filed on March 1 that seemed to fit the unknown female from the motel. At this point, Officer Hutnik was thinking he was closing in on the ID of Fifteen, but his "Pat" would prove to be someone else.

On March 22, DPD brought the thirty-seven-year-old Lonnie – unemployed, residing with his mother in Highland Park – to the station for a talk. Sergeant Danny Maynard took his statement. He and Valerie grew up together, Lonnie said. He had known her since she was a little girl. They were friends, but a couple years earlier they had been intimate. He last saw her in September. Was she having any trouble with anyone? No, Lonnie said. She just had a baby. Yes, she was walking Woodward, he said, and sometimes she would go into vacant buildings with tricks. No pimp. He didn't know of any boyfriend.

When did you find out Valerie had been killed, Maynard asked. He ran into a friend named Bookie – real name Raymond – in the first week of January, and Bookie told him about it. "Yeah, she was supposed to have AIDS, and some n——er killed her," Lonnie quoted Bookie as saying. "I said I hoped he was bull-shitting because I didn't want AIDS," Lonnie said. But they couldn't find the body, Bookie told him, adding that he thought Lonnie should know this since he and Valerie once "kicked it." It was a trick who killed her, Lonnie said Bookie told him. Lonnie denied ever telling anyone he talked to a guy who killed Valerie. The only person he told about this conversation with Bookie, he said, was his ex-girlfriend April, to see if she ever got an HIV test.

So somebody was lying – either Robyn or Lonnie. Somebody knew more than they were saying. Did Lonnie talk directly with their serial killer? Or was Lonnie possibly their guy? He knew Valerie. And he didn't seem fond of this HIV rumor. Police grew more suspicious.

On March 24, it was Lonnie's buddy Raymond, aka Bookie, who took a turn at the station, talking with Officer Hutnik. The thirty-three-year-old man was self-employed in "hair and nails," he told Hutnik, and living with his girlfriend in Highland Park. He drove a blue '91 Thunderbird. Like Lonnie, he knew Valerie, had known her for about fifteen years. But he knew her from church and school – she was never his girlfriend. She used drugs, he knew. He last saw her on Woodward in Detroit in September or October. She was pregnant at the time but looked bad, looked like she was strung out. Raymond only heard that Valerie was dead when they reported it on the news, though everyone suspected she was one of the three Monterey girls, since her poster was up all over town.

"The talk on the streets was that she probably had AIDS and gave it to some guy who then came back and killed her," Raymond said.

He mentioned Valerie's boyfriend, named Bones, who he said was the father of her ten-year-old. Hutnik asked Raymond if he saw Lonnie between Christmas and the day the women were found at the Monterey. Only on the street, Raymond said, but he didn't talk to him because Lonnie was always begging for money. So you didn't talk to him about Valerie's murder, Hutnik asked. Nope, he didn't talk to him at all – the guy always had his hand out.

So now police had two people contradicting Lonnie's story about Valerie.

"Is Lonnie a scandalous person?" Hutnik asked.

"Yes, he is very scandalous," Raymond said. "You name it, and he will do it."

The idea of Valerie having HIV is, of course, unsubstantiated, not reflected anywhere else in the case records, though the HIV factor will come up later in the story for our perp. At the end of their conversation, Raymond asked Hutnik if Valerie was the "one who had her leg missing," illustrating how tales can get twisted on the street. It was even reported in the media at one point that Valerie's family had been told the rumor, amid their circulating the numerous fliers around town, that she was being held captive in a building.

At the same time Hutnik was pursuing the Lonnie angle, he was continuing to try to connect the "Pat" these folks kept mentioning to one of the Jane Does of the case. His work led him to Celestine, sister of Patricia Cannon George. He spoke to her on March 24. She said the last time she talked to Patricia was the day before Thanksgiving; Pat was supposed to come to the family dinner the next day but didn't show up. Pat would be gone from time to time, having been involved with drugs for about ten years now, but she had never disappeared for this long, Celestine said. Her checks were piling up – in fact, she was removed from her assistance program. Celestine mentioned Pat's boyfriend, Larry, and her current address, and she said Pat had a lot of dental work done. The next day Hutnik contacted the clinic at Fourteenth and Philadelphia to get her dental records.

A few days later, Hutnik got another tip from Celestine. She had received a call the night before from a woman named Verline, who knew Pat and said that she had heard on the news that Pat was dead. Hutnik knew this was not the case – there was nothing released publicly identifying Pat. Verline told Celestine that she had smoked crack with Pat and another woman named Geraldine (not Pat's sister by that name) on the night before Thanksgiving in a basement on Kenilworth. That night, Pat left with a tall Black man around age forty, wearing a tan coat, and no one had seen her since.

Hutnik got with his contact C. Kish at the Wayne County Medical Examiner's office to have Pat's dental records compared with the case's Jane Does. The WCME called in Dr. Warnick, who had assisted with ID'ing the Monterey women. Warnick determined – noting no inconsistencies – that the records matched the woman who was found at the torn-down house on Kenilworth. Hutnik had found his "Pat" – Patricia Cannon George. It must have been pretty rewarding for Kish, as well, since he had worked tirelessly in January fielding inquiries from area residents with missing family members, comparing fingerprints and records with this Unknown Female No. 1, to no avail. Hutnik asked Kish to keep the ID under wraps a couple days while DPD kept working these leads. DPD notified Celestine on April 2, as well as HPPS.

Hutnik had Robyn back down to the station on March 29, showing her some photos. Did she recognize them?

"Yes, one of them is Valerie," she said. "The drawing looks like Pat, and the one with the head wrapped in a white sheet looks familiar."

Hutnik asked Robyn about the things she had told Myles. He asked her about any strange tricks she had encountered. She mentioned a tall, thin guy, maybe forty, who wore glasses and carried a plastic bag with a change of clothes. That guy was picking up girls in taxicabs. One night last summer, the last time she saw Valerie, this guy had taken both her and Valerie to a motel (though evidently not the Monterey). He brought a bunch of other people to the motel room, too. "He would sit in a chair naked and masturbate while he watched the other people have sex," Robyn told Hutnik. "He was very quiet and rarely said a word. He kept taking showers." Soon the others left, she said, and she and Valerie stayed behind with this trick, who wanted the two women to have sex together. Robyn wasn't into that, so she got ready to leave. The guy went crazy, she said, grabbing a towel and starting to choke Valerie and ripping up her clothing. Robyn ran out.

Does Lonnie know this guy, Hutnik asked. In other words, could this be the guy who told him he killed Valerie? He might know him, Robyn said, since everyone knows everyone else in that area. The guy, who was clean-shaven and always had lots of crack, wore a wedding ring and had a pinky finger that was crooked; she thought it was his left pinky.

Hutnik showed Robyn a photo of Lonnie and a girl. That's April, she said, Lonnie's girlfriend. In and out of the hospital a lot. Is she dead, Robyn asked. I don't know, Hutnik replied.

Next Hutnik talked to Geraldine, a thirty-eight-year-old Detroit woman with a pierced nose who was living just a couple blocks east of where Pat was found. She had known Pat since 1987, had seen her on the streets hustling for crack. She corroborated what Celestine had reported from Verline, that Pat was at her house a day or two before Thanksgiving, smoking crack in the basement with Verline and a tall, thin man Geraldine didn't know. Geraldine was upstairs cooking, she said, and she didn't want to smoke that night, so she just let them do their thing downstairs. She recalled all three leaving together, though, not just Pat and the man, and she never saw Pat again. Hutnik showed Geraldine a photo, and she said yeah, that could be the man, but she wasn't sure. But she had definitely seen the guy in the photo with Pat before.

On March 31, Lonnie was arrested for suspicion of murder.

Lonnie took a polygraph test on April 1 and failed. Police drew three vials of blood from him. They searched his home with his consent. They asked him where he was on the night before Thanksgiving, and if he knew a woman named Pat George. No, he said, and he was with his girlfriend April and another friend named Dorothy on the day before

Thanksgiving. He said he smoked crack but did not know Geraldine and had not been to the Monterey since it closed.

On April 2, Hutnik talked to Lonnie's ex-girlfriend April, who said she had heard from Lonnie that Valerie got strangled by a trick. AIDS came up in Hutnik's short conversation with April – he asked her if Lonnie had ever talked to her about getting tested, and she said yes.

The next day, Hutnik again spoke with Celestine. She said Pat's boyfriend Larry had told her he last saw Pat on November 30. She reiterated what she had said before, from the phone call with Verline.

There were things about this Lonnie guy that looked good to police, and they must have felt pretty good to have him in custody. But as the weeks wore on, they would find that some very important pieces just didn't fit.

***

It got warm on April 7, so Ernestine took her coat off and put it in the tote bag she had with her. She knew the house on West Grand was empty. People slipped in and out of there a lot, getting high. So she went inside the house and left her tote bag there. She didn't feel like carrying her stuff around while she was out doing some business and hanging with folks in the neighborhood. The forty-three-year-old woman stayed over on Washburn in Detroit, to the west, but today she was here. She hid the bag in the corner of one of the rooms of the house and left. No one else was around.

A couple days later, she went back to the house to get her bag. She noticed there was a mattress folded over in the room, and it had a sock sticking out from under it. She looked on the other side of the mattress and saw a foot, then part of a leg. That was about all she wanted to see, at that moment. She ran on out of there, to West Grand and through the alley. She found her friend Sheila over by the party store.

"There's a dead body in that house," she told her.

"Where?"

They both went back to the house so she could show Sheila what she was talking about, making sure not to touch anything, then they ran back to the party store, which was at West Grand and Woodward, Bill's place. Bill called the police.

It was five-thirty p.m. when the call came in to Highland Park Public Safety. Sergeant Ted Mixon, the patrol supervisor, responded to the scene, followed by Officers Don Storball and Kevin Maclin. Mixon first met Ernestine and Sheila on Woodward, then they took him to the boarded-up, two-story, four-bedroom house at 26 West Grand, just west of Woodward, a house that had been abandoned for some time. They went inside the house, to the living room, where he saw the mattress in the northeast corner. The mattress was bent over, and there was a box spring on it, too. Mixon flipped over the bent part of the mattress, shining a flashlight on what was hidden underneath. Sure enough, another body. Nude from the waist down, maybe thirty, maybe a hundred forty pounds. She wore dirty white ankle socks and a yellow sweater with a beige shirt under it, ripped open. She was lying on her right side (according to one report – the medical examiner on the scene said she was face down) with her head pointing east. Blood had come from her nose. Her face looked like it had been beaten. There was a gold-colored ring on her left pinky finger. The M.E. noted "skin poppings" on her neck and both legs.

In the northwest corner of the room, about five feet away from her, was a pair of blue jeans with a pair of pink panties still tucked inside them.

"Do you know her?" Sergeant Mixon asked Ernestine.

She had a good look at the woman's face. "Yes, that's Brenda, Dianne's sister," she replied. Sheila concurred.

Ernestine didn't know Brenda really well – she knew Dianne better. But she had seen Brenda around for about three years. She recalled spotting Brenda getting out of the car with her mother and going into the Hotel Granwood at the first of April when Brenda got her check. Sheila had only known Brenda for a week or two and had just seen her the Saturday before. That would have been April 4.

The officers ordered everyone out of the house. In all the shuffling about, Sheila said something to a guy standing nearby, and he took off running toward the house next door. Minutes later, another man came to the scene. His name was Frank, brother of Dianne and Brenda. That might be my sister in there, he told police. Storball and Maclin took down his info. Dianne came to the scene later that night, as well as brother Fred. Police also talked to their mother, Maggie.

Detectives Morris Cotton and Willie Taylor arrived. Evidence techs processed the scene. They found human feces all over the room, on the back of the vic's left ankle, and in the kitchen of the house. There were other mattresses and box springs around the house that looked like people had been sleeping on them. The rear door of the house was busted open, and you could get in through the basement. There was a brown Samsonite suitcase sitting next to the body with an Amtrak label bearing a name and an address in Benton Harbor, on the west side of the state. Officers observed blood on the wall of the living room. The evidence techs collected samples of the blood, as well as latent prints from the sliding door in the living room, and they gathered up the suitcase, the blue jeans and panties, the gold-colored ring, a beige coat, and a pair of blue cloth shoes and gray (some reports say green) pants also in the room. Besides that, the usual trash was everywhere in this abandoned place.

Medical examiners took Brenda Mitchell's body to the morgue around nine-thirty that night. Hair and fingernail samples were taken from her, along with a blood sample and rectal, oral and vaginal swabs. Her identity was confirmed via fingerprints.

So make that one more kick in the teeth for the Highland Park detectives. It was back to the cold morgue the next day. Detective sergeants Larry Beller and Jim Dobson recalled what that was like, reporting to the Wayne County Medical Examiner the day after a body was found. How foul it was.

"That old building," Beller mused. "When we would have a homicide, it was mandatory that you go down the next morning for the autopsy. The detective in charge of the case had to go to the autopsy. So the medical examiner had the information for him. You'd go down there, and the autopsy room was in the basement, down these long stairs. And you'd open up that door, and the aroma that'd come out of there ... You'd walk in, and on any morning, there were ten, fifteen bodies they were doing autopsies on." This included Detroit and the rest of Wayne County. "The ventilation was terrible down in the basement."

Dobson said, "We were required to go down there because they might want something from us, or they would share information. Cause of death, manner of death. And we kinda worked together. But the numbers were overwhelming. And they'd open up drawers – there would be people everywhere."

This was in the old building on Lafayette near Beaubien Street in Detroit, a rather grand 1925 structure styled after an Egyptian mausoleum. It stood in the downtown's revered Greektown area right across from a big tourist hotel, a "top-notch hotel," as Dobson put it. At one point, leadership at the hotel complained because of all the bodies being taken in and out in view of their guests. A little later in the 1990s, the medical examiner's offices moved to Warren Avenue.

Though the manner of death in Brenda's case was ultimately determined to be homicide, there was some confusion at first. It was assumed to be a drug overdose, and that's how the media reported it. Her toxicology analysis showed positive results for alcohol, cocaine and benzoylecgonine, negative for several other substances like morphine and barbiturates. Later, semen would be detected on her rectal swab but not the vaginal or oral. No semen was found on the blue jeans or panties. Blood was detected on numerous items: the ring, her fingernail clippings, the gray pants, the coat and the suitcase. Brenda had type A blood, and that's what was found (not the type O blood her killer would be revealed to have). No prints would be found on the suitcase.

The month of April would prove just a little more deadly for the crew at Highland Park Public Safety.

April 15, six-thirty a.m. It would be cloudy and cold that day, thirty-five degrees. A thirty-four-year-old man named Maurice lived in an apartment at 111 Highland and wandered next door, to 121 Highland, which was another apartment building but vacant, to see if he could find anything for his place, which he had just moved into a couple weeks earlier. In particular he was looking for some usable furniture. He went around the south side of the building to the back door, climbing over some furniture to get inside and go up a few stairs to the first floor. He went into the apartment on the right. He found a chair he liked and threw it out the window to the ground. Then he went across the hallway to the apartment on the left. At the front of the apartment he found another chair and threw that out a nearby window, too. In that same room there was a mattress on the floor, and it looked to Maurice like someone could be living in this apartment. He went into the bedroom in the rear and found a third chair. That went out the window. "I then looked to my left," he told police, "and I saw something on the floor. I looked closer and I could see that it was a body, and it was a Black girl."

He scooted out the apartment, out the back door of the building. He first took the chairs he had thrown out the window back to his apartment, then he went to the apartment of his cousin, who also lived at 111. She called the police.

The call came in to HPPS at seven-ten a.m. Body in a closet of an abandoned apartment building at 121 Highland Street, west of Woodward Ave between Second and Third streets. Apartment 106, southwest corner of the first floor. The building sat between Highland Park Community College (which would close four years later) and Cortland Elementary School. Ferris School, a former elementary that was a middle school at that time, was also nearby.

Officers Sheila Herring and Frank Ross responded to the scene, joined by several others from the HPPS crew. They found the back door open, but the entranceway stairs blocked by a couch and some mattresses. After moving the couch, they searched the basement of the building at first, thinking that's what Maurice meant by the first floor, then proceeded upstairs.

Like the other scenes, there was all kinds of damage to this vacant building, from both scavenging and vandalism. Doors and windows were damaged or missing. Debris was everywhere, like broken glass, garbage and construction materials. As they stepped in and out of the rubbish, it was Officer Craig Pulvirenti who actually spotted the body, he and his partner Willie Woodruff up in that room while Officer Deana Smart, who had arrived with her partner Brenda Perkins, was at the southwest side of the building with Ross.

The windows were boarded up in this heatless, powerless apartment except for one window on the south side, which allowed some emerging sunlight to stream into the den. Officer Ross pulled up the top piece of clothing lying on the woman's body. She was nude, face down, in the closet of the apartment's den, with her head pointed to the south and feet pointed north. Her right arm was extended above her head, with the hand and wrist partially inside the sleeve of a black coat and a shirt, and her left arm down by her side. Other pieces of clothing lay on top of her. She had a blue sock on her right foot. And around her neck was a black belt like from a trench coat, Herring wrote in her report, not knotted. She was wearing pink nail polish, as well as two rings on her left ring finger.

Officer Smart advised the others to vacate the room and secure the building, and HPPS called on the Michigan State Police Sterling Heights crime lab again to process the scene. Sergeant Herbert Bell, patrol supervisor, put in the call to the detectives, and Willie Taylor and Richard Hartman reported to the scene. Taylor notified Jim Dobson on his way. The HPPS officers made a check of the whole building, including the roof. They also notified officials at the two nearby schools, Cortland and Ferris, that police, and no doubt media, would be there all day, so the schools agreed to keep kids inside (despite that, *The Detroit News* would report children at Cortland watching behind the fence as the body was taken out of the building). HPPS Director John Mattox came to the scene, as well as a couple city council members and former Highland Park Mayor Martha Scott. Scott and one of the council members immediately crossed the police line to check things out but were asked by officers to leave. Mattox "loaned us his portable telephone to use at the scene," one officer's report noted.

A team of three from the MSP lab arrived at ten-thirty a.m., photographing the scene, and Taylor and Detective Morris Cotton took their own photos, as well. MSP collected all kinds of clothing from the apartment: white uniform dress, brown corduroy jacket, gray jeans, black jacket, blue short-sleeve knit shirt, floral print jacket, blue jean skirt, blue jean cutoffs, more blue jeans, tan and blue coat, the blue sock she was wearing, maroon jersey shirt, a pair of brown shoes – one of which was in the living room with a blue sock tucked in it matching what was on her foot, and the other lying next to her body. What might belong to this woman, or what might belong to the perp, or what might have just been left here by others? They also grabbed a couple empty matchbooks from the pockets of the black coat, along with a tube of lipstick, a Menthol Lights cigarette pack with one cigarette in it, and a partially smoked cigarette. They took a stool specimen from the room. The black belt around her neck was taken up by HPPS, also to be analyzed by MSP.

She was transported to the morgue shortly after noon. The customary samples were collected: Hair, fingernails, blood, and oral, vaginal and rectal swabs.

Officers talked with some of the folks in the neighborhood, like staff at several Woodward Ave businesses: a bookstore, a motel, an arcade and a "peep show," where they spoke with a twenty-eight-year-old dancer. They interviewed residents of 111 Highland whose apartments faced 121. No one saw or heard anything of note, except one twenty-two-year-old male resident who had observed another guy from his building, someone he had always found shady, walking with a female the night before, when he had never had a female companion before (the suspicious guy had a nickname reflecting his sexual orientation – not to be included here). The man was hanging around outside the vacant apartment where the body was found, the resident told officers.

A twenty-three-year-old prostitute named Frances, petite at just four-foot-ten and one hundred five pounds, told police about an incident a month earlier with a john who picked her up in front of the Cavalier Motel. He drove a small burgundy sports car, she said, with burgundy interior, and had been circling the block awhile before he stopped. He drove them down Colorado Street to John R, turned, went a couple more blocks. She tried to make small talk; he said nothing. He parked the car, looked around, turned the car off and let out a big sigh.

"I hate to do this to you," he said, then began to choke her. In the midst of it, Frances said, this guy talked about the Monterey Motel, though she couldn't really make out what he was saying.

A nearby porch light then came on, and the man released her. She managed to grab a soda bottle and hit him with it.

She had not screamed – she was too weak, she said. She got out of the car as a couple guys came out to the porch. She told them she had just been choked. They merely looked at her.

Her attacker was a white guy, Frances said, young twenties, about six foot and two hundred to two hundred twenty pounds, sandy blond hair, blue eyes. Wearing blue jeans, a sweatshirt and white gym shoes. She took police to the locale, which was on East Buena Vista. So HPPS had another guy to throw into their mix – was he the one? Or just another random guy attacking a prostitute?

Police also checked out Maurice pretty good, searching his apartment with his permission. Nothing of interest found. Maurice was characterized in the police reports as having a mental handicap. He had been assigned a case worker and had done a two-week stay in a state psychiatric hospital a couple months earlier.

"Gory rerun in Highland Park," the *Free Press* headline read the next morning. *The Detroit News*' story that day said Highland Park's council president pledged to get some of the city's vacant parcels boarded up, as residents continued complaining. "I don't care if we've got to take all of the money out of the contingency fund," he said. An angry parent near the scene at 121 Highland shouted, "Our children play here!" as police tried to wave away onlookers.

That day, Unknown Female No. 30 became Vicki Marie Beasley Brown, ID'd by her fingerprints, with alternate names reflected on some of the case records: Denise Linda Beasley, Denise Brown, Sandra M. Beasley. HPPS learned she had a missing person's report filed on her in Detroit. Her mother, Gloria, confirmed her identity at the Wayne County Medical Examiner's office. With abrasions on her neck and hemorrhages consistent with ligature strangulation, the manner of death was, once again, homicide. She also had abrasions on her back and legs and a cut on her right eyebrow. All five-foot-five, one hundred nine pounds of her (though another report would peg her as five-foot-three and one hundred ten). Yung Chung, assistant medical examiner, did her autopsy and would go on to examine victims of serial killer John Eric Armstrong a few years later.

Vicki's tox screens came back negative for alcohol, barbiturates, morphine and cocaine.

Police spoke with Vicki's family members, including her estranged husband, Jerome. They looked at the schedule for the place where Jerome worked, a security company. On March 24 and 25, the time period it's believed Vicki disappeared, Jerome was on the schedule for midnight to eight a.m.

Gloria, who had filed the missing person's report in Detroit on April 2, told police that Vicki had a troubled relationship with John, a man she knew on Trowbridge Street in Detroit. Gloria last spoke with her daughter three weeks earlier, at midnight on March 25 (whether the eleven-fifty-nine p.m. was March 24 or 25 is unclear), when Vicki told her that if she heard about a man being killed, it was her shooting John, whom she said was abusive toward her. Even Jerome had assaulted Vicki right before Christmas, Gloria said.

Police also questioned John. And they continued to pound the pavement in the search for clues, going right to the homeless on the street. "Some are very cooperative," Mattox told *The Detroit News* a couple days after Vicki was found. "Some are hesitant to talk to us. And of course, a lot of them are asking, 'What's in it for me?'"

Later in the month, the MSP crime lab had the results of what was taken up at the scene: No semen detected on the clothing from the room, but blood found on the black coat. Hairs were recovered from some items that could be tested against future suspects. The partially smoked cigarette also could be analyzed for A, B, O (H) blood group substances in the future, the lab noted. No semen was detected in the samples taken from Vicki. Nothing of evidential value was found on her fingernails.

On April 22, 1992, Ron Gotowicki, a forensic chemist in the Detroit Police crime lab, sent a few samples for analysis to Cellmark Diagnostics in Germantown, Maryland:

- A seminal fluid stain detected on a coat found near Bertha Mason
- The condom and tissue paper from the Valerie Chalk scene, on which seminal fluid and H blood group substance were found
- Two tubes of blood from suspect Lonnie

Lonnie was their guy at the moment. He had failed a polygraph test. So now they were trying to match his DNA to the fluids found on these items. "Check for high molecular weight DNA in the unknowns prior to extracting the knowns," Gotowicki wrote in the letter, also mentioning both DPD and HPPS as wanting these results. Perhaps the two departments were working more in tandem at this point.

It was around this time that the two jurisdictions would get some much-needed help – both in handling the workload and in drawing more attention to the case. The Detroit office of the Federal Bureau of Investigation, in the form of agent Paul Lindsay, came on board to help move things forward.

"Jim Harrington was able to set up a meeting where the state police, the FBI, Detroit police, and Highland Park police could attend," John Mattox recalled. "And that was at Domino's Farms," referring to the Ann Arbor office park of Domino's Pizza founder Tom Monaghan.

Mattox didn't remember the exact date but said the meeting took place before the FBI and the state police officially came onto the Atkins case. Right after the meeting, help arrived from FBI Director William Sessions, and there were several more meetings to follow as the agencies coordinated their efforts around the investigation. Then special agent Lindsay jumped in.

Lindsay, a twenty-year veteran with the Bureau, was in the midst of embarking on a writing career, penning a few novels drawing from his time in the Detroit office and featuring a smart, daring special agent named Mike Devlin. The FBI wasn't particularly fond of these novels. Lindsay departed the FBI not too long after the first was published.

"He was brought in to coordinate the case for us," Larry Beller recalled. "He was assigned to us. We weren't computerized at the time. Our filing system for tips was a shoebox with cards in it. And he brought a technician, or a guy who wasn't an FBI agent, a kid with a laptop. And he got everything into the computer. Lindsay had the contacts to get help, outside help, also."

Sessions connected with the Highland Park mayor, with a little help from HPPS Director John Mattox, and on May 6, the Detroit office met with HPPS. The Bureau got entrée into the case with kidnapping laws that give it jurisdiction when a person has been missing at least twenty-four hours. The connection of these women being "kidnapped" might have seemed a bit loose at the time, but whatever. It worked. Also joining the case that week: the Wayne County Sheriff's Department. Two detectives and a crime tech were loaned out. The mayor had made an appeal to Wayne County Sheriff Robert Ficano. Slowly but surely, as the bodies surfaced, so did the help, allaying the frustrations Mattox felt early on.

Lindsay's assistance was felt right away. "He made arrangements with the Chrysler Corporation that was in Highland Park on Oakman," Beller said, "and he got us an office over there, so we could be away from things – Jimmy and I would go over and type warrants up, they'd give us a private office and the best typewriters and everything, to do the typing."

Dobson said of Lindsay: "He was very different. A well-decorated war hero, well-decorated FBI agent. But Larry will tell ya, he was different." But, "he had everything. When it came to something, money, our department was kinda poor. We'd go somewhere, he'd find an informant that wanted to help us, he'd give him a couple hundred dollars. I'd say, 'hey, you're ruining it for everybody else! We don't have that resource available to us.' He says, 'I do!'" Lindsay's good connections in Detroit included the local constables. Whereas Dobson and Beller had a hard time getting through to DPD, "when Paul went down there, because of his background and all the times he had operated with them, he was kind of the glue that tried to bring stuff together."

The deal with Chrysler helped immensely, Dobson said. "Chrysler took good care of us. The problem was the news media would follow us everywhere. So we'd go over to Chrysler. There were different gates we could go in and out of. And we had freedom."

Chrysler also provided a graphic artist to help with charts, sketches and any other artistic tools. Mattox remembered the assist from the automotive giant, and the challenge of working the case with everybody watching you. "Chrysler on the QT did that," Mattox said. "That was not my connection. That was Larry and Dobson that got that. They asked me about it. I said sure, go with it. Because we had to get out of the police station. You couldn't use the telephone because of the other police officers looking and gaining information to their advantage. Thought they were going to solve the case."

Lindsay also helped with the processing of evidence, backed by federal clout and connections. The speed with which DNA can be analyzed has changed a lot since the early 1990s – back then it could take quite a few months to get results. With how fast their killer was moving, police couldn't afford to wait that long.

"I remember Lindsay was cutting corners," Mattox said, "and it would take about maybe three, four months then, maybe longer. And I mean, normally they would tell you six months, but you could have an individual in your custody and released several times, until you got the results back."

In early May, the Wayne County Sheriff's Department – specifically Sheriff Ficano – enlisted the help of Dr. Bruce Danto, a forensic psychiatrist based in Los Angeles at the time but with Michigan roots, who was also involved in the investigation of the notorious 1970s unsolved case of the Oakland County Child Killer. Danto called the Woodward Corridor Killer obsessive and organized. "He stages who he is looking for," Danto told Corey Williams for *The Detroit News*. "He creates the opportunity and makes sure he doesn't leave a clue."

Along with forensic consultant Thomas Streed, Danto developed this sketch of the killer:

- Early thirties
- May have been abused as a child
- Uses drugs to lure the victims
- Collects things from the victims like underwear or jewelry
- Hasn't changed his M.O., meaning he might subconsciously want to be caught
- Lives in or near Highland Park

Danto believed the perp was driven to kill because it felt good to him, and that he strangled because "there is a special way of venting anger through your hands. You can watch a person slowly expire. It's a more gratifying form of control or torture." Danto said if this guy was subconsciously wanting to be caught, it was because there's only so far you can go as a wrongdoer. "After they have killed a certain number of people, they become very unhappy. They can't sleep and can't stand themselves anymore. They show remorse in different ways. One way may be by pulling a traffic offense with a police car behind them, or by letting someone glimpse their memorabilia."

Police were continuing their appeal to local residents. HP offered a two-thousand-dollar reward for tips. "This guy is going to blend right into the background," the *Free Press* quoted MSP Detective Sergeant David Minzey in a May 6 story that all these years later has many eerie truths ringing through it. "He says very little; he's just always there." The killer probably has bad social skills and finds it difficult to establish relationships, Minzey said. "He may not be perceived as a threat." Lieutenant Donald Roberts of HPPS echoed the sentiment: "It's got to be somebody that basically they would trust." Police were assuming at this point that the killer operated on foot, and that he may have even been watching them from the crowd at the crime scenes. They felt strongly that there was someone seeing these news reports who knew this guy and could give him up.

Well, yeah, there was. But police didn't listen to her a couple months earlier.

To this day Agent Paul Lindsay is credited with discovering Darlene Saunders' March incident report in the files, wondering if anyone had followed up on it, thus bringing her onto the case to help, which led to the arrest of the true perp. But Darlene's son, Rashad, said that's not exactly how it happened. His uncle was the one who brought it to the forefront, he said. His dad's brother Daniel, who was a well-known veteran. He called police in May and insisted they listen to what Darlene had to say. That she knew who was attacking these women. It also took an HPPS officer named Donna, who knew Darlene, to really get her report some attention. Donna, who would go on to work for the Wayne County Sheriff's Department, wanted to make sure Darlene did not get overlooked. Donna, along with Jim Dobson, then spoke to Darlene further and learned more about her attack, Rashad remembered.

Still, it would be a few more months before Darlene would help get her attacker arrested. As the investigation continued spinning, other bodies turned up around town that were determined to be unrelated. In May, a couple days before Dr. Danto was quoted in the paper, an eighteen-year-old woman's body was found in a parking lot in Highland Park. She was bludgeoned to death and run over by a car, however, and she was white whereas all of the strangling victims were Black. She was left out in the open, not hidden. An unidentified Black female turned up in the Detroit River in mid-April on the city's east side. Also unrelated. Another serial had been operating in Metro Detroit at the time: Leslie Allen Williams was convicted of killing four females between September 1991 and January 1992. He was apprehended in May 1992. And Paul Lindsay was investigating a different serial killer in the nearby city of Inkster just after this case, according to a profile on him that appeared in *Vanity Fair* magazine in 1993. This perp was raping and strangling Black women and leaving them in abandoned buildings, as well. Michigan State Police were investigating that case in not only Inkster but also nearby Romulus and Ypsilanti, the *Detroit Free Press* reported when the Monterey discovery was made. There were ten unsolved slayings dating back to 1985, at least three of which were prostitutes.

Apart from Detroit just being Detroit, there was a fear out there on the street at the time that was palpable. Former cop Melvin Toney remembered it. He grew up in southwest Detroit and spent years with DPD. He knew a lot of people. He worked Vice, he worked projects, he worked over in Housing and in other areas. He worked Precinct No. Two. He loved working the street. "I was a street person. Everybody couldn't understand how I did what I did. But I just wasn't afraid. I grew up on the streets, so I knew the streets."

But at the time of this case, Toney said, especially for the women who worked the trade, "there was a lot of fear. A lot of fear, because some of them were so afraid that they always had somebody that was in the area that was monitoring them. They were walking the street. OK? And that's when they set up other places where they took the johns and everything. That way they weren't out there. That's what they did. And then they started the thing where they became 'call girls.'"

The term "call girl" has become synonymous with prostitute or hooker, but there is a difference, Toney pointed out.

"Call girls do not walk the street. You've got a number that you call. That's the difference in a call girl. And you make your arrangements and then you just – the arrangements are made; you just meet up. You're told where to go."

So a slightly safer way to do business, rather than a john picking you up on the sidewalk. The women started to carry pagers, perhaps even coyly worded business cards, as retired DPD officer Mark Bando will tell you. He would hang onto the cards when he spoke to the women on the street; he kept them in an album. Tried to keep tabs on these girls when he could, as they navigated the stormy sea of the inner city. Some of these females had madams, too. In Toney's work patrolling for the Detroit force, he watched that shift to the "call girl" approach, and much more. He and his comrades learned where people hung out, who they were noticing, what they were doing, as they hunted a killer on the Woodward corridor.

"We were in the street most of the time," Toney said. "We could go into those areas, and we could get a lot of information. And everybody that was out on the street, basically they were involved in something illegal. But we built a rapport with them. We used to write the names, numbers and addresses, and I knew where everybody hung out. So I would go find them. I could only find them at night, because I worked the midnight shift."

Toney remembered another killer operating in the area around the time, but killing prostitutes who were transgender. It was happening up in the Twelfth Precinct, he said, near Palmer Park at Seven Mile Road and Woodward, but it was largely kept out of the news. Everything was political up there, Toney said, with big houses and things remaining quite hush-hush. That area of the city has been in the news in more recent years for its unofficial "red-light district," particularly where transgender prostitutes are concerned and the murder of at least one of them. Back then, though, Toney said the serial killings just stopped, and he would give no further detail, just saying "there's a lot to this story. It's a lot to this story. OK? I know that for sure."

Survivor Margie Osborn also remembered a serial killer operating in the Woodward/Palmer Park area, from her own time on the streets, but she remembered it as happening a few years later. Possibly a different case? "They never caught him, and the kicker about that is," Margie said, "the killer is a transsexual himself and he's Caucasian. I remember how he looks. He never bothered real women; he always murdered people of the same sexual orientation. And this was going on in 2008-2009. It's so strange that street people have more knowledge about crimes than the police."

Apparently, that's a tale for another book.

John Mattox recalled a particular prostitute who used to frequent Woodward Ave. "I was talking to her one night. I said, 'What is going on around here?' She said, 'I don't know, but people are disappearing.'" And this was before things started happening with the Atkins case. "I said, 'What are you talking about?' And she looked at me, she said, 'You should know, not me.' She was saying, you know, girls were disappearing. She didn't tell me how many, and after that when things got hot, she vanished. I never saw her after that."

Every region of prostitution in Detroit has had its own feel, over the years, and it remains true today. A few years after this case, the aforementioned John Eric Armstrong hunted prostitutes on Michigan Avenue. He would hunt by car, not on foot. He had a family at home. He had a job. He had been in the U.S. Navy. He was the boy next door. And he chose the strip-club-laden Michigan Ave. Then there's the Cass Corridor, where the serial killer nicknamed Bigfoot hunted in the 1970s. A guy never caught, murdering seven female prostitutes on the Cass between February and October 1975, and before that raping four others who were able to give a description to police. This author has a reporter colleague who wants to write a book about that case; he grew up in the area, hearing about it as a kid. I hope he does do the book.

Then there's the historic Woodward.

"There were pockets of Woodward that there was no activity in," Everett Monroe pointed out. "And then you go a little bit further, and then bam, you've got all this different activity going on. As opposed to Cass, it was just wide open. Now, what would happen is a lot of the girls would work different areas. They would be over in the Cass Corridor for a while. If things were not going good for them at that time, then they would go over to Woodward, because you're only talking two blocks over, and they would be on Woodward Avenue. But they would bounce around. But Woodward was a lot different than Cass. I mean, it was areas that there was no activity like that going on, and then all of a sudden, now you've got it. Woodward was unique in its own way and totally different from Cass Corridor, totally different from Michigan Ave. It had its own culture."

Was it more the drugs, or how was it different?

"Depending on what you're looking for," Monroe said. "I mean, if you're looking for the drugs, there were certain areas of Woodward Avenue that it was plentiful. If you wanted prostitution, there were certain areas that it was plentiful. Especially around the north end, around Clairmount and Woodward, that was the popping area. Everything was jumping. Whatever you need, you could buy. And then you go over further north, it was a little bit different. And then it was a dry area up until you got around … closer to Highland Park things kind of changed a little bit. But people knew where to go on Woodward for what they wanted. If they were looking for drugs, they knew to go around the north end area, go on back south, a little bit north. And looking for prostitution, well, it was readily available."

The different areas of prostitution varied by the price that would be paid, as well, Mattox said. "The ones that worked Cass would get less money," he said. A lot of Woodward Ave has been cleaned up since then, but Mattox remembered that even back at the time of this case, Wayne State University was largely "skipped," as he called it, where crime and prostitution were concerned. The campus, plunked right down there in the Cass Corridor in the thick of things, didn't suffer the same ills as the surrounding area. The biggest concern of the Wayne State security force was the activity at the bars, he said. And then there was Hamtramck, Detroit's other enclave like Highland Park. The small town with Polish roots located just a few blocks east of Woodward Ave and southeast of Highland Park didn't seem to share its crime with anyone. It's not that there was not prostitution there, Mattox said – there was. But you just never heard about anything happening there. "Nobody went to Hamtramck!" he said with amused surprise, still, after all these years. "The ones who worked in Hamtramck, they stayed in Hamtramck."

And untangling all of that, making sense of the beast that was Woodward Avenue – beautiful in some places, ugly in others – was made all the more challenging with a serial killer who was on foot but definitely had his foot on the gas.

"The case kind of took on a life of itself," Monroe remembered. "I mean, it was just growing. And because of the seriousness of it being a serial killer. And he had such a jump on us, you know, because leadership, especially in Homicide, didn't want to say, OK, yep, we got this serial killer. They wanted to keep things down. Things being numbers, down. And it was a lot of things going on behind the scenes that a lot of people weren't privy to hear or to read or so forth."

***

"Mr. President Bush, could you please help us? Our children are growing up, our young ladies are growing up, right next to where we find victims of a murderer. Please, can you stop the killing?"

Those were the screams of a forty-five-year-old resident named Caroline, as reported in the *Detroit Free Press* on July 9, not long after another body turned up attributed to the killer. Even worse, that July find was not one of Atkins' victims – it was (evidently) the victim of some other killer. This one — a man, not a woman — was also found by a scrapper in an abandoned building.

The neighborhoods were feeling it. Fear. Chaos. Disgust. And it had been several months of frustration for law enforcement from two different cities, who knew, deep down or right on the surface, that the serial killer case happening in Florida at the same time was getting a lot more press and care than their cities' murders. The victims down there? White. College students. "Good" girls. The perp was white, too, Danny Rolling, nicknamed the Gainesville Ripper. The injustice was glaring. Heartbreaking.

Adding to that were the occasional comments of local folks like the pastor of a church on Woodward, who told the *Free Press* of the victims, "They were already among the walking dead." Whether it was out of compassion or disdain was unclear, though he added, "Nobody deserves to die that way, but they were already dead in a sense."

At least the discovery of Joanne O'Rourke, the final victim found before Atkins' arrest, would make the front page of the local paper.

Folks living in the area had been noticing a foul smell coming out of the building at 12223 Woodward, between Cortland and Richton in Highland Park. The doors and windows were mostly boarded up, but the two rear doors of the structure had been open for a couple months, said a man who lived on Richton, and he noticed the odor beginning around Memorial Day. People were coming in and out of that building all the time, he said. The building had two levels with vacant apartments upstairs and three commercial units downstairs, two of which were vacant at the time with the third occupied by a soup kitchen. It was mid-June, and the warmth of the approaching summer was settling in, cooking whatever else was in that building. On this particular day it was seventy-five to eighty degrees.

Craig Pulvirenti was early on in his law enforcement career. He was in the midst of the six years he would spend with Highland Park Public Safety before moving on to the eastern Detroit suburb of Roseville. He was a cop for three decades in all, and he was also in military intel and the Green Berets.

"I started off, and they were working on the case, and I was attached to the DB *[detective bureau]* in the unit I was in," Pulvirenti recalled over the same lunch where his former HPPS brothers Larry Beller and Jim Dobson were interviewed for this book. "At this time, the city was really in bad shape, and one of the places that we were called to was the former campaign headquarters for Martha Scott. It was this abandoned building. So we got dispatched there." Whether or not the building was actually Scott's campaign locale is unconfirmed – and it would be painfully ironic, given that she had just visited the prior crime scene – though the building was reported to be the office of former state Rep. Ethel Terrell.

The call came in just before two p.m. on Monday, June 15, 1992, from Thomas, a worker at the soup kitchen. A smell had been emanating from the building for weeks. That may seem odd, that the smell would go uninvestigated for so long while a high-profile serial killer case was in the news. But it was not unusual to detect odors from buildings in this town. "Highland Park had not picked up the garbage for quite a while," Pulvirenti said. "So everybody was taking their garbage and throwing it into this building. You can imagine what the smell was like. We walked in the building, we got about ten steps in, they said, no, no, it's just the smell of the garbage. So I said, let me go a little further in. So I walked in further and I saw a leg sticking out. I remember I yelled, 'Lieutenant!'"

He and the HPPS crew had, of course, gotten calls to buildings with foul smells before and they had come away empty-handed. But this time, Pulvirenti said, the odor was overpowering. "Livid," as he put it in his report.

Thinking of the years he spent in HP, he recalled the city being a dumping ground for dead bodies on numerous occasions outside of this case. "We were literally a tiny precinct inside of Detroit. We didn't have the officers of Detroit." There was less likelihood the perp would be caught because they didn't have the manpower to handle it. At least that was the thinking of the criminal mind. "But the good part is, as small as we were, we had a lot more specialties in the people we had," he said.

The building at Woodward and Richton was one of three of the case's crime scenes Pulvirenti responded to. He and his partner Frank Ross, along with Sergeant Bell, gained entry at the rear (west) side of the structure, finding the rear door lying on the ground at the entranceway. The center unit on the first floor had three rooms: the westernmost room had been used for storage, the middle room used for preparing food by the restaurant that once occupied it, and the easternmost/front room was a serving and storefront area with display windows. Flies swarmed everywhere and the odor grew stronger as the officers neared the northeast corner of the front room of the center unit. There was a pile of garbage there that included a bunch of cardboard boxes. Pulvirenti picked up one of the boxes to discover the body.

She was wearing only her black (which Atkins had remembered as blue), velvet, high-heeled, ankle-length, fur-lined boots and the black socks underneath them. She had her wrists tied behind her as she lay on her side. A pair of panties was around her left ankle; police and the coroner surmised the underwear had been used as a binding for her ankles. Fly larvae were in and around her – her clavicle was exposed for the maggots. There were two plastic bags secured over her head and tied around her neck, a white bag inside and a black bag outside. The white bag read "Adult Education – Detroit Outreach." The left sleeve of a dark shirt was tied around them at the woman's neck. A bra had been used to tie her hands. Amid the garbage were a couple pairs of pants: blue jeans and gray corduroys. Larry Beller hand-wrote in his notes that grass and other plant life was found inside her boots and on the socks. He reported to the scene along with Jim Dobson.

Police secured the scene then searched the whole building, including the basement, as Beller also included in his notes. They canvassed the neighborhood, talking to several people. They learned that just before they arrived, a Detroit Edison utility worker had been there checking out the building, having noticed the odor, but left before police got there because he didn't want to get involved. The media reported that he had gone inside the building with Thomas from the soup kitchen. An area prostitute also came by as the scene was being processed, saying she knew of a woman named Beverly who had been missing. Maybe it was her they found? She wondered.

The Sterling Heights crime lab of the Michigan State Police again sent a team to process. Four people in two vehicles arrived around four-forty p.m., wise enough to be armed with battery-powered lights. They photographed and sketched the scene. They lasered the walls for blood and fingerprints and searched everywhere else for fingerprints. They did find prints on some glass near the body, with one usable latent print added to the case files. Among the items they collected: the black boots and black socks, the pair of white panties, the soiled bra tied in a knot, the black shirt with the left sleeve tied in a knot, a blue sweatshirt that had been lying on top of her, and four cardboard boxes.

The woman was taken to the Wayne County morgue just after seven p.m., and the next day, Beller and Dobson were off to that stenchy building once again. "Manual force was applied around the neck of the decedent to obstruct blood flow to the brain and therefore depriving the brain of adequate oxygen," Dr. Laning Davidson wrote in the autopsy report. "The force applied around the neck was enough to also fracture the hyoid bone (a bone that is just above the larynx or voice box). Possibly contributing to this asphyxial death was action of suffocation caused by two plastic bags tied around the victim's neck." Tox screens were positive for cocaine and barbiturates, negative for alcohol and morphine. Five-foot-three and about one hundred three pounds, the report said.

"It's like somebody dropped a hammer on us and knocked us down again," the Highland Park mayor was quoted in the June 16 edition of *The Detroit News*. The woman who ran the soup kitchen told the paper she had reported the odor to police a couple weeks earlier and they did not investigate. "The smell got worse after the weather turned hot," she said.

At this point the police were hesitant to publicly attribute this latest find to their killer, but HPPS and Wayne County Sheriff's deputies did plan on going door-to-door to talk with area residents. And, of all things, a horseback patrol was planned for the streets, ordered by Sheriff Robert Ficano to help the cash-strapped Highland Park, which laid off several officers in June. Their elusive killer was already being recognized as operating at a high speed, though he had not yet officially earned his monikers of the Woodward Corridor Killer or Highland Park Strangler.

The woman, whom police realized could have been dead as long as February 20 when the building was last included in a sweep of abandoned structures, was too decomposed to obtain vaginal or rectal swabs. Her mummified hands were removed in similar fashion to the victims at the Monterey, and the lab report noted that the hands were clutching hairs, which were also tested. At the end of June, after the elimination of other missing women, a print from the woman's right pinky finger ID'd her in AFIS – the Automated Fingerprint Identification System. Joanne Mae Ollie, aka Joanne O'Rourke. Dr. Warnick also examined the dental records, as profiled in a June 19 *Free Press* story, where he noted Unknown Female No. 51's slight gap between the two front teeth and the congenital defect of never having developed two teeth in her upper jaw. The two teeth normally fit between the pointed canines and the front teeth, but the canines had taken their place, closing the gap. It's an inherited defect only affecting five to eight percent of the population, the dentist told the paper.

On June 25, the MSP determined there was no semen on the panties found at the scene and nothing of evidentiary value found on the other clothing items. The two plastic bags that were tied on her head were tested for prints; negative. On July 6, the lab completed its analysis of the cardboard boxes found at the scene; no fingerprints. The hairs collected from the woman's hands were determined to be her own, not from any possible perp.

So not much to go on, with this latest find. And though the media noted the boldness of her body being left across the street from the Monterey Motel, it's likely that from the killer's perspective this was merely a convenience, not a statement.

On July 8, as the man's body was found at Highland and Hamilton streets and initially attributed to their serial, the HPPS officers were being spread pretty thin, despite getting a hand from other agencies. The city cut three and a half million from its sixteen-million-dollar budget on July 1. Even the secretary of the detective bureau was laid off, leaving the officers to answer phones. HPPS had forked out eighty thousand dollars in overtime for police since the Monterey Motel discovery. The mayor and Chief Mattox were also catching heat because none of the primary officers investigating the case was Black, while all the victims and many of the folks interviewed in the neighborhoods were. How were residents going to find it easy to talk with white officers? Mattox pushed back on that in the media: "I think the most important thing is that this case gets solved."

HPPS finally connected with Darlene Saunders on July 18, then Detective Sergeant Dobson sat down with her on July 27, giving her the audience she had long deserved. She remembered her attack as happening sometime after the kids had gone back to school, late September or October. She was working the street over by the library, around four-thirty to five a.m., she said. She described Tony this time as five-foot-three to five-foot-four (his height would later become a point of contention in court) with a fade type haircut. His arms seemed a little long for his body, she told Dobson. He was clean-shaven at the time, but the last time she saw him, in May, he had a light moustache. In this account, she mentioned an additional person on the scene. After Atkins had run off, Mario (whose name was actually Demerio) only stayed a couple minutes while she got her clothing from the building, she said, then he had to catch the bus for work. Another man in a tan pickup truck pulled up and shined his headlights into the building for her while she continued to gather her things. Darlene gave another interesting detail in this July report with Dobson: She said that when she later told her friend Donna about the incident, Donna said she had been attacked by the same person, so they decided to report their incidents together at the police station. Could Donna be an additional attack by Atkins? Or was this the Highland Park cop who helped draw attention to Darlene's report, and the details just became confused over the years? The files give no explanation.

It was around this time that a man described as a "rogue drifter" in his thirties came on police radar. Multiple prostitutes had pointed this guy out to police. He was a former patient at a local psychiatric facility and had lived in the Monterey and other abandoned buildings in the area. He spent a lot of time up and down Woodward Ave. The women claimed he had paid them for sex then tried to choke them. Police questioned him in June but had nothing concrete to hold him. They released him and kept an eye on him. They then raided the home of his family on the east side of Detroit in mid-July, taking a couple boxes of stuff and figuring they might find some of the effects of their case victims. It was not a fruitful search. By this time, police were better acquainted with Darlene Saunders' account and the fact that she knew her attacker as Tony. This man's first name was Anthony. But the thirty-five-year-old man was presented in a lineup in early August, and Darlene told them that wasn't their guy. She knew this Tony, too, but he wasn't the person who attacked her. Dobson had his DNA tested against the seminal fluid stain found on the coat at the Bertha Mason scene; negative.

They also realized by this point that Lonnie wasn't their guy, either. Cellmark Diagnostics in Maryland got back with

DPD in mid-May with their reports: It was not Lonnie's DNA in the coat stain from the Mason scene or on the tissue paper from the Valerie Chalk scene, though they could not obtain DNA from the condom. The man who discovered Vicki Beasley, Maurice, had his palm print tested against the Monterey print with negative results.

In early August, another suspect emerged, with the first name Evie, and his DNA was tested against the tissue paper at the Chalk scene and the coat stain at the Mason scene, again with negative results. Still, Evie's fingerprints, like those of Lonnie and Anthony, would show up later in testing after the true perp was arrested. Even Atkins' breaking-and-entering buddy from the year before, Diosdado, got his fingerprints tested after Atkins was in custody.

To complicate things a bit more, in July police released a composite sketch to the media of a different man they were tracking, based on two other assault reports from prostitutes. One of the women was not actually sexually assaulted, and the other was not seriously injured. The sketch, looking nothing like Atkins, was of a man described as in his thirties like the drifter mentioned earlier in the news (Anthony), but it was reported this was not the same man. Was this the man with the first name Evie? Or someone else they did not yet know the name of? Were either of these assault victims Darlene? Unclear, but unlikely. Confused? Yeah. Police were, too.

ARREST

Royce Alston tended to get the jobs that nobody else wanted.

Born and raised on the east side of the city of Detroit, he had become streetwise. In his nearly twenty years with the Michigan State Police, that quality had served him well. Especially when Detroit cops didn't necessarily want the state police on their turf, as they were in this case. Alston started with MSP in 1977 and spent most of his career there, having previously served in the U.S. Air Force as a security officer. A onetime partner of DPD's Everett Monroe on the Violent Crime Task Force, he had learned to sail the rough waters of law enforcement politics, to step in and assist where needed. But not to take over. To lend expertise. But not step on toes.

And so it was, in the summer of 1992, that he found himself riding around incognito in an old raggedy car with the sole known survivor of a yet-to-be-apprehended serial killer.

Alston got along well with a supervisor in Detroit's Homicide division, Bill Rice. They were friends. So Bill figured since Royce was from the city of Detroit, he'd be a good one to help on this fast-moving case, this very high-profile case where the media was breathing down their necks. To take this female, whose story they now had no choice but to believe, around on Woodward Ave. See if they could finally lay eyes on this perp.

Maybe you could say Detective Sergeant Alston drew the short straw. Because it was a bit of a challenge.

"Didn't nobody want to be bothered with Darlene," Alston recalled when contacted for this book in 2022. "That was the bottom line. That was the bottom line."

Alston, who had retired to Florida when we spoke but still did some work in security, had surgery in more recent years that left him with good days and bad days. But those days on Woodward Ave have not faded from his memory. His unit of the state police was based in Livonia but traveled all over Metro Detroit for its work. Sometimes up to Pontiac in Oakland County. Sometimes down to Flat Rock in what's referred to as Detroit's downriver area. And definitely into the city.

MSP had to carefully step through the lines where Detroit was concerned since the police didn't want them there, Alston said. "But we always had a detective unit, an undercover unit, that worked the drugs in the city of Detroit, and everything else, you know. They used to tell us, 'You guys ain't in Detroit,' but you have to realize Detroit's in the state of Michigan. So I could go anyplace I want to in the state. So there was some conflict. There was some animosity between us. In cases like Benjamin Atkins and other cases that we worked together. And then we joined their basketball league. That brought us together. They realized that we were just like they were. Half of the [MSP] troops were born and raised in the city of Detroit. We were all for the same thing. So well, a lot of us developed really good relationships with officers in the city of Detroit. Once we got to know each other, we respected each other."

As the others working the Atkins case investigated suspects like Lonnie and Anthony and Evie and anyone else coming onto their radar, Alston was the one who spent a lot of time with Darlene, largely unaware of, or at least uninvolved in, the other work being done. He was simply pursuing that particular angle – the Darlene angle, one of several they had, the angle nobody else wanted, though the crew did not realize it would turn out to be their key lead. Jim Dobson had gotten to know Darlene pretty well from hearing her story, and he also met her son Rashad, who remembers the HPPS detective well to this day. But it was Royce who spent many evenings with Darlene over several weeks in the summer of '92 — as many as ten to twelve hours at a time, he would later testify — roaming the streets of Highland Park and Detroit, peering into dark crevices, going places he didn't even know existed. That was the thing – she took him to locales inside Woodward Ave's underbelly that law enforcement did not know of. She gave him access no other officer would have. All the while with Royce posing as a homeless person, just another guy on the street. They were hunting the hunter, looking just like him. Trying to be like him. Was it believable? Would it work? Time would have to tell.

"I would get Darlene like every day that I worked," Alston recalled. It depended on his schedule. "So I would say I had Darlene probably five or six days a week with me. We only went out at night or early evening because that was his time. That was his time. His time was when the prostitutes were out. That's when Benjamin came out."

It proved to be a rather fascinating experience for the MSP officer. "We would ride around, and Darlene, she would tell me war stories. She would tell me things that she had been involved in with her dates, and how many times she had jumped out of cars, and hotels, out of hotel rooms. And then on top of that, she still had a drug habit, too. So I had to make sure that when I got her, she wasn't high. I mean, some nights, some nights as I recall, it was a real challenge for Darlene. I could recall one night she was really acting goofy. I kind of swore and I said, 'Darlene, damn, look at these people out here.' 'OK, OK, OK, OK,' you know. I mean, to be with Darlene, we had our good nights. We had our nights that I had to really get her to focus."

Where others on the case were tougher regarding Darlene, perhaps seeing her chosen line of work first and foremost, Royce was more of the "good cop."

"I would have to calm her down. And it worked out well. It worked out well for us because she trusted me, you know. She trusted me. And I would tell her, 'Darlene, the nights you ride with me, you better get high before you get with me, and you better be calmed down because I'm not going through your bull.' And a lot of nights, she got in and she wouldn't be high. Yeah, she wouldn't be high."

The car they rode around in was "a little bitty midsize Pontiac or old blue Chrysler Cordova," Alston recalled. "It was a wreck, because it wasn't nothing that even looked like a police car." But they only spent part of their time in the car – a lot of their hunting was done on foot. It was an eye-opening experience for Alston. Bars. Dope houses. Seedy, hidden pockets. Hiding in plain sight.

"She was taking me places that police officers weren't entitled to go," Alston said, "unless we were on raids. You know, I was walking into whorehouses that we didn't even — as I recall, I was walking into places with illegal activity with Darlene. And I would wait two or three days, and I would call it in for them to raid it."

Though Alston was taking these kinds of measures to avoid blowing his cover, he still had to wonder if word was getting around. It had to be, right? Since people on the street generally knew everybody else on the street? Saw folks around? Nevertheless, he and Darlene forged on.

"We went into a couple abandoned buildings that we thought victims were in there," he said. "We went a lot of places that, like I said, we didn't, as law enforcement agencies in the metro area, we didn't even know they existed. ... In the Cass Corridor, you go in one building, out of one door, across the courtyard and into someplace entirely different."

One night, their mission bore fruit.

"We would be riding through the Cass Corridor, and she'd be telling me war stories, and I would be laughing," Alston remembered. "And I would have to get serious. I'd say, 'Darlene, look at these fools out here. Stop playing and look.' 'I'm looking, I'm looking.' And the night that we spotted him, she was in one of those moods where she was talkative and telling me about the war stories and how she had to put a razor blade in her mouth and would hide razor blades everywhere. And I'm like, 'Darlene,' and all of a sudden she started to hyperventilate."

They were in the car – along with Alston's partner Detective Sergeant Morris Brown – near Woodward and Alexandrine, close to the Cass. It was August 19, 1992, about a quarter to midnight. And there was Tony. Standing on the west side of Woodward. At a pay phone.

Darlene was reacting, clearly agitated, unable to speak at first.

"And I called her a couple of names," Alston recalled. "And I say, 'What the heck's going on with you?' And she kept saying, 'Ah-ah-ah-ah!' I said, 'Darlene.' I think I recall grabbing her on the shoulder, getting her attention, and that's when she told me, she said, 'Royce, that's him.'"

"Darlene, are you sure?" he asked her.

"Royce, that's him," she repeated.

They had to wheel the car around so she could get another look. "Darlene, you've got to be for sure."

For a third time: "Royce, that's him."

The tension inside the car was high. "I had to swear to her, seriously, calm her down," Alston recalled. "And I wasn't really nice. 'Damn it, Darlene, you can calm down,' you know. And the fact is, what I was trying to explain to her, is she needed to calm down to be sure. Because I told her I might have to kill this man. And she did calm down. I said, 'Darlene,' and I think I might have grabbed her, said, 'calm down.' Because her reaction, to me, she'd seen the man that attacked her. It was no doubt in my mind that she believed that was that man. But I had to be sure, too."

Alston called for backup. Their quarry out there on the street, he could see, was moving.

"And if you've ever been in the Cass Corridor at nighttime, back then there were so many nooks and crannies. This is the only chance I had. And I took it. I took it."

Alston told Darlene to stay in the car. She was happy to oblige. He got out. He pulled his weapon and hid it behind his back.

He walked up on Atkins. "Tony," he calmly said.

"Yes, sir," Atkins said to him.

"Do you know who I am?"

"Yes, I know who you are."

"Who am I?" Alston said.

"You're the state trooper that's been looking for me."

Unfazed, Alston told him, "You have two choices."

"What are my choices?" Atkins asked.

"Lay on the ground or die."

"I choose to lay down," Atkins said.

Alston continued to carefully watch his suspect, taking in the details. Yes, they had the guy who attacked Darlene, but would he prove to be the killer that law enforcement had been searching for these many months? "His demeanor, his dress, his appearance, wasn't the best. You know, individuals like that, you don't see in too many places but an area like the Cass Corridor because he would stand out. Even in the city of Detroit. I mean, even in a decent neighborhood. If Benjamin was in a decent neighborhood, he would have been probably labeled the neighborhood drunk or the neighborhood crackhead. That's the way he carried himself."

Calls were placed to Detective Sergeant Dobson, and Agent Lindsay. DPD officers Samuel Guy and Terry Greene arrived and assisted with the arrest. They conveyed Atkins to Highland Park. Oddly enough, he initially used the name of his brother (which is not Tony, just to clarify) – even his brother's birthdate – but that wouldn't last long; he would soon be on record as Benjamin Thomas Atkins, aka Tony.

After the apprehension, Alston was pretty much done with the case, except for his testimony at trial, although Darlene's son Rashad remembers him keeping in touch with his mom, stopping in from time to time to check on her. But at the time of the arrest, his captain in MSP, James Gage, told him to wrap it up because he needed him somewhere else.

"Everybody had a part," Alston said. "And when the FBI came in and Detroit and Highland Park, they were the lead agencies. Our thing was, we would go in and assist other agencies. And that's what we did in this case. I went in to assist. We didn't go in to take over. My thing was this: I could provide technical support for any evidence they had. For the FBI and Detroit to get processed would take them weeks. I could get it tested within a couple of days, because we had labs right there in the metropolitan area. So that was always our function."

Alston remembers this as the biggest case he had worked on. It upped his cred and helped his career with the MSP.

"In fact, as I recall, another little city had, right after that, they had some women being attacked, and they called and asked if I could come down and be an observer. And it was so funny because it wasn't nearly an extent as Highland Park. I think maybe one or two girls that got beat up and robbed. But yeah, the Atkins case boosted my career. It was really good for me."

'LET'S CUT TO THE CHASE'

A day and a half after his apprehension, Atkins was taken to a low-key building that had been converted from a school near Brush Street and Mack Avenue in Detroit. Detroit Police didn't want him at the precinct downtown, at least not for this questioning. Highland Park Public Safety really couldn't accommodate the interview. The task force quite literally snuck him out the back door to this other location.

"I don't think most of the people knew that the police department was utilizing that building," said former HPPS Director John Mattox. "The news media was ready to blow this off the roof, and you didn't want them to know that you were interviewing somebody for these homicides."

Mattox joined some other officers in one room of the building. "We went in there, and we were sitting in one section, and they were interviewing him in another. And we were watching it on closed-circuit."

Atkins was advised of his rights at around eleven-forty-five a.m., and DPD's Bill Rice began the questioning. It was slow-going, however. Rice asked why he had lied about his name when picked up; Atkins said he had a couple warrants out for trespassing. Have you ever hurt anyone, Rice asked. Not without cause, he replied. Do you have any enemies? Some. What's that on your arm? I was shot. Is there any reason why someone would say you hurt them? Not that I know of. If you've never done anything to anyone, why would someone say you have? I don't know.

This suspect, who had waived his right to have an attorney present, wasn't giving anything up. *What to do ...*

Enter Ron Sanders. He had hired on with Detroit Police in October 1969 and spent his law enforcement career there before a stroke cut it short in 1993. He did a little bit of everything, over the years. Spent a decade in Homicide. Did uniformed precinct patrol and supervision. Did citywide plainclothes work. Had a turn in Internal Affairs. Worked with the state attorney general's office. Worked a special detail here and there. Was a member of what was called Squad Six back then, a unit dedicated to dope killings. Served on the Wayne County Task Force. And one thing he was known for was his skill at interrogation.

When contacted, Sanders was out for a haircut, getting ready to go on a vacation in Chicago, but that didn't matter. Police had what they believed to be the Highland Park serial in custody. This was kinda big.

"I got a call from the inspector to come in to interrogate him," Sanders recalled via phone in 2022. "Because they weren't getting anywhere."

Sanders immediately headed to Brush and Mack.

"When I got there, Bill Rice was laying — how can I say it? He was laying his head on the table talking to this guy. In other words, it was like casual. I couldn't believe it. It's like, what is this guy doing? What is he doing? Well, for everybody it's different, so I won't criticize. But I'll never forget that when I came, him in there with his head. I'm talking about the homicide investigator had his head like laying on the table in the crook of his arm, talking to this guy. So that just struck me as odd."

Sanders went into the room and went right to work.

"How did you get those scratches on your face?" he fired at Atkins.

"My boyfriend did it," Atkins replied.

It was a lie, Sanders knew. "Your boyfriend didn't do that," he countered. "The women did that."

"I was very confrontational," Sanders recalled decades later, "but then again, that was my style. Now, I'll be honest with you. I've been doing it for so long. When I interrogated, I mean, for the first hour, basically every suspect that you get for a homicide will lie for the first hour. 'I wasn't there. I didn't do nothing.' So I learned some kind of maneuver. In other words, let's cut to the chase. I mean, that was my style. In other words, I'm not going to listen to your lies and denials for an hour or two hours. We're going to get to the meat of the story." It was one strong aspect of Sanders' interrogation style over the years, sticking to the details. "Just the facts," a la the old *Dragnet* TV series. He never wanted to fall into what he called a "Ring Around the Rosie" mode.

In Atkins' own account of the questioning, handwritten later on a yellow legal pad for his defense attorney, he recalled Sanders having him take his shirt off, no doubt noticing the marks on his neck, his arm and other places, then asking, "Do you know why you're here?"

"No."

You're a suspect in a rape, Sanders explained, asking if he'd ever heard of a Ms. Saunders.

"The name sounds familiar."

"Why did you rape her?"

"I never raped anyone."

"You're lying."

"I'm a homosexual. I don't like women."

"So why would someone say you raped them?"

"I don't know."

Sanders was figurin' that Atkins was figurin' he had this whole thing beat, sitting talking so casual-like with the police. All he had to do was lie and he would skate. But as his conversation with Sanders continued, Atkins was learning that his stories of boyfriends and whatever weren't going to cut it. The two men discussed their upbringings – Atkins with no father figure, Sanders with a mom and dad and siblings and dinner on the table every night. Atkins talked about his experience in foster homes and in a Detroit home for boys, where he said he had a homosexual experience with a staff member. Sanders was getting a sense about this suspect. He was picking up on a troubled past. And a troubled present. He made it clear to Atkins that he was from Homicide, that he was questioning him because of those murders in Highland Park and Detroit, and he mentioned other murder cases he had recently dealt with, which involved sexual abuse and other ugly details.

"Are you familiar with the movies *Three Faces of Eve* and *Sybil*?" Sanders asked him, operating on a hunch. Throwing it out there. "Am I talking to Ben Atkins?"

"Yes."

"Am I talking to any personality other than Ben Atkins?"

"I have no other personalities," Atkins replied. "I'm sane."

Sanders brought up another movie exploring multiple personalities he had just seen the day before, *Raising Cain*. "I don't have that problem," Atkins assured him.

"I'm police, not a psychologist," Sanders told him. "I don't like you personally, just concerned about you and your soul."

Mattox recalled watching the interrogation on the closed-circuit TV. "I had met Ron one other time. Not on this case; at a party I met him. And he was a very good officer, strait-laced. A strait-laced, good officer. Could manipulate from the street to the academics very easily."

Mattox was struck by Atkins' demeanor during questioning, and also by Sanders' technique.

"I was listening more or less to what Ron was doing," Mattox said. "He was like talking to him. And Ben, his demeanor and response was like very flippant, and 'Oh no, that's not me.' I remember one time, one question that came up, and he was saying, 'Oh no, I don't like women; I'm gay.' And I remember the response. I don't know if it was Sanders or the other officers, they didn't buy into it. It was just like something that came up, and it just like went right up in the air. That was it. They didn't pursue that. But you know, we heard it. I heard it. Like, come on now. And I think at one point Ron was getting kind of disgusted with him. Like, 'You're sitting here lying to me.' Like, 'You think this is my first pony ride?' or whatever. He was just trying to convey to him that he wasn't being truthful with him. 'Come on, you got to do better than that,' you know. What he was saying was unbelievable."

Assuming the gay thing was at least one part subterfuge, Sanders charged on in his questioning. "And he hit a nerve some kind of way and got a relationship going," Mattox said, "and that was it. And the case came rattling together very quickly. I give Ron a lot of credit. He showed enough patience and concern, but he wanted to get to the crux of it. And he wasn't going to take no for an answer."

It was reported in the media that the confessions that came forth from Atkins were fueled in part by cheeseburgers. Mattox remembered something along those lines, just as Sanders had Atkins on the edge of admitting to the crimes: "He asked for a cigarette. I remember him asking for a cigarette. I don't know if it was a cigarette first or hamburgers. This guy is talking about homicide, and he wanted a hamburger!" Mattox was sitting with the head of the detective bureau as they watched from the other room, feeling incredulous at what he was seeing. "I didn't understand it – you want a damn hamburger? And a cigarette? And here we are talking about all these bodies, of these women, and I mean he's just sitting there just as calm and emotionless as you would be talking about a checker game or a card game, a sporting event, you know. 'Well, let me have a hamburger.' This guy was sitting there talking about homicide like you would be talking about a tennis match."

There was a central theme of Sanders' approach with Atkins. He could tell this suspect was having issues. Atkins was mentioning things that clued him in to a conflicted soul. He told Sanders about his mother. He told him that when he was about four years old, his mother put him and his brother in the back seat of a car, and she turned tricks in the front. The Woodward and Canfield area, he said. He didn't know what oral sex was back then. Another detail he remembered for Sanders: His mother only dated white men. And he himself had girlfriends from time to time but preferred men. He didn't know why.

"The key to my interrogation," Sanders said years later, "what you got, was — follow me, now – redemption. That was the key factor. In the example that I told him, I said, 'Look, those women are dead; you can't bring them back.

You've gotta look out for Ben Atkins now. You've got to save your soul.' Because he was telling me he was taking Nyquil and he was seeing the women, all the dead women, come at night. He was having nightmares and stuff like that. So I used that and turned it around. In other words, well, hey, you can't do anything about bringing the women back. They're dead and gone. But you're still here. Redemption. Redemption."

It worked. "Well, OK, I'll tell you," Atkins finally said. "I did them all."

The details of the crimes came spilling forth. Sanders began writing. And kept writing. His style would later be noted by defense attorney Jeffrey Edison as being overly large and drawn-out, with his pointed cursive script engulfing each page in huge fashion, just a few written lines per page to increase the page count, as Edison saw it. Nevertheless, Sanders captured everything, page by page, statement by statement, carefully noting for each and every murder account how Atkins had reviewed and OK'd the text. How Atkins was approving everything included in the written statements. Repeating that verbiage over and over, to make sure there was no misunderstanding. Atkins signed his full name to every page. The sessions were not recorded, by most accounts including to the defense attorney's knowledge, a point that would later come up in court.

The first confession was for the killing of the long-missing Valerie Chalk, written at one p.m. on August 21. The statements lasted until around midnight, all afternoon and evening, twelve of them in all, rounding out with the one who survived, Darlene. Atkins had attended Southeastern High School in Detroit until the ninth grade, the first statement noted, and could read and write just fine and well-understood what he was reading in the legal language of the statement template as well as in Sanders' handwritten transcript. Police made sure he had food and cigarettes, that he was not sleepy or in need of medical attention, and that he stated this for the record.

"Why did you kill and rape this woman?" Sanders asked after hearing the Valerie Chalk account.

"I never really planned to kill her," Atkins replied. "But in the process of things happening the way they did, I ended up killing her. I said that to say this. After raping her, having sex and hating her for being a woman, I had the desire to kill her for being a woman. I just wanted to hate her and cause her harm."

A couple questions later: "It's not that I hate women; it's something relating to prostitutes. Female prostitutes."

When Sanders asked if he had killed other women, Atkins remembered nine others at first, then revised that to ten others. Sanders asked if there were any victims that police had not found yet. Atkins said yes, two. He was under the impression that Patricia George had not yet been discovered amid the demolition rubble at Kenilworth. But the other one he said had not been found was a surprise to police – an unknown victim – and it sealed the deal with Atkins. It showed them definitively that, past the false-starts of several other suspects and leads, they had their man at last.

"This girl I knew," he said, "CC, they called her, Cecilia or Ceilia. She hung out on Grand and Woodward in Highland Park. I think this was the end of June this year."

We know it was the first of June. And CC would be the point at which he paused, ultimately his last victim. Did he get nervous, seeing the hunt splashed all across the media, knowing that multiple law enforcement agencies were on his tail and even the FBI had been called in? Or did he have some kind of epiphany or attack of conscience? Maybe something else changed in his life? Whatever the reason, there were a couple mysterious months there on idle, after his spree of such a frenzied pace. A couple months, we surmise, anyway. It's always possible there were other victims.

After hearing Atkins' horrifying account of CC's murder, even of his leg injury treated at Detroit Receiving Hospital – something concrete that police could check, and they did – Sanders asked for the location of this building where he left her. Behind Popeye's Chicken off Woodward and Grand, he told him. The garage behind the house where another victim was found. "You go inside the side door of the garage," he instructed. "About twelve steps to the stairs. Her body should be on the steps, near the bottom."

As the questioning progressed, Atkins wanted to clear up some confusion. Valerie Chalk had not been his first victim, as had been implied at first. His first murder was in Detroit, not Highland Park. But he didn't want to talk about that one just yet, the one he thought had not yet been found. "I'd rather tell you about the second and third murder that I did in Detroit," he said, then launched into the account of Vickie Truelove.

"How do you remember the details of each of these murders you've told me about?" Sanders asked.

"I remember them because it come back to daily *[sic]* about what I did. Plus I got a real good memory."

After they had both signed the Truelove confession, Sanders then returned to the statement with another question: Do you remember putting anything in the mouth of this victim? (A sock was found in Vickie's mouth.) "I don't think so," Atkins replied. "I can't remember. I'm telling the truth as best I can remember."

For the fifth statement, Sanders then coaxed out of him the story of Patricia Cannon George. He had left her under the stairs in this house, behind a closet door, and he knew the building had been torn down later but didn't know she had been found. He didn't read the paper, he said, just watched TV.

By now Sanders and the other officers watching were becoming acquainted with Atkins' technique of strangling each woman, sometimes with an object like a piece of clothing, sometimes with his bare hands over her "Adam's apple," as he put it, then checking for a pulse, pressing against her chest, pushing any remaining air out.

That evening, for the sixth statement, Detective Sergeant Lee Caudill stepped in to transcribe and assist with the questioning. Now we were at the Monterey Motel with the story of Juanita Hardy. The account with Fifteen followed.

"Did she say anything to you?" police asked.

"She asked, 'Why me,' and I said, 'because you bitches deserve it.'"

"Why did they deserve it?"

"Just because that's what they wanted because they are dirty rotten bitches."

For the second-to-last statement, the account of Vicki Beasley Brown:

"Did you rip any of this woman's clothing?"

"I believe only her shirt she had on."

"Did you put anything in this woman's mouth?"

"No. She went out pretty quick when I choked her the first time, so I didn't have to use anything in her mouth to keep her quiet."

"So why did you strangle this woman?"

"More or less because I didn't have to worry about them or her to go pressing charges against me. So I strangled them, killed them all, eleven of them."

"Explain what you just answered," police said.

"I killed all eleven of them so I didn't have to worry about them pressing charges. If a person can't go and tell that I raped them then I wouldn't have to worry about the police or retaliation from any of their family members since I was walking the streets."

Another person who was watching it all that day was FBI Agent Paul Lindsay. He had been instrumental in diverting

Sanders off his vacation plans and into the interrogation room. What then ensued that afternoon and evening, Lindsay would tell *Vanity Fair* magazine the following year, was an astonishing performance. "Not a third-degree interrogation," the mag paraphrased Lindsay, "but the spiritual seduction of a serial killer," then quoting Lindsay as saying, "It was the most exciting thing I've seen in twenty years."

It took Sanders only thirty minutes to crack Atkins, Lindsay told the mag. "He began by going head-to-head with Tony and ended up going soul-to-soul, shifting in that brief time from cop to shrink to preacher."

Sanders' approach was contrary to what the FBI had always advised, Lindsay said. Agents were taught to minimize the victims, like "they were just hookers." Say they meant nothing. Instead, Sanders spoke from an assumption of their value in his confrontational approach – and he didn't let Atkins get away with lying.

The detective raised the tension in the room super-high, Lindsay said, and goaded Atkins about his homosexuality, trying to get his macho vanity to betray him. There was a certain degree of homophobic self-loathing going on here, to play on.

What was Sanders' impression of this perp? Like if he met him somewhere else, in some other context? At the grocery store, or at a party? "Weird," he told this author. "Weird. Let me give my layman's opinion, OK, because that will tell you a whole lot. See, he was like he would be gay during the day, and at night he would come into this killer mode." A sort of dual life. When everything was said and done with the case and many more facts had been brought to light, particularly via the examinations by a few different psychiatrists in prep for trial, Sanders would speculate that this man was killing his own mother, over and over, with these women.

"I want to emphasize that this is my layman's opinion," Sanders said. "I'm no psychologist by a long shot. No training, nothing of that sort. But I was able to determine that that was a connection. He was killing those women, killing his mother."

Ironically, Atkins didn't want his mother to know about these crimes, he said during the interrogation. But he also told Sanders that he had planned to turn himself in when he heard that police had arrested another man (the other "Tony"). He got to the Thirteenth Precinct but then turned around and left. He was relieved to be telling someone about all of this now, however, he said to Sanders, who included in his own separate handwritten notes of the interrogation that Atkins' eyes got watery at that point.

Sanders recalled the CC Waymer revelation. At that point early on in the statement spree, he had told Atkins, what if you're just fooling with us? What if you're just giving us details you read in the paper? So Atkins gave them something they didn't have. Something big. A body better hidden than the others. A body undiscovered.

Dobson recalled it well. They were up against a whole lot of splashy news reporting from the previous months. Many details were out there, swimming around in the urban ecosphere. "Paul Lindsay brought up the fact that the media was just looking for sensationalism. So they planted an idea. We said, can you tell us where any other victims are that we can't find? That's when he gave us the one in the garage on Woodward, in the basement. And then we knew. We said, well, here, this was something that wasn't out in the public and everything else. So that lends credibility. That was the last victim."

Everett Monroe was also watching the questioning. He was in the same room as Atkins for a short time, not watching on closed-circuit TV. He recalls being in Squad Room 6 of the Homicide Division, though, not in the repurposed building, and we do know that Atkins was moved at some point during the day. Monroe remembered Atkins' demeanor:

"He was willing to talk. He didn't hold anything back. Ron would ask him questions and he would answer them fully. So I feel he was ready. You know, it was over. He had run his course. And from interrogating other homicide [suspects], they want to talk about it. You just have to get them to that point where they want to talk. But they want to talk. They want to talk."

Monroe was struck by certain aspects of the conversation. "I remember Benjamin saying why. Why he did it. And he had this hatred for prostitutes. And I remember him saying that his mother was a prostitute. And she would take him out with her when she would do her tricks. And he would be in the back seat while his mother was performing. And he just developed this great disdain for street women. And so that's when he came up with this idea of eliminating them, you know. And he talked about this one particular girl that he had strangled, and she was just about ready to pass out, and he revived her, and then went back to strangling her again. And he thought that was kind of humorous. He was a different kind of guy."

Monroe recalled the revelation of where CC was, too. "I remember they were interrogating Benjamin, and he said, he asked them, did they find the body, his last victim. And they were like, no. He said, yeah, she's over on – there was like a vacant barnlike garage over there on Davison and Woodward area. And it's like the first street just north of Davison. And that body was found in there. So that was a body that we were unaware of. I think that was the eleventh person that was found."

John Mattox remembered that big moment, as well.

"They were interviewing him, and Atkins made mention to Sanders that, 'Well, you know they forgot this one.' And we're like, 'Forgot one?' And so quite nicely – Sanders was not aware of what he was speaking of – he said, 'What are you talking about? Which one?' He said, 'The one over there right off of Davison.' He kept on saying Davison.

Sanders didn't know the streets in Highland Park, so he was kind of quizzing him to find out a better location, along with giving the idea to Ben that he knew what he was talking about. He said, 'Oh, yeah, yeah.' He said, 'Right there on Grand.' Well, I knew the place, when he said Grand and Woodward, I knew the garage that he was talking about, because I walked that beat when I was a new officer. But I didn't know that this place, it was actually a garage that they used for cleaning cars. The Granwood hotel was right there, and in the back was this garage. You had a lot of guys who would come up from Kentucky and Tennessee that would purchase cars. They would clean them up in this. This guy had a kind of a cleaning service of cars, and they stayed in the hotel and then they left. But I didn't know that this garage had a double basement. What I mean by that, it had a basement, and then after that it had a basement under that. And this goes back to the prohibition days. And I walked that beat. I walked that beat for a number of years. I never knew it, nor anyone that was active on the Park department when we were there was aware of that."

While Sanders was keeping it in high gear with Atkins that afternoon, Mattox, Beller, Dobson and Lindsay headed over to the garage, which was at the rear of 20 W. Grand (sometimes listed as 18 W. Grand, but long since torn down). They found an enclosed staircase in the southwest corner of the building that led to the bottom level, which had a dirt floor. There they saw her body lying face up at the bottom of the stairs. Just where Atkins said it would be. It was four p.m.

"We went down there, and he said that he took the body down," Mattox said. "And the body was down on the basement floor right next to the steps. And the condition of that place was, the temperature was ideal to preserve the body. It was cool, just an ideal temperature to preserve your body."

This crime scene stands out to Mattox, decades later, for this reason, as well as for another reason that made it different from the other Atkins crime scenes. This scene did not have the same challenges as the other abandoned structures where they had found victims.

"I remember that one more so than the others," Mattox said, "because there was nothing else found in the basement, nothing. You know, no furniture, no debris. Because no one knew it, no one had access to that but the people who'd worked there. And I don't even know how he [Atkins] found out about it."

As they beheld this final murder scene of the case, the officers could see ample confirmation of other gruesome details Atkins had offered up. Strangulation, they could tell from the electric can opener cord around her neck. There was the dark-colored belt he mentioned he had used to bind her hands behind her back, still in position. Though she was fairly well-preserved for having sat there in the heat of summer for over two and a half months, she was still rather skeletonized, the medical examiner would note, unable to tell her race or even her gender at first. Her body was facing east, her head at the base of the stairs. She had a white sandal on her left foot, and the matching shoe was lying in the upper level of the garage. The M.E. noted flies on her right foot and piles of maggots nearby. When her body was removed that evening, her lower jaw fell off and was placed in the body bag with her.

A lab scientist and two specialists from the Michigan State Police's Sterling Heights crime lab arrived at six-forty p.m. Several items were taken for evidence: The two sandals, the belt, other bindings, the gag from her mouth. And of course, the can opener and cord. Officers took Polaroid and thirty-five mm photos of her and the scene.

They had a first name to go on for Unknown Female No. 63, since Atkins said he knew her as CC, Cecilia or Ceilia. Through her dental records, with the help once again of Dr.

Warnick, she became Ocinena (CC) Waymer. She had a missing person's report filed by her grandmother in June, where it had been noted that CC was "unstable - maybe using crack." She had a record, too, taken in by Craig Pulvirenti at Woodward and Sears Street on February 11, 1992, noted as resisting arrest.

Later that night of the questioning, after police moved their suspect to headquarters, Atkins' mother had arrived at the station.

"After the interrogation, we then went back over to 1300 Beaubien," Sanders recalled. "It was myself, his mother and him. We took pictures and laughed and joked and everything. I got Polaroid pictures of the three of us. I've got pictures, after the confession and everything, where I was standing there, you would think it was my little baby brother. I gained his confidence. I was his best buddy. I was big brother. You'd think like it was a family reunion."

At this point, Sanders was basically done with his part. Like Royce Alston, he had one discrete role to play in the case of Benjamin Atkins, and that was it. He got back to his life, and he did get to take that trip to Chicago that had been interrupted.

The following year, 1993, was a big one for Sanders. He was interviewed along with Paul Lindsay for the *Vanity Fair* magazine piece discussing the Atkins case. He was talking to a Hollywood studio about a movie on his career, with the name of Denzel Washington being tossed about. But in May, the month after the *Vanity Fair* story, he had a stroke that would not only force his retirement from DPD but also prevent him from testifying in Atkins' trial. He fell into a depression. And admittedly indulged a certain measure of anger.

Sanders was nearly three decades recovered from that stroke when contacted for this book, though, also like Alston, still having good days and bad. But with certain details of the case and its perp forever etched on his mind. He wrote a book of his own, *Concerned But Not Consumed*, which is a personal testimony about his faith. "I've tried to capture the essence of the message that one must not be CONSUMED by anything in or of the world but should be CONCERNED about God and establishing a personal relationship with Him," Sanders said on the book's website. "The central theme of this book is aimed at helping others to cope with and not be CONSUMED by everyday life problems. It is put forth as an instrument of encouragement and hope as they progress along the way to becoming more CONCERNED with establishing a deeper and more personal relationship with God."

He had other books in him, he said, and he planned the next one to be about his career with DPD. He was once part of a nearly all-Black unit in the 1970s, and that was significant. "I could tell you some stories, I'm telling you."

Sadly, Ron passed away in September 2023.

His fellow writer Paul Lindsay's second novel, *Code Name: Gentkill*, includes a recreation of Ron Sanders' questioning of Atkins as a small side plot, a way to introduce the character of Jerome Wicks, who in the book is a homicide inspector with DPD. Lindsay did alter some details about the case and the interrogation, but it's pretty unmistakable, there in Chapter 3.

Lindsay died in March 2022.

CONFESSIONS

Here is the order of Benjamin Atkins' statements to police on August 21, 1992. (The numbering of the Jane Does by the medical examiner was for all of Wayne County. So for instance, Valerie Chalk was the fourteenth unknown female found in Wayne County in 1992.)

1 p.m.: Valerie Chalk, Unknown Female No. 14 for 1992

3 p.m.: CC Waymer, Unknown Female No. 63 for 1992

4 p.m.: Vickie Truelove, Unknown Female No. 10 for 1992

5:30 p.m.: Bertha Mason, Unknown Female No. 52 for 1991

6:45 p.m.: Patricia George, Unknown Female No. 1 for 1992

7:45 p.m.: Juanita Hardy, Unknown Female No. 16 for 1992

8:20 p.m.: Fifteen, Unknown Female No. 15 for 1992

8:55 p.m.: Debbie Friday, Unknown Female No. 48 for 1991

9:30 p.m.: Joanne O'Rourke, Unknown Female No. 51 for 1992

9:50 p.m.: Brenda Mitchell, Unknown Female No. 28 for 1992

10:20 p.m.: Vicki Brown, Unknown Female No. 30 for 1992

11 p.m. : Darlene Saunders, survivor

Benjamin Atkins at his arrest in August, from DPD files.

TIMELINE

The most likely timeline of Benjamin Atkins' crimes, based on an examination of the case records and personal testimonies.

	Attacked	Found	Location
Margie Osborn	December 1990	Survived	Highland Park
Darlene Saunders	October 1991	Survived	Highland Park
Patricia George	Nov. 30 – Dec. 5, 1991	Jan 3, 1992	Detroit
Valerie Chalk	Nov / Dec 1991	Feb 17, 1992	Highland Park
Vickie Truelove	Dec 5-10, 1991	Jan 25, 1992	Detroit
Debbie Friday	Dec 13, 1991	Dec 14, 1991	Highland Park
Bertha Mason	Dec 19-29, 1991	Dec 30, 1991	Detroit
Juanita Hardy	Late Dec 1992	Feb 17, 1992	Highland Park
Fifteen	Early Jan 1992	Feb 17, 1992	Highland Park
Vicki Beasley	March 25, 2022	April 15, 1992	Highland Park
Joanne O'Rourke	Mar/ Apr 1992	Jun 15, 1992	Highland Park
Brenda Mitchell	Apr 7-9, 1992	Apr 9, 1992	Highland Park
CC Waymer	Jun 1, 1992	Aug 21, 1992	Highland Park

Atkins worked very fast from fall 1991 to early January 1992, then had cooling-off periods in January to March, mid-April to early June, then after early June. Possibly his arrest for sleeping in an abandoned building caused his first cooling-off period? Impossible to know.

Another name has been associated with the Atkins case in sources online, LaTanya Showanda Smith, but there is no mention of her name in any of the case records or from any of those interviewed.

THE PATH TO COURT

The day after Atkins' arrest, on August 20, Detective Sergeant Jim Dobson interviewed Demerio, aka Mario, the man who had likely saved Darlene Saunders' life. Age twenty-eight at the time of the encounter, he would catch the Woodward bus between Cortland and Richton south toward downtown Detroit on his route to work. That early morning, between four-thirty and five, he told Dobson, he was heading toward the bus stop but diverted to the gas station on Glendale to get some change. That was when he first saw Darlene that morning, shortly before the attack. She was on the same side of the street, he said, and she asked him if he had a cigarette. He had seen her around, knew her by the names Darlene and Debbie. It was a short time later, then, after he had gotten the change, that he heard a woman screaming as he about to wait for the bus.

"The voice was coming from across the street, from the area of the old Howard Johnson's," he told police. "I walked across the street to see what was happening and this is when I kept hearing the voice calling for help. I came through the park next to the restaurant, and this is when I saw the woman I know as Darlene; she was butt naked and there was this guy all dressed in black with his hands on her. He appeared to be wrestling with her. She ran out of the back door of the restaurant, and he followed her into the place where they parked the cars before it was closed. He grabbed her again and as he did this, she called out my name. I was coming through the bushes, and the guy ran down the alley toward Oakland."

He continued, "The guy was a male Black. He was just slightly taller than me and he was wearing all dark clothes. He had on a hooded sweatshirt, but the hood was not over his head. I think I would know the guy if I see him again."

After the man ran off, Demerio said, Darlene asked him if he would help her get her clothing, but he was leery of going inside the building. He said he would wait outside for her. He asked her how she ended up naked, and she said this guy forced her to take her clothes off. After she gathered up her things, he saw his bus coming down the street. He hopped on it and headed to work, but later that day he told his mom what happened. She attested to police that he had given her the account of the incident.

Demerio didn't remember what day this was but did remember he was wearing a jacket and that it was right when his job moved to Romulus, a city on the southwest side of the metro area where Detroit Metro Airport is located.

Two days after Demerio's statement, and the day after Atkins' confession spree, the news was out. "Man confesses he's serial killer," splashed across the front page of the combined Saturday edition of *The Detroit News* and *Free Press* on August 22. Above the fold. Front and center. Atkins was not identified yet but described as a part-time laborer in his twenties from Highland Park. He was emotionless as he relayed the details of the murders, the story said. He had been arrested on a misdemeanor charge of trespassing on Wednesday night, the media said.

The next step was imminent. "The arraignment was, you present a portion of your case to the court to prove or present to the court that a crime has been committed," John Mattox said. "You don't go into everything, but you go into some facts of the case to have this individual bound from a lower court to the next court, because felony cases are held in circuit courts, not municipal courts. We were a municipal court at the time, which means you present it at this level and if the judge feels that there's enough information to bind this individual over to the circuit court, that is done."

So on August 22, Atkins was arraigned in Detroit's 36th District Court for two of the Detroit murders, Patricia George and Vickie Truelove, and was also arraigned for one of the Highland Park murders, Debbie Friday. He was held without bond pending a September 1 preliminary exam in Highland Park and September 2 preliminary exam in Detroit, to be delayed if a psychiatric evaluation was requested. The initial charges were for first-degree murder, but police weren't telling the public what other crimes he would be charged with.

Now that his name was out, the next day's media coverage brought up friends and acquaintances of his from the area. People who fed him on occasion. People he ran errands to the store for. People who said that when he did crack, he became a different person. He was described as nomadic, living in various abandoned buildings, working an odd job here and there. His brother and brother's girlfriend were reached but had no comment. A neighbor of theirs told *The Detroit News*, "The Benjamin Atkins I knew was a very personable, nice guy. I considered him a friend. He would come into my apartment and bake a cake or brownies. He really didn't seem the type who would kill somebody."

Like others who knew him, this neighbor was aware of his crack use. "He would always be in denial," she said. "He would say, 'I'm so proud of myself. I haven't smoked crack for a week.'" He also regularly drank malt liquor, said others who were interviewed. He told police he was sexually abused when he was younger, another story said. The murders began right after Atkins' lost his job at a pizza parlor, the story also said (there are conflicting accounts of when Atkins lost that job – one person said October, another December). "I was never really comfortable with him working here," the pizza-parlor manager told *The News*, suspecting drug abuse at the time. Stories that followed over the next few days provided more details: the heroin-addicted mother who was a prostitute, the childhood in foster homes, the hatred for prostitutes. Pieces like this were coming together, in the sometimes-unspoken but always-understood quest to ascertain the "why" of it all, as we'll discuss in a later chapter when we examine Atkins' short life in greater detail.

And even though this perp was now behind bars, those touched by the case were still feeling the sting.

"If it is him – and I hope and trust it is – then at least he won't hurt anybody else," Valerie Chalk's mom Jessie told *The News*. "But I don't feel this has put an end to anything. We're living in very sinful days."

Concerns were still there. Area residents were saying they still didn't feel safe. Fingers were pointed. As reported in a late August 1992 issue of the Michigan Citizen newspaper, a Highland Park council member claimed she had been stalked recently by two different men and police largely dismissed it. One of the men, she said, may have been Atkins.

Back in July when the other suspect, the other "Tony," made news, he was identified by full name on one of the local TV news stations, and this brought ethics into question. Would he have a legal case regarding this? Experts were saying there should have been more restraint in reporting on this high-profile investigation.

John Mattox recalled the big news of the case, even on the national level. Who was talking about it. The politics of the case. Who was trying to take credit, who surprisingly did not.

"You had all these groups that was crying, concerned citizens and politicians," he said. "And you've got to remember that the politicians, they were right in on this. I remember Ficano was running for re-election, and he was talking about he was doing so much."

This included deputies riding on horseback through Highland Park. "I really got ticked off at him because he sent the Mounties to ride up and down the street," Mattox said. "And I said, how in the hell is this helping us? You're out here riding a horse. But he was up for re-election. And it was just a real donnybrook. Everybody wanted a piece of the pie."

And Larry Beller recalled the two detectives loaned by the sheriff's department. "You could just tell they weren't really interested," he said. "They were just there because they had to be." He gave them several tips to follow up on at the time, about ten different tips as he recalled, and never heard from them again. "Maybe they're still working on the case," he joked in 2023.

Mattox said, "But I give the governor credit that he never, never mentioned it, never. He never used it, never talked about Highland Park publicly. Neither did Sessions. And they knew what was going on, because their officers had to report and keep them aware of this. I know I called him a couple of times and he said, 'I'm getting briefed on this just as well as you.' He said, 'You know that, don't you?' And I said no, I wasn't aware of that. He told me that he was being briefed on this once a week. And I had the names of all the state troopers that were working on that case. A lot of people weren't aware on how many people it was. Matter of fact, I kept all those officers' names, and we had a party, you know, a gathering. And they were all invited. And I was starting with all the evidence techs that worked on it, the people from the morgue, the people from the prosecuting offices, the city attorney."

The August 24 edition of the *Detroit Free Press*, in a front-page, above-the-fold story, called Atkins the "Woodward corridor serial killer" in its lead paragraph, perhaps the earliest mention of one of the monikers he would come to be known by. The *Freep* repeated the phrase, this time capitalizing the "Corridor" in a follow-up story three days later. *The Detroit News* called him the Highland Park Strangler in a May 3, 1993, story, then in a splashier, multi-page story later that month. Before Atkins' arrest, in a June 1992 story, the Saturday Sun in Canada dubbed him the Crack City Strangler. And in April 1994, when the trial wrapped up, *The News* called him the Woodward Strangler.

Did Mattox think it was possible there were additional victims in Detroit that were never attributed to Atkins? "My gut feeling, I think so. I don't have any firsthand knowledge of this, though, because they weren't sharing any information. And anything we learned was through offices that we had dealt with."

August 25 and 27 brought more charges for Atkins, now for the murder of Bertha Mason and the attack of Darlene Saunders. At his arraignments, he stood mute, with not-guilty pleas entered for the record. Additional charges followed on the first of September: CC Waymer, Joanne O'Rourke, Vicki Beasley Brown, Brenda Mitchell and the three Monterey victims. First-degree murder, felony murder, first-degree criminal sexual conduct, attempted murder, and assault with intent to murder. Police were speculating at this point that Atkins' failure to kill Darlene led him to choose smaller-statured women as the attacks continued. He was reported inaccurately to be about five-foot-seven and one hundred forty pounds (perhaps drawing from Darlene's description to police), though Atkins was actually taller and weighed more. He was strong and muscular, as those interviewed described him in the media.

"He was like kind of an average-sized person," Larry Beller recalled. "He was a little husky, but average size. But I've got large hands, and his hands were like larger than mine. We used to transport him around a lot, and I would be driving, and he would be in the back seat with Jim Ayers or somebody else, and I was worried about those hands getting around my throat." Still, Beller never really felt threatened by him, describing him as "Gentle Ben."

For her part, Darlene geared up to face her attacker in the legal proceedings that would follow. She could have been scared. For the most part she wasn't. "I'll be in court," she told the *Free Press* a week after the arrest. "The Lord saw me through that rape. He'll see me through this."

The post-arrest process continued on. On August 28, Judge L. Kim Hoagland of the 30th District Court in Highland Park ordered a diagnostic evaluation for Atkins, as did Judge Vesta Svenson of the Recorder's Court in Detroit on September 2, to determine if he was fit to stand trial. A warrant was issued in early September for blood, saliva and hair samples from Atkins. Also in September, the FBI had the results of comparing the shower wall palm print from the Juanita Hardy scene at the Monterey with the palm print of Atkins. For good measure, the print was also run against those of prior suspects Lonnie, Evie and the other Tony. The print was identified as that of Atkins. On October 22, the Michigan State Police crime lab reported that it found no identifiable fingerprints on the white Hoover can opener taken from the CC Waymer scene. Then, in December, Cellmark Diagnostics had the results of the DNA comparison between Atkins and the tissue found at the Chalk scene and the black coat from the Mason scene. The seminal fluid on the coat did not match their suspect, but the DNA on the tissue did.

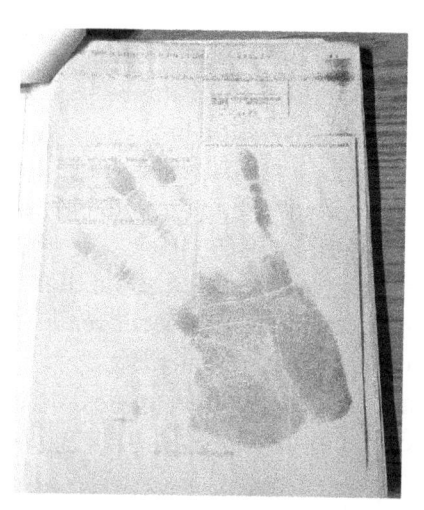

The palmprint of a strangler – with large hands – from files faxed by prosecuting attorney Michael Reynolds to defense attorney Jeffrey Edison in January 1994 just as the trial was getting underway.

Atkins, meanwhile, was running into some trouble behind bars. A fellow inmate filed a report in November that Atkins attacked him. The following March, this same inmate reported that Atkins had attacked him again, this time aided by another inmate – one who had served as a witness to the first attack, actually.

As the officer in charge of the case for Highland Park Public Safety, Jim Dobson was sure of a couple things. He was going to treat Atkins fairly, probably the most fairly of anyone, as he told a European news channel that came to Michigan to do a story on the case. But he also was going to make sure, as he told the perp himself, that Atkins never saw the light of day again.

"He was probably the most interesting character I've ever talked to," Dobson recalled decades later, in a second interview at his home in 2022. "He'd say, 'Jim, I want to talk to you.' We'd put our heads down."

And as the details of Atkins' background unfolded, as more and more questioning took place – by both law enforcement and those in the psychiatric field – all kinds of things were dredged up. Multiple personalities and voices, for example. Though it's an aspect many people remember from the Atkins case, and something that came up during Ron Sanders' questioning, Dobson never recalled any mention of multiple personalities or voices in the considerable time he spent with the killer.

"I don't ever recall him talking about voices. For the lack of a better term, I think he was half-assed honest with me. He wouldn't tell me everything, but he would tell me things. ... I kept asking him, why? Why? I was just curious. And he said that he used to sit in the back seat of the car while his mother turned tricks in the front seat. He could sit here with us, right here now, and talk, and you would never guess anything was going. This is what I'm getting out of the whole thing. But the minute he got near hookers, or that crack cocaine, that's what set him off. Because people would talk to him, and they'd say, 'Are you sure? Are you sure?' 'Yeah, I'm damn sure!'"

Years later, as Jim Dobson thought back on the case, a couple things stood out to him.

"I didn't feel threatened by him. The only people that should have felt threatened were women, and crack cocaine prostitutes. I just remember people approaching us: 'Why are you trying to put this guy out of business? He's killing hookers. He's killing people that are a menace to society.' And I would always say, they are people. They have families. What happens the one day when he doesn't get a prostitute? He makes a mistake and gets a secretary? The people would come to me, and they'd say, 'Well, you ought to be run out.' Hey, this is a job; I'm doing it, and this is what I said I was going to do. They'd look at it like, 'Oh, this is another one off the welfare rolls' or something like that. Honest to God. ... I never understood the people. There were people, they were pissed off at us, because we were working on this case, you know?"

LEGAL COUNSEL SUITS UP

Assistant Wayne County Prosecutor Michael Reynolds had been involved with the case since before Atkins' arrest, and with the arrest, he labored furiously to bring charges and convictions for every female whose life had been lost, plus the one they knew of who had survived.

In his late thirties at the time, Reynolds had been with the prosecutor's office since May 1980, a 1979 graduate of Wayne State University's law school. In the early 1970s he earned a bachelor's degree in history from the University of Michigan.

In his fourteen years with Wayne County before going into civil litigation right after Atkins' trial, Reynolds often handled the high-profile cases. He worked successful prosecutions in People v. Anne Vincenza and Timothy

Markham, a fatal car bombing in the western Detroit suburb of Garden City; and People v. Charles Fisher, the duct-tape murder of a woman in Canton Township, also west side. And even after his years in the civil arena, he evidently missed the thrill of the homicide case. He returned to the prosecutor's office, assigned to the homicide unit, and worked on some additional higher-profile murders. As evidenced in the Atkins case, Reynolds, who died at age sixty-seven in spring 2022, not only had an affinity for these cases, he had a skill for them, as well.

Former Highland Park Public Safety Director John Mattox recalled when the longtime attorney came into the investigation, after Mattox's appeal to then-prosecutor John O'Hair that secured the cooperation of the office.

"So then we got Mike," Mattox said. "Mike, you know, this was thrown in his lap. And he was a young prosecutor at the time." Mattox remembered Reynolds sharing with him that he didn't have a lot of experience on homicides at that point. "Don't worry," Mattox told him. "Don't worry about it; you'll get there."

Reynolds developed a reputation for fighting hard but always fighting squarely. "He was a fair and decent man — nothing underhanded, everything aboveboard," a fellow lawyer said at the time of Reynolds' death. Another remarked, "You could always rely on his word." He was also known for his trademark "uniform": rumpled blue blazer, white shirt, red tie and khakis.

One person who worked with him at the time of the Atkins case was Dana Nessel, who would go on to become Michigan's attorney general (serving in that post as of this writing in 2023). She was an intern in law school at the time, and she assisted Reynolds in court by helping survivor Darlene demonstrate the stranglehold Atkins put on her. A picture of Nessel and Darlene in this demonstration made it into the 1994 newspaper coverage of the trial. "I started passing out and the last thing I saw was Mike smiling,"

Nessel recalled for the *Detroit Free Press*' March 2022 obituary for Reynolds. "Afterward, I told him I could have died. He said 'Yeah, but we're gonna totally win this case.'"

Reynolds' adversary in the courtroom, however, was going to put up a heck of a fight and was going to be well-remembered decades later for making the most of what he had to work with. Forensic evidence, confessions, a survivor's account – it didn't matter. Defense attorney Jeffrey Edison, appointed just days after Atkins' arrest, threw all he had at this representation, every bit of his expertise. That much is evident decades later when he speaks about the case, and when others speak about him. Especially those from the opposing side, like law enforcement.

At the time of the case, Edison was a pretty young guy, too, and he was still practicing when interviewed for this book. In fact, this author spoke with him at his offices – in the beautiful, historic Guardian Building downtown Detroit, then at the office he moved to in the city's Eastern Market a few months later in 2022. He was marking 46 years in practice when we spoke.

He was asked by Dalton Roberson, the chief judge of Detroit's Recorder's Court at the time, to defend Benjamin Atkins. Edison didn't flinch, already having years of criminal defense under his belt and feeling a pull toward those poor and of color. His career path was driven by what he once told the media were "typical" experiences for a young Black male – guns pulled on him by police as a teen. What he told this author was that he grew up near the Birwood Wall, a one-foot-thick, six-foot-high concrete wall stretching a half-mile near the infamous Eight Mile Road in Detroit. It was put up in 1941 to physically separate Black and white residents in that area of the city, at Pembroke Avenue between Birwood and Mendota streets. Though the wall still exists as it was originally constructed with one foot buried in the ground and five feet above ground, it is no longer a separation. Local folks have worked to change that, and parts of the wall have even been turned into a mural.

"When we came up, we didn't call it like Birwood Wall. It was just the wall," Edison explained, the reality of social injustice woven through so many of the thoughts he presented during my visits. His terminology reflected that, like how he described the wall so succinctly: "Everything west of the wall was European. Everything east of the wall was African."

He went on, "My family moved out there in the '50s, in '52, '53, when that racial difference had, I guess, stopped to some extent. At any rate the neighborhood – we just referred to growing up in the neighborhood, Eight Mile. And that's different from the Eight Mile that was popularized with Eminem; that's the east side."

Like Reynolds, Edison graduated from Wayne State's law school. He also graduated from Howard University cum laude. He worked for the Legal Defender's Office in Detroit in the latter 1970s. He has awards from the Detroit chapter of the NAACP, the National Conference of Black Lawyers and the Wolverine Bar Association among others. He has taught criminal advocacy workshops. At least one cop interviewed for this book remembered him as taking the Atkins case pro bono, but Edison clarified:

"They say pro bono probably thinking that, well, he wasn't retained, which I was not retained. I was appointed. And although there was compensation, it certainly would not have been the same degree of compensation if there was a source that could have sufficiently hired me for this type of case. I wasn't complaining about it. That's what I do. That's what I did."

He was a criminal defense lawyer from day one, he said. And how was this case different from others he worked on over the years?

"I don't think my approach was any different than any other. You know, a lot of times you're asked over time or at any given point in time what case stands out more or whatever. And for me, my kind of response to that is that each person that comes through the door, or who I represent, to them, each of them, their case is the most important case that I have. So I try to relate to each person the same way in terms of my preparation, my advocacy, my perspective on those who are accused and their relationship to the system. I try to, you know, to bring to the table, bring to the case, the same degree of advocacy, because each person's freedom is crucial. I mean, it's a no-joke business. Where one day, one hour, incarcerated and loss of freedom is too much if you're not supposed to be there."

Edison knew exactly what he was up against, in this case.

"The government, the prosecutor has to, in terms of its burden and responsibility, has to prove on one hand the charges," he said. "On the other hand, they have to prove that who they have charged committed it, or who did it. And therefore what is the connection between the person charged and the crime charged. And in this instance, Ben Atkins was the connection. Or how can the government, or how does the government, intend to establish the connection between Ben Atkins and the women. And there are a number of ways that that might be established. But then that's the first phase of the analysis. Then it just does not stop there, particularly in a case that is involving this type of allegation. If there is a connection between Ben Atkins and these women, a sufficiently established connection, then what is his state of mind? So in order for the government to prove the charges, and I believe it was first-degree murder, let me give you that analysis. The killing of a person is — well, the act of killing is not a crime. What makes the act of killing a crime is the state of mind of the person responsible at the time of that act. The intent.

"We kind of, from a lay perspective, kind of think motive. But technically it's intent. So from a law school perspective is the act, or they call it the '*actus reus*,' and the state of mind, the '*mens rea*.' And the *mens rea* has to be present at the time of the act. So the medical examiner basically said, well, it's a homicide, which is that the death is caused by another person. That's the basic fundamental definition of a homicide. But homicide is not a crime. The crime is when you attach the state of mind to it. Is it first-degree, second-degree, manslaughter or whatever? So second-degree murder is the unlawful killing with an intent to kill. There's the state of mind and intent to kill. And there's three different states of mind for second-degree. One state of mind for second-degree is that you just outright intended to kill the person, and they die. Another state of mind is you intend to commit great bodily harm to that person, and they end up dying. The third state of mind is your conduct creates such a risk, if you will, that death is likely to result.

"In order for there to be first-degree, you have all of the second-degree plus an added intent of deliberation, premeditation, or that the death occurred during the course of another felony. That's felony murder.

"So the connection between Ben and these charges can take different forms. DNA can be a connector. Identification is a connection. And this is like all cases, any kind of case. Identification. A person's statement, or a person's words, is a connection. And obviously now today, if there was surveillance footage of the area that captures the incident or the before and after the incident. Phone records and that sort of thing. We didn't have that back then. So the connection between Ben and the women, identification, DNA and his statements were these three."

Detroit's Recorder's Court, which went away in the late 1990s, was a different kind of beast. A different element for this criminal case.

"Recorder's Court's jurisdiction was all criminal cases arising within the city of Detroit," Edison said. "You have Wayne County Circuit Court that has jurisdiction over criminal matters within Wayne County except for the city of Detroit. And right after this case, soon thereafter, because of political and historically systemic racism, Recorder's Court was abolished, and the jurisdiction was merged into Wayne County Circuit."

Jeffrey Edison at his office in the Guardian Building, 2022. Photo by the author.

He elaborated: "The merger was a result of systemic racism, at least from my perspective, because the court had evolved from the '60s to the '90s to be a predominantly African-run court in terms of the first Africans being elected to the bench were in the late '60s and then by the '90s it was predominantly African on the bench. And because it was a jurisdiction of Detroit matters that arose in Detroit, also at that time within the city of Detroit the population had morphed into a majority African population. You had more representation in electoral positions across the spectrum, and there was an enhanced quality of justice for the African community, if you will, that was not the same prior to the mid-'60s, in terms of what African residents would perceive as justice in the system.

"And so not only did you have an increase in the African representation on the judiciary, you also had an increase in African lawyers, prosecutors, I mean, just across the board. And it's important to understand at the same time that during the height of this African representation on the bench, that Recorder's Court was acknowledged nationally as being one of the, if not the, best administratively run urban courts in the country.

"So they received awards. But then in the late '80s going into the '90s there were a few racially charged cases where there were European complainants, African defendants, African judiciary. And the results of those particular cases did not reflect perhaps justice to the white community. There were a couple of juvenile cases — well, young guys charged with murder, and the decedents were white, the defendants were Black, and there was judicial discretion as to whether those persons should be treated as adults or as juveniles. And if as adults, they would have received natural life or significantly long periods of incarceration, but treated as a juvenile they would not. And at the time, there was public, at least within the white community, outrage that they weren't treated as adults. And then it was the perception that African juries, or Black juries, predominantly Black juries, would render verdicts favoring Black offenders when the victims or complainants were white. And it just wasn't supported statistically because African juries convict African defendants the same way they convict anyone else based on their perception of what's being presented in court. The Black community wants to be secure and safe.

"So all that dynamic was going on at and about that time, about the time. So I'm giving you the background in terms of Recorder's Court. Because Recorder's Court is, or was, an anomaly in terms of the state, but it was an exception that was created back in the 1800s."

So for the Benjamin Atkins case, it meant two jurisdictions – Recorder's Court for the Detroit cases and Wayne County Circuit Court for the Highland Park cases. There would be a jury for each court, but the two juries would hear the cases concurrently. So essentially one trial, but two sets of people in the same courtroom listening to the same thing at the same time, except where there were some items that came up specific to Detroit, for instance – then the Wayne County jury would be dismissed. And when some HP-specific stuff came up, the Recorder's Court jury would be dismissed. It was a configuration you don't see every day in the legal system, and it was the only such case Edison had ever seen. And in a situation like this, with twelve known victims, things can get a little complicated. The twelve incidents were also combined into this single trial instead of being tried separately, by the prosecution's motion for what is called a joinder, a motion that Edison objected to unsuccessfully. Factors in determining joinder could include not only the similarities of the charges and the defenses for them, but also the time and expense involved in separate trials versus a combined trial, and any possibility of prejudice against the defendant.

"You also have a thing of similar action," Edison said. "There's also an evidentiary process where the prosecutor is allowed to offer – well, you start from a premise that other bad acts are not admissible in the trial of 'A.' That's, you know, you charge me with this act, then you rise and fall on this act, all right. That's the foundational premise. Then there are circumstances where a prosecutor will argue that there are certain acts that are so similar that it is relevant towards identification, motive (although you don't have to prove motive), scheme, plan, design. And because these acts are so similar to the case of 'A,' that the court should allow them in to establish or to argue identification, scheme and plan, in case 'A.' I just don't remember whether they used similar acts. But I do know the statements were not before the same juries. So Ben's statements about the Detroit *[cases]* were not in on *[Wayne County's cases]*. ... Whether the arrest and circumstance, there were these other cases, because the juries knew that there were cases in Detroit. I mean, they're sitting up there. I just don't recall how specifically we dealt with that."

That is a lot to keep track of. Seems like that would lend so much confusion to the proceedings. "Well, that's the defense argument," Edison said. "In a typical case that's exactly what the defense would say. Actually, to give you a contemporary example, that's exactly what the Supreme Court in Pennsylvania said in the Bill Cosby case. That the evidence of these other acts should not have been admitted because it potentially confused the jury. So just from a legal perspective, you know how they're always referencing, 'Well, he's out on the technicality'? OK, that's how people used to say, 'Oh, so he still is guilty; they threw his conviction out on a technicality.' Well, the reality is, *but for* that other evidence coming in, he would not have been convicted. See, because of whatever — the social dynamic, the political dynamic, the racial dynamic, the celebrity dynamic, or — how should I say — the sexual abuse of women dynamic. Whatever it is, the reality is, and the way media handled it, the reality is, *but for* that abuse of discretion that the judge used to allow that evidence, he would not have been convicted. And so that's the standard that the court uses in reviewing that type of evidence. That '*but for* that evidence' it's likely it would have been a different outcome. In order for them then to overturn what happened, OK. So people say, 'Oh, he just out, he still did all that shit; it's just, you know, just a technicality.' Yeah, it is, *but for* that, it would have been a different outcome."

Where Atkins' statements about the crimes were concerned – and Edison sticks to the term "statements," not confessions, pointing out that it's standard for the defense perspective and even the jury instructions – he had a long road ahead in his prep for trial. The statements weren't recorded, for one thing. "Even back then they could have had a tape recorder going. Ron was too slick for that," Edison said. So the question arises, are these really Ben's words? Even though Sanders meticulously had Atkins read and sign each page (each very *largely* written page – that other big concern Edison had), he still took on the task of poking holes into these statements.

Everything is video-recorded now, Edison pointed out. "So back then you didn't have that. It was a whole different context for the government or the prosecutor advocating what somebody said, and the defense advocating that that's the product of the detective as opposed to the person."

And you don't know, when the person signed each statement, if they actually were provided enough time to read through it, he said. "But even if you do, just the subjectivity of it. I mean, even if you give them time to read it, whether they are reading it, whether they understand what they're reading, whether they're reading it and saying, 'Well, damn, this isn't exactly what I said but kind of what I said.' And so that's more to why I say we don't reference it as confessions. Particularly back then. See, we're in a different age now than at the time Ron Sanders and them were interrogators.

"It's like, how do you say, 'Well, Ben, do you know about A, B, and C,' and 'Did you have any contact with her?' 'No, man, I don't know what the fuck you talking about.' And then the interrogation continues, and then it morphs into 'Well, I might have seen her, but no, I didn't have no contact.' And then it morphs into, he said, 'Yeah, I had some contact with her; we just was smoking, but that was it.' Then to ultimately, 'Yeah I had contact, we were smoking, I had sex, and then I killed her.' I mean, you know, that whole transition, all that conversation, and that ends up being this written document. But none of that development or process or interaction is there to see, whereas now with video, you see all of that.

"But back with this, you just had that written statement. So there might be an hour, and I say hour, could be — there's a period of time where the interrogator and the person are just talking. Chitchat. Not just chitchat, but that's the preliminary part of it, chitchatting. Then it gets into talking about the incident and they're just talking about the incident. And then at some point, it's a reduction to writing what has been said and talked about. So it's not like for the first time you're talking about it and I'm writing it down. It's not like a contemporaneous recording, written recordings."

So it's not necessarily verbatim, Edison said. And then with the mode of stretching the handwritten text out across more pages than it would normally take up, totaling eighty-seven pages for Atkins' statements, he said, "This is my spin, in terms of one of his techniques. Or yeah, that's how I take it, all right. You're saying the same thing, but it ends up being five or six pages when you could have done that shit in a paragraph or half a page. So when you're before this jury, 'Yeah, I got this,' you know. So yeah, it's in Ron's writing. And you just have the detective's rendition of what supposedly the person said, notwithstanding the fact that they signed it. But this still is, so I'm saying to you one thing, but what you're reducing to writing is not verbatim. It's what you are interpreting from what I've said and putting it down. You had all those kinds of dynamics. So now all of that is minimized because of recordings. You see what I'm saying? Back then they didn't have it."

IS THIS SUSPECT CRAZY?

The month following Atkins' arrest, he was evaluated for competency to stand trial. Todd Rosen, staff psychiatrist at the Recorder's Court Psychiatric Clinic, issued his report on September 28 from sessions with Atkins on September 9 and 10. This certified forensic examiner determined him fit for trial. Rosen found no medical issues, and no real history of psychiatric treatment except for some sessions Atkins had with his mother and his brother in the mid-1980s as part of his probation for the two boys trespassing in a Detroit building on Christmas Day 1982.

The evaluation included a battery of psychological tests. Atkins' IQ test came out in the low-average range – he didn't seem to have benefited from his schooling, Rosen noted. "His social commonsense judgment is also low," the report said. "There were no indications from his verbal test responses of a disturbance in thought and his projective drawings did not reveal any psychotic signs. However, marked ego impairment is evident from the testing. In particular, his actions are poorly organized, impulsive and unplanned. His controls are significantly impaired. Mr. Atkins is easily overridden by his impulses. Judgement is very poor."

Rosen noted the scars on his body. A bite mark on his left shoulder Atkins said he got at age fifteen from his brother. Scratch marks on his chest he said he got from a male lover. Two scars of two and a half inches each on his lower left abdomen, which he said came from an older woman he dated in 1990 who cut him with a knife. A skin graft on his left forearm from multiple surgeries following a shooting incident with another older woman, earlier, when he was just seventeen. She shot him four times at that point and then in another incident before that, he said. With both of these older women, he told Rosen, the injuries occurred when he was trying to leave them.

And here the idea of multiple personalities or voices showed up: Rosen noted, "He claims to experience auditory hallucinations of a male and female voice commenting on his behaviors on a daily basis." (About a week after he spoke with Rosen, on September 18, Atkins also noted to Wayne County Jail staff that he was hearing voices.) Beyond that, though, Rosen found Atkins to be pretty normal, in his order of thoughts and communications, his tone, his word usage, his mannerisms, his memory capabilities for recent and remote events, his attention and concentration.

Rosen did believe Atkins to be malingering, however. Faking some things. In the testing, Atkins checked off more symptoms than was probable for his condition. He reported his mental and physical symptoms as extreme, not moderate or a little bit. Depression, anxiety, hostility toward others, phobias. A whole host of ailments. Rosen was skeptical. Plus, Atkins during these sessions said he did not recall making the confessions/statements to police. "He claims he did not commit the murders he is accused of," Rosen wrote, though he would cop to sexual assault. Atkins told the psychiatrist he had lost periods of time and sometimes would meet people who called him by a different name, people he did not remember. Malingering, Rosen felt.

All in all, this subject had an adequate understanding of the legal process he was undergoing, of the judge and jury he would see in the courtroom, of the attorneys who would fight over him. He was in the here and now, connected with reality, Rosen said.

In the first week of October, both Highland Park's 30th District Judge William Bledsoe and Recorder's Court Judge Vesta Svenson determined Atkins was fit to stand trial. *The Detroit News* and *Detroit Free Press* filed motions for access to Rosen's report that was the basis for the decision, but the two courts denied it, instead providing the newspapers with an edited version of the nine-page report that left out the meaty section on Atkins' history. But Detroit's two daily newspapers still wanted the full report, every page, and they legally challenged the decision for months afterward.

The prosecution, the defense and the Recorder's Court Psychiatric Clinic all opposed the idea of the media having access to the report. Edison was quoted in the newspaper saying that the report's release could prejudice the public before a jury trial. Indeed, Judge Bledsoe raised the issue of the subject matter Atkins discussed with Rosen, and doesn't the defendant have a right against self-incrimination? The papers argued for the public's right to know the information, saying that this court-ordered report used for the decision was not doctor-patient privileged information, but that it was part of court record and as such was open to the public. No, Edison argued back – the report was not actually entered in as court evidence. He and Reynolds had made what's called a "stipulation" on the report – an agreement based on the report's conclusions – and that was what was entered into court proceedings. The judges' decisions were based on the conclusions of the report, but the report also contained content not addressed in the competency hearings, and that content spoke to the defendant's state of mind, an issue yet to be brought up at trial. And, Edison argued, if it was established that reports such as this could become public knowledge before a trial opens, how honest is any defendant going to be while talking to the psychiatrist? The Recorder's Court Psychiatric Clinic sent its own representative to the hearings, since its staff member was the one who produced the report, and among its arguments asserted the fact that when a court-ordered evaluation is being done for a defendant, the defendant is advised that the report contents will be shared with the court, the prosecution and the defense, but he or she is not told it will be shared with the public or the press. The clinic at the time was reviewing some four hundred to five hundred individuals a year for competency and agreed that if it was known this kind of report could be shared publicly, it would have the effect Edison cited, described in court as a "chilling effect."

There were less-restrictive means to assuring a fair trial, the papers argued, such as careful selection of jury members, sequestering of the jury, even change of venue.

The legal battle raged on, with the judge who was to preside over Atkins' trial, David Kerwin, saying at one point that yes, the full report could be released to the media, but not until after the jury was chosen at the least, maybe later. The issue was not resolved, ironically, until the end of March 1994, just before verdicts were reached, with the papers losing their appeal before the Michigan Supreme Court.

A preliminary exam for Atkins was held on Thursday, October 15, 1992, before Judge Bledsoe, wherein the court not only heard the lawyers for Detroit's two dailies arguing for access to the Rosen report, but also addressed a couple of the charges that had been leveled against Atkins thus far. John Mattox attended and remembered the courtroom being packed: "You had the family members, you had the news media, you had concerned citizens, and just people who wanted to see the trial."

Darlene Saunders, who at this point had been kept under lock and key to preserve her testimony, confined in a jail cell and even doing disgruntled interviews with the media from there as she was detoxing, gave a full retelling of the encounter with the man she knew on the street as Tony. Her attacker scowled at her as she spoke at the hearing, the *Free Press* reported, and continually drummed his fingers on the railing in front of him. Demerio, who asked the court for his identity to be minimized – to not have his face on camera, for instance – also gave his account of breaking up the scene between Darlene and Atkins that morning.

Whether she was coached by the prosecution or not, Darlene held her own. She listened carefully to the two attorneys' questions, corrected them if she had to. Did she know a person by the name of Benjamin Atkins? Edison asked. No, she knew him as Tony. She would see him around, like at crack houses? At an apartment building. Yes, but in the apartment, buying and smoking crack? Yes. And you call that place the crack house? I call it an apartment building because I live in that building. So, I call it an apartment building, she said.

"You're not familiar with the term 'crack house'?"

"I'm very familiar with it," she retorted.

"But because this particular place where you buy and use cocaine is in the same building that you reside, you choose not to call it the crack house?" Edison pressed.

"Well, like I said, it's an apartment building because we purchased in the lobby. We didn't go into a particular apartment. So I wouldn't call it a crack house."

"And that's the distinction you make?"

"Well, it's not a crack house. A lobby."

Edison spent considerable effort on the timeframe of the incident – the fact that she couldn't remember what day it was or perhaps even what month it was – and her crack addiction, as well as how she described Atkins to police, particularly how tall she said he was. She corrected him on several points, like where she made her police report, or which jurisdiction she called when she saw Tony again, Highland Park or Detroit. She clarified that she had crack on her that night so was not needing any crack he could offer her (she told Tony she could use a hit but was not asking for his crack).

"So you just decided to see," Edison asked, "when you saw him walking down the street at four-thirty in the morning, you said, 'Hey, Tony, why don't we go hit this crack pipe,' right?"

"No, you said that."

She was guessing at Tony's height, she said, just knowing he was taller than her own five-foot-three.

"But you knew this person," Edison said.

"Yeah."

"This wasn't a stranger, right?"

"Which is true. I know a lot of people, but that don't mean I have to know everybody's height."

Why didn't she call police the next time she saw him, at the crack house, but she did when she saw him at the same crack house on a later day?

"Well, it was night. And at nighttime when I'm smoking crack, I get paranoid. And I was paranoid that night. I wasn't paranoid during the day."

Edison swung hard at that easy pitch. "So you're saying that depending on the sun being out will determine whether or not you're paranoid from smoking crack?"

"Yes, that's what I'm saying."

The defense attorney spent several more questions on that before moving on to the issue of what assistance she received from law enforcement for her cooperation. Darlene said she received two checks from law enforcement for groceries: one for sixty-eight dollars and one for eighty-seven dollars. She went to the store to use them with family members, one of which was a sister who was a cop, and she provided receipts.

At one point in the testimony Edison asked if Darlene was "fading out" on them, and she said no, you're just upsetting me.

After Reynolds redirected with a few clarifying questions, Demerio took the stand. "Frightened, scared, crying, excited," is how he described Darlene when he came up on the two of them that morning. It was about twenty to thirty minutes after the first time he'd seen her, and he was going to the gas station to get change. Edison had only a few questions for Demerio but did make the point that when he asked Darlene what had happened, she never mentioned Tony's name.

Detective Sergeant Ron Sanders was scheduled to testify next, but Edison and Atkins waived the right to hear the rest of the witnesses for this preliminary exam. Atkins was bound over on the charges, and the arraignment-on-the-information was scheduled for October 29. The judge also raised the issue of two other charges that day, for the murder of Debbie Friday, and Atkins waived his right to a preliminary exam for those. That arraignment would also be on October 29.

"I love you, Mama," the *Freep* quoted Atkins as saying to his mother as he left the courtroom.

Darlene told the paper, "I wanted him to feel the hurt and the pain and the anger – I wanted him to feel it in my eyes."

There were seven cases in Highland Park still to be addressed at that time, and on November 5, Atkins was bound over for trial for them, as well, having waived the preliminary hearings.

A few other psychiatric evaluations followed for Atkins in the year leading up to trial. In all, Atkins was seen by four different psychiatrists and multiple jail personnel before his trial: One psychiatrist for the defense and one for the prosecution, Rosen from the Recorder's Court along with a colleague, Dr. Dexter Fields, plus medical staff at the jail.

Dr. Fields did his evaluation a few months after Rosen's, in 1993, issuing his ten-page report on April 2. He spoke with Atkins about each of the women, and Atkins mentioned details that often matched but sometimes were not included in the statements written by Sanders and Caudill at the time of the arrest. Sometimes the details just seemed jumbled. Atkins, of course, had trouble with dates and times.

Still, Fields wrote, "His associations were coherent and relevant with no signs or symptoms of a psychotic process." In this evaluation, however, one of the voices in Atkins' head got a name: Tony, ironically (or perhaps appropriately). This "Tony" influenced his decisions and sometimes helped him out of trouble, Atkins said. Sometimes he would be fed up or tired and not listen to Tony, though. And Tony was not the only voice he heard. There was another. But Tony was not an imaginary friend, he told Fields – he was a person. Tony had been around since Atkins was seventeen years old, and he would urge him on when Atkins was with someone sexually. Tony told Atkins to use his name as his alias. Atkins took a lot of time, Fields said, to explain that he would "become" Tony, that Tony was often around – even in interviews with law enforcement or other personnel – but that Atkins was hesitant to mention him. And: "I don't know if he became me, or I became him."

Dr. Charles R. Clark, who practiced in Ann Arbor, was tapped by the prosecution to evaluate Atkins for criminal responsibility/insanity and diminished capacity. He interviewed Atkins for nearly four hours on July 16, 1993, then again on November 10 for close to two hours, plus he administered about two hours of psychological testing. Clark issued his report on December 11, 1993.

In determining criminal responsibility, Section 21a(1) of Act 180 of the Public Acts of 1975 says that a person is legally insane if, as a result of mental illness, as defined in Section 400(a) of Act 258 of the Public Acts of 1974, or as a result of mental retardation, as defined in Section 500(g) of that same act, that person lacks substantial capacity either to appreciate the wrongfulness of his conduct or to conform his conduct to the requirements of the law. We know Atkins was not retarded, so that leaves mental illness. The definition of mental illness requires a substantial disorder of thought or mood that significantly impairs judgment, behavior, capacity to recognize reality or ability to cope with the ordinary demands of life.

So there is this issue of impairment – mental illness or the effects of substances, drugs and/or alcohol, which it was well-established were part of Atkins' life. In either case – a claim of diminished capacity can only be applied to crimes where specific intent is an element, as it is with charges of first-degree murder and murder in the commission of a felony as in this case. Fields had already determined that Atkins' intoxication from cocaine did not impair his ability to form intent to commit the crimes.

In the sessions with Dr. Clark, all of the voices in Atkins' head got names, and there were now three instead of two: Mayolla was a motherly figure who would comfort him when he was down, Mary was another female persona who would sometimes try to protect him, and then there was Tony, the dominant voice/persona. Mary and Tony were friends, but Tony was foul, asking Atkins to do things that disgusted him. Atkins even gave them last names: Tony Smith, Mary Jane, Mayolla Brown. He was seeing them before his arrest, he said. (In one of his first jailhouse visits with his attorney, just a few days after his arrest, Atkins gave Tony's full name as Anthony Jerome Smith.)

Tony was the one who told him to commit the crimes, Atkins told Clark. Tony was the bad one. He was disgusted with Atkins, disgusted with his homosexuality, always demeaning him. "A side of me hated I was indulging in homosexuality," Atkins told the doctor. Tony hated him and Tony hated the women, too, seeing them as worthless and deserving to die, egging Atkins on to kill them. "It was his revenge on them," Atkins said rather tellingly.

At this point, Atkins had been reading a Bible in jail, had been drawn to "religion," as he called it. With this, Tony was visiting him less. And the visions of the women he had killed that had been haunting him, they didn't come anymore. Atkins said he also had been seeing visions of a staff member from the home for boys where he lived for a time with his brother. He called this staff member Mr. Winfield and said the man had sexually molested him when he was a teen (sort of agreeing with, yet differing from, the account he gave Ron Sanders upon his arrest). Then Tony started appearing after Atkins became involved in homosexuality.

The way he explained it to Clark, Atkins didn't understand what brought on the offenses, his killing spree. "All I know, one minute I'm getting high, smoking cocaine, had a date with a guy, go take a walk, and it's at this time Tony would appear ... and I would say what do you want? ... And along with him would come a woman. ... To get away from Tony, I would see a woman, I would ask to spend some time with her." Atkins felt having an encounter with a woman would help him "overcome" his homosexuality, overcome his guilt, and shut Tony up.

But Tony criticized him for being with a woman, too. Atkins told Clark he wanted to smoke with these women and talk to them, ask them why they were out there degrading their bodies. "The same question Tony would ask me," Atkins said. He had also said these "dates" with men tended to be paid encounters, so he was prostituting himself, as well, receiving thirty-five to fifty dollars a date, which he would then put into drugs and alcohol. All the while Tony challenged his manhood, taunting him to prove he was a man. Atkins didn't roam the streets looking for a woman every time he smoked crack, he said. "I never knowingly or willingly went out wanting to be with a woman. ... I had a girlfriend."

He described how he choked the women. He described beating the women, as he said Tony told him to. He even described lighting a match and putting it in a victim's hair. But he didn't hate women like Tony did, Atkins said, though he did admit to some dislike for them. He had been shot by them. One of them aborted his child, he claimed. Another one left him for another woman in 1989. "I don't believe 'em," he told Clark.

There's a lot to unpack here, and some of what Atkins told Clark goes around in circles and contradicts itself. Unlike in Rosen's examination, Atkins told Clark he did remember all of the offenses. He jumbled a lot of details, though, thinking the first murder occurred at the Monterey. He was sleeping there because his brother had put him out due to his drug usage. It didn't bother him to be at the same motel where three of his victims lay. He just shut the doors, he told Clark. It was Mary and Mayolla who convinced him to tell police what he had done when he was arrested. "First time Mayolla ever ruled over Tony," he said.

After the first murder, "Mary and them took control," he said, and he quit crack and his encounters with men. But then an argument over the phone with his brother brought Tony to the forefront again. He resumed prostitution, got some money, went back to crack.

In the five months between his first and second session with Clark, Atkins had lost some of his faith, stopped reading the Bible, struggled to regain it. Tony came back. Tried to get him to commit suicide. But then he got back into the Bible and was receiving visits from pastors, and thus Tony again receded.

Clark asked him about the months that passed between his last killing and his arrest, and Atkins said he was trying to get things together, that he had quit the drugs, had started going to church. He still was doing some prostitution, he said, but was also doing other legit jobs. He wasn't as depressed, as Mary and Mayolla pointed out to him.

In this second session Clark re-asked a lot of the questions he had asked in the first. He got very similar answers (though in the second session, for instance, Mary and Mayolla did not have last names, but Tony still did). He also went over what Dr. Fields had written in his April 2, 1993, report on Atkins, and Atkins took issue with a lot of what the report contained, saying it was just a "written transcript from the state" and didn't reflect what he actually said. He claimed he told Ron Sanders about Mary, Mayolla and Tony during the questioning after his arrest and Sanders just didn't write it down. Clark wrote in his report that Sanders had asked Atkins about the movies *Three Faces of Eve* and *Raising Cain*, and Atkins denied having multiple personalities, told him he was sane. As Sanders had pressed on, appealing to his need to unburden himself from the guilt, Clark wrote, Atkins reportedly said, "I'll tell you, Sergeant Sanders, 'cause I see them every night at my bed. I take Nyquil and Tylenol so I can sleep because of the women. They be standing at the foot of my bed every night."

Clark examined jailhouse records for Atkins and noted that he had brought up the voices on September 18, 1992, claiming he had been hearing them for the previous two weeks. He repeated it on October 13, but staff saw it as a manipulation. He went into more detail about Mary, Mayolla and Tony with jail personnel the following July, a week and a half after his first session with Clark. Two days after that, he was found hanging in his cell but was taken down before he could be hurt. The following month, August, he continued to talk about the voices with jail staff.

Clark noted the differences between the report of Dr. Fields at Recorder's Court and his own sessions with Atkins. He had told Fields about Tony but didn't blame the offenses on him, merely saying Tony sometimes tried to influence him but often he resisted Tony.

While Atkins presented himself well to Clark, who noted his politeness, his coherent and relevant speech and his orientation to the correct time and place, he also appeared to have poor judgment skills. In Clark's administration of psychological testing, he noted Atkins' endorsement of too many symptoms – as with Rosen, suspecting malingering.

The bottom line for Clark: Atkins was not mentally ill, either during the commission of the crimes or during this evaluation. Clark doubted Atkins' visions and hallucinations, saying they were inconsistent. He had not told friends or family about the hallucinations. He had not had contact with mental health professionals before his arrest. And even though he was engaging in risky behavior like prostitution and drug use, Atkins still was capable of taking care of himself on the street. Even with the egregiousness of the murders and rapes, Clark said, there's no indication he was mentally ill. Abnormal, but not necessarily mentally ill. And even if this perp seemed "off," it didn't mean he lacked the capacity to understand the law and conform to it. To know his actions were wrong. In fact, he made some pretty good efforts to hide those actions. And that idea of Tony pulling his strings? "It is difficult to imagine how Mr. Atkins could have remained at large as long as he did," Clark wrote, "all the while committing more of the same kind of offense, if he did not have substantial ability to control his behavior."

Regarding the issue of diminished capacity, Clark said this was not the case for Atkins. Not his unusual hatred for prostitutes, the sexual sadism, his background of sexual abuse, or anything else in his background. Even the crack and alcohol as possible factors were reported inconsistently. His similar actions in each incident – taking the woman to an abandoned building, choking her, having sex with her, hiding the body – indicate goal-oriented, purposeful behavior. So no, on both these counts, concluded Clark's twenty-eight-page report.

Then the other side got a turn. For attorney Jeffrey Edison and the defense, Dr. Michael F. Abramsky, practicing on Woodward Ave in the northern Detroit suburb of Birmingham, took his own shot at Benjamin Atkins, interviewing him several times in latter 1993: November 7 and 27, and December 6, 13 and 20. It was ten hours total in these two-hour sessions. Abramsky looked at Atkins' personal background and history and questioned him on the current charges to try to ascertain his mental state at the time of the crimes. He gave Atkins a battery of psychological tests, some of the same tests that he underwent with the other psychiatrists. He also interviewed Atkins' mother and brother via phone on December 19. And he reviewed the Rosen and Fields reports.

In talking with all three family members, Abramsky discovered a strong bond among them. While the two boys were in foster care over the years, they would try to run away, thinking they could be back with their mother, Ben in particular wanting to be reunited with her despite the fact that she admittedly was a heroin addict who engaged in prostitution. There was the feeling that the three of them together didn't need anybody else, as Abramsky's report put it. Ben idealized this scenario in a bit of childhood fantasy.

In Abramsky's sessions, he also uncovered more of the story of Ben's allegations about sexual abuse in the home for boys where he and his brother were placed. His brother went to another unit, and as a result Ben became close to a male staff member as a sort of substitute for his older brother, Abramsky explained. "He had someone to himself and did not have to compete with others for attention," his report said. Then another boy at the home came along who started to gain more of the staff member's attention. Ben told Abramsky that the staff member asked him for sexual favors, and he complied in an attempt to maintain an exclusive relationship with him.

As their stay at the home progressed, the two brothers began to have weekend visits at their mother's home. Their mother often wasn't around, though, and the boys were left to their own devices. As his brother saw it, Ben adapted to this situation with some homosexual liaisons to get cash. *"[Brother]* and Ben both paint a picture of almost feral children alone and having to cope through their own resources," Abramsky said. Both boys were then returned to their mother's care, and things got worse. There was a drunken, abusive father figure to deal with (their own father was removed from the picture when Ben was only two), fighting at school, and skipping school as Ben increasingly fell into prostitution. He also began using marijuana and psychedelics, moving on to cocaine.

In his late teens and early twenties, Atkins tried to quit both the homosexuality and the cocaine, getting more stable jobs at restaurants and staying with his brother and his brother's girlfriend. Ben maintained relationships with both men and women during this period, the report said, though he felt more comfortable with men and felt he had to "pretend" with women.

His brother recalled putting Ben out at Christmastime 1990 because of the drug issue. Drugs were something he was getting over himself, and he didn't want to get pulled back into it with Ben's usage. From Ben's point of view, it was more his brother's girlfriend's manipulations that turned him out. Both could have been true, but either way it left Ben homeless. For Abramsky, Atkins elaborated a bit more on the cycle he was immersed at this time: stay out until six a.m., sleep until noon, go out and eat and play some basketball, go back to sleep, then at night go out again until six a.m., engage in prostitution and visit crack houses. Later in the nineteen-page report, Abramsky restated this cycle, or perhaps just the portion of it that related to the overnight hours: get a homosexual date, collect cash, feel remorse, hear voices calling him names, get angrier with himself, go to a crack house, buy crack, smoke crack, walk the streets, encounter a female.

"The bond between mother and child is the psychological foundation of personality," Abramsky wrote, clearly attacking this angle more than the other psychiatrists. The loss of both his parents thwarted Atkins' development, he said. He developed aggressive feelings toward women. He was ridiculed in school and got into fights, losing control so deeply that it often brought on a dazed state, his brother said. "It was as if some demon inside of him had taken control," Abramsky paraphrased.

Abramsky saw Atkins as knowing what was real and not real, having a good sense of reality. Like the other doctors, though, Abramsky noted poor judgment. He chronically entered into self-defeating behavior, the report said. He had difficulty delaying his impulses; he often lost control. Abramsky also pointed to something he called depersonalization – an alteration in the perception or experience of the self in that the usual sense of one's reality is changed. Sometimes he thought he was Ben; sometimes he was Tony. Sometimes he saw himself as male, sometimes female. His memory was great at times, poor at others. "The world often appears to be hazy to him, perceptions are vague, and people appear in less than human form, generally simply as objects." This was illustrated when he had sex with his lifeless victims – he was not seeing them as human beings.

Abramsky did not find Atkins to have multiple personalities, but he did recognize what he called "splitting." This condition was evident in his two different first names and in his attitude toward his sexuality, and even the fact that he could feel deeply protective toward children, refusing to go to a victim's house if there was a child there, but at the same time could viciously murder that victim and deprive her child of a mother.

Atkins really did hear the voices, Abramsky said, but they seemed to be diverse parts of his personality. He had an internal contradictory dialogue going – to kill or not to kill, to smoke crack or not, to engage in sex with a man or a woman. His splitting further manifested in his selective memory – sometimes remembering the crimes, sometimes not, often being bewildered that the person who did the crimes could possibly be him. Atkins attributed the murders to Tony as a defense mechanism. He even told Abramsky he would hear about the discovery of the bodies on the radio or television and not even put it together that it was him who was responsible. It seemed unreal. But Abramsky clarified that there was not an amnesia state – this was not a case of one "voice" doing the killing and the other "voices" being unaware of it.

"Benjamin is like a puzzle that does not fit," Abramsky wrote. The doctor's own experience with the subject on a personal level was that he was unfailingly polite and docile – another contradiction. Abramsky contrasted him with other killers he had spoken to: Ben was not aggressive, never intimidated him or gave him the feeling he could reach across the table and grab him at any second. Quite the contrary.

Crack can bring on violent rage reactions, Abramsky pointed out, and these crimes were precipitated by crack usage. Beyond that, though, Abramsky saw the murders as serving a dual purpose for Atkins: He was indeed killing his mother over and over, as others have surmised, and he was also killing the drug-using, prostituting part of himself that he despised. Atkins even described feeling a calm after each murder.

Where the insanity question was concerned, Abramsky said, the defendant would have to not only be deemed insane, but it would also have to be determined that his crimes sprung from his insanity. Atkins' mental illness was not typical, not acute like schizophrenia. It was essentially a failure of development. A personality grossly traumatized at an early age and the traumatization reinforced by other factors so that normal development did not occur. Bottom line: Abramsky felt Atkins was mentally ill – though not insane by the definition of the statute. As Clark had observed, Abramsky noted that he took great pains to conceal his crimes, clearly knowing the difference between right and wrong. Abramsky considered Atkins in the category of an "organized" serial, repeating his pattern of taking the women to abandoned buildings, killing them by the same method, hiding their bodies. Atkins denied any plan to kill each victim, but his actions pointed to planning, if only perhaps on a subconscious level. This indicated a certain level of control, Abramsky argued, a level of control that mitigated even the impairment of cocaine. And the rage effects of cocaine would tend to create a more disorganized killer rather than an organized one.

Not necessarily what Edison wanted to hear, but he would still endeavor to use it for what it was worth. If Atkins were found guilty, Abramsky suggested a determination of "guilty but mentally ill." So that's what Edison would need to run with. But perhaps he could still poke holes in the prosecution's evidence of guilt.

"Our position was that Ben traditionally was insane," Edison said. "But at the time, the jurisprudence did not reference that state of mind as insanity. It's called criminal responsibility. OK. So legal jurisprudence kind of discarded that terminology of insanity maybe in the '70s or early '80s or something like that. And it evolved into a terminology of criminal responsibility.

"So it is presumed that everyone is responsible for their conduct. There's a presumption of that. So if somebody comes in and takes my money, it's presumed that they're responsible. They have the state of mind to come in and take it. There's an assumption that Ben had the state of mind to sexually assault and kill these women. That's that state of mind. Our challenge now, because the challenge to whether he is the person is not as viable, although it's still argued. But more critically from an advocate's perspective, we've got to still deal with his state of mind. Even if we might say, well, the evidence is lacking to show that he actually is the person, because A, B and C. Even if you think that he is the person, he's not criminally responsible. And so to get to that, or that in other words even if you think he was the person, he was insane at the time. ... In order to raise the issue of criminal responsibility, first you have to be mentally ill. And there are definitions for mental illness. But being mentally ill does not negate your criminal responsibility. People are mentally ill, but they know the difference between right and wrong. So our position was because of his mental illness, he couldn't conform."

Edison did file a notice with the prosecutor's office in November 1992 of intending to pursue a defense of insanity and/or diminished capacity.

Edison recalled meeting with Atkins' mother Judy in his prep work. She was present, she was concerned about her son, Edison said, and the effects of long-term drug abuse were all-too evident about her.

Adding to the info gathered on Atkins leading up to trial was an interview with his former manager at the one legit job in particular that gets referenced a lot in his background details, the job at the pizza place (though he evidently worked in multiple restaurants in the two or three years leading up to his arrest; this particular pizza place was in the western suburb of Westland). In April 1993, a law intern interviewed the manager, first name Dan, via phone. Dan considered Ben a friend, had even partied at his brother's place. In many ways, Dan backed up what others had been saying about Atkins – he didn't find any sign of mental illness, never heard him talking about voices or anything like that. But Ben would act "out of whack" sometimes, usually when he was drunk or high. He would get in a "bad moody state." Dan did not know that Ben hated prostitutes. He also figured Ben was gay, just based on the guys who would call for him at work. Ben was a hard worker, when he was there, but the problem was he didn't show up a lot of the time. And he would disappear for months without any notice or explanation. He would return needing money, so he would drop right back into his job. Dan learned of Ben's crack problem through Ben's brother's girlfriend. Also, Ben stole some cash out of Dan's jacket pocket and denied it when Dan confronted him about it. Their boss compensated Dan for the missing cash and had Ben work it off.

TRIAL

It was the end of an era for the City of Detroit in January 1994 as Dennis Archer took the mayor's seat. After twenty years and five terms, Coleman Young was gone, having dropped out of the race due to illness before endorsing Archer's opponent. Archer took office at the beginning of the year, and both of Detroit's dailies – normally taking different positions along the political spectrum – lifted him up in their coverage and wished him luck.

The investigation into the attack on Olympic figure skater Nancy Kerrigan at Cobo Arena in downtown Detroit dominated the front page in the first month of the year. Jack Kevorkian was in the local news, and Lorena Bobbitt was on trial for so gruesomely dismembering her husband.

Also in January 1994, it was the People v. Benjamin Thomas Atkins, Case Nos. 92-12314 and 92-12315; 92-12375, 92-12376, and 92-12377; and 92-13111, 92-13112, 92-13113, 92-13114, 92-13115, 92-13116 and 92-13117, charged with eleven counts of first-degree murder, eleven counts of felony murder, two counts of first-degree criminal sexual conduct, one count of attempted murder, and one count of assault with intent to commit murder. Judge David Kerwin, a Wayne State University grad who had been with Recorder's Court since 1979, was set to preside. He was born and raised in Detroit; in fact, he had grown up in the same area as defense attorney Jeffrey Edison and they both attended Mumford High School and Wayne State Law School.

The first day of the proceedings was January 10, on which Kerwin ruled, over Edison's objection, that the prosecution could introduce evidence of the other charged offenses in each of the individual incidents (mentioned earlier as "similar acts," which could show a common scheme or method, like how the women were killed: smoking crack, strangulation, gags, bindings, abandoned buildings). Kerwin was obligated by a recent Supreme Court decision for that. The judge did have some cautionary instruction for the juries, however, which were about to be chosen in the *voir dire* procedure, about the limited admissibility of this evidence. Then Kerwin made the ruling to combine the twelve separate incidents into a single trial – nine for Circuit Court and three for Recorder's Court – the motion for joinder. The prosecution had cited many prior Michigan cases with joinder under similar circumstances.

"Families weep as Highland Park murder trial starts," said *The Detroit News* atop the Detroit/Wayne section of its January 11 edition. Brenda Mitchell's brother Frankie was one of those family members in court the day before, as Michael Reynolds and Jeffrey Edison argued the pre-trial motions and Atkins sat listening with his hand pensively over his nose and mouth for *The News*' accompanying photo. "He needs to be where the rest of them are at," Frankie told the paper. "He deserves to be in the grave, too."

Bertha Mason's mother Rosemarie was there with her husband. "Whenever I look at this guy, it tears me apart," she said. "No matter what she did, what her lifestyle was, my daughter had a right to live."

That same day, the *Free Press* ran a photo of Bertha's family in its own coverage of the trial's start. "They should cut his hands off," the *Freep* quoted Rosemarie outside the courtroom. "He killed my daughter with those hands."

And while the print media was doing its coverage, the TV media was noticeably absent. At least it was noticed by Judge Kerwin. Court TV had submitted a request to televise the whole trial, and CNN had requested to bring cameras into the courtroom, as did the local TV stations. But where were they now? Though plenty of cameras had been there for the preliminary proceedings, as John Mattox recalled, where were they now? Court TV had televised the Jeffrey Dahmer trial in 1992 and the Menendez brothers' trial in 1993. "This case was so hot at first," Judge Kerwin told writer Toni Swanger for her own story on the Atkins case in the Metro Times weekly paper. But by the time the trial rolled around, Kerwin said, "there was Lorena Bobbitt, then there was Tonya and Nancy, then the Branch Davidians down in Waco, Texas." Unlike the serial killer case in Gainesville – Kerwin also had to draw the comparison – this case in Detroit was not getting the attention. (This author's inquiry to Court TV/truTV about their request to televise the Atkins trial, by the way, did not get a response.)

In the pre-trial motions, Atkins' statements to police were entered into evidence, despite Edison's best efforts. Reynolds had drawn up a four-page memorandum of law citing prior Michigan cases where similar written documents were admitted, noting that he had law enforcement witnesses ready to testify to the confessions and the interviews that produced them, and that he could have the signature on the pages authenticated. Edison would, of course, spend a lot of time on the statements Ben made to Ron Sanders at the time of his arrest. Were they really Ben's actual words? No lawyer was present – was it possible there was any intimidation or coercion or even what some attorneys would term "indoctrination" on the part of police? All issues to consider. Edison was still going to push it for all its worth. (Though Atkins had detailed his encounters with the women when talking with Dr. Fields, his statements to Fields could only be used to determine criminal responsibility and diminished capacity and could not be used as evidence at trial to show he committed the crimes.)

Sanders expressed his own views on that in his interview for this book. He explained that one of the techniques he developed in his years of interrogating suspects was to purposely make a mistake on each page then have the suspect sign or initial it.

"It might be the misspelling of a word, or a word inserted that wasn't said," Sanders recalled. "But the point of the mistake was to get the signature or initial of the defendant, so later when it goes to court, he couldn't say, 'Well, Sergeant Sanders just wrote this thing down, and I signed it.' It kinda gives – what's the word, *prima facie* evidence? That he read what it was, what I put down."

Though Sanders was not able to testify at the trial because of his stroke the year before, he was not concerned about how the statements he took from Atkins would be perceived or portrayed.

"See, they knew that I was an excellent statement taker. They knew that. But I mean, you're a defensive lawyer, so you've got to poke holes." Edison was simply doing what a defense attorney does, Sanders asserted, even noting it was common knowledge he wrote his statements in large cursive.

When I spoke to Ron Sanders on the phone in April 2022, I had already sat down with Jeffrey Edison at his office in downtown Detroit a month before, and I had heard Edison speak well of both Sanders and Royce Alston, in terms of this case. They were two cops Edison respected. I could not help but relay that to both of them later, in my interviews with them, and where Sanders was concerned, it lent a bit more context to this discussion around the confessions vs. statements.

"If he thought I was an out-and-out liar," Sanders told me just a touch glibly, "do you think you would have had a cordial visit with him, or he would have been so cordial about, 'Ron Sanders is a nice guy'?" Upon hearing of Edison's regard, Sanders laughed and said, "Read between the lines!"

Indeed. Edison indicated to me that he'd had to watch Ron back in the day, that he knew Ron had certain "techniques" you had to look out for. But there was certainly no resentment. They *both* had a job to do. And they both did it.

"His job was defending," Sanders added. "Defending. But you can't defend the undefendable."

So with the admission of the statements, along with the similar acts, Edison was coming out of the gate with some disadvantages. As Reynolds held his more than one hundred witnesses at the ready for the prosecution, along with many exhibit photographs and giant detailed charts, would this back Edison into an insanity corner?

With the trial's start, Edison told the media he was not sure he was going to put forth an insanity defense, but that he had filed notice of it so Atkins could be examined by mental health experts. An insanity defense could mean admitting Atkins did the crimes but was not criminally responsible because of his mental state. A jury could choose a guilty but insane verdict under Michigan law, but like a regular guilty verdict, it could send Atkins to prison. A verdict of not guilty by reason of insanity could send him to a mental health facility.

Jury selection began on January 11 and continued through the end of the month. In all, thirty-two jurors were chosen, including four alternates for Wayne County Circuit Court and four for Recorder's Court. On the Detroit side, it was fourteen women and two men. On the Wayne County jury, it was nine women and seven men. One potential juror excused was a fourth-grade teacher of one of the victims.

As opening statements began in the first week of February, mental health did key heavily into Edison's presentation. Darlene Saunders' allegations were too incredible to believe, he asserted, Atkins' statements were made two days after his arrest and were not recorded and were therefore suspect, and Atkins' troubled childhood led to arrested personality development and insanity. Edison brought up the voices in his client's head. *The News'* coverage of the beginning of the trial described the defendant as incessantly rocking in his chair. Atkins' mother Judy sat in the first row of a courtroom packed with spectators as Edison described her life of prostitution, how she performed oral sex for johns while her two children watched.

Former HPPS Director John Mattox said, "I was impressed with the attorney. He did everything he could to win the case. But I mean, you can't — one thing about the law, some cases you cannot win. You just cannot win. There's just too much evidence against you."

Still, Mattox said, "Even the police officer said this guy did everything he could, legally. He did his homework. Most of them, they don't — a case like that, you know, 'This guy's guilty, shit, I'm not going to be busting my butt behind this.' 'Hey, he's going to be found guilty; there's nothing I can do.'"

For his own opening statement, Reynolds compared Atkins to the fabled Pied Piper, luring women to their deaths with the promise of crack. He mentioned the palm print found on the shower stall at the Juanita Hardy scene, linked to Atkins. He mentioned the semen found at the Valerie Chalk scene, linked to Atkins. He mentioned the fact that Atkins gave the color of the condom from the Chalk scene – yellow. "He was the first safe-sex serial killer we've seen," Reynolds told the court.

Atkins concealed the bodies of his victims, Reynolds went on; he knew the consequences of his actions. Taking victims to abandoned buildings showed he was in control of his actions. And strangulation takes time – premeditation. Prior to trial, Reynolds' own case notes identified these five facets for his approach to establishing Atkins' guilt:

1. Darlene's testimony
2. DNA evidence
3. Fingerprint evidence
4. Similarity of the crimes
5. Atkins' confessions

Reynolds further identified these four items he would use to show that Atkins was not insane nor acting with diminished capacity:

1. The testimony of three experts
2. The way in which each crime occurred
3. Observations of those who had contact with Atkins at the time of the crimes
4. Atkins' confessions

On Tuesday, February 8, Demerio was the first to the stand. As he retold the tale of that morning of Darlene's attack, Edison went for the fact that he couldn't actually identify Atkins in the darkness, didn't see his face, and that he remembered Darlene's attacker as just a little taller than Darlene, and taller than himself. Darlene was only five-foot-three, and Atkins was five-foot-ten (though he called himself five-foot-nine). Demerio told the court he was five-five or five-six. As Edison listened to Demerio's testimony, he noted on the yellow legal pad in front of him, "did not say Tony raped me," "don't know date, year, month," "did not see injuries, scars, scratches on back."

After his cross-examination of Demerio, Edison reinforced the height difference in his questions for Detective Sergeant Jim Dobson, witness No. 2 for the prosecution. "You say Mr. Atkins is five-feet-ten inches," he asked Dobson, "and she describes him as five-foot-three or four? That didn't pose any problem to you?"

With Dobson's testimony, the prosecution added exhibits of maps and charts of the areas of Woodward Avenue that Atkins frequented, plus photos of Darlene. Dobson talked about when he first spoke with Darlene, as well as the arrest of the other "Tony" who proved to be a false lead. He talked about the decision on where to interrogate Atkins, which personnel were present, the fact that they didn't want the press to get wind of it. Exhibits were entered for Atkins being advised of his constitutional rights. Dobson spoke to the general progression of the case, who was working it, whether or not Atkins was advised of the specific charges when being questioned, the fact that it was not recorded. "Cannot say statement is Atkins' actual words," Edison wrote on his legal pad.

Edison also probed about the reward money Dobson had discussed with Darlene. Dobson spent most of Wednesday under Edison's cross. He discussed his desire to be fair to the suspect and to not appear to be intimidating him, again the fact that the questioning wasn't recorded, and what happened on the day between the arrest and the questioning (which, by Atkins' own account to Edison, was simply that he was fingerprinted and then waited around in a holding cell). Atkins' prior arrests on misdemeanor charges like trespassing came up, putting Dobson even more on the defense, as well as DPD's Gerald Stewart, who tried to explain to the media that they had no reason to hold Atkins after his January 1992 arrest.

Darlene took the stand to tell her story on Thursday of that week, crying as she shared the details. Again, Edison took on the question of Atkins' height in her description of the perp. "I didn't carry a tape measure with me," Darlene said. When Edison pressed about the reward money, she shot back, "Get this straight. I didn't turn him in for no reward. I turned him in because he killed those eleven women."

In her testimony, Darlene talked about how when she walked the streets, she would often have razor blades in both hands. She had known Tony for years before encountering him that morning. He did not appear to be responding to any voices, she said.

Also testifying that week were officers Lindsey Pace and Terry Greene, the latter of which assisted in Atkins' arrest and recalled him giving his brother's name at the time. Pace noted that Darlene appeared to be high when police first spoke with her, something Darlene herself admitted on the stand. Debbie Friday's mom Sadie, Uncle Herb and boyfriend Calvin testified about when they last saw Debbie and what they knew of her lifestyle.

Atkins was calm during most of the proceedings, though he muttered angrily under his breath as Darlene testified. He also made an outburst during Edison's opening statement: He yelled across the courtroom for one of the jurors to wake up, that this was his life on trial; the female juror had been sitting in the back row with her eyes closed. She said she had not been sleeping – just trying to listen while her eyes were burning – and even sent an apology to Atkins through his attorney.

On Monday, February 14, Officer Judith Norwood of Highland Park Public Safety talked about the October 1991 trespassing arrest of Atkins, that he did not appear mentally ill. Also that day, Reynolds presented further evidence in the Debbie Friday murder. Among the people's exhibits were autopsy diagrams of Debbie and numerous sketches and photos of 170 Elmhurst. Theodore Cadwell, Michael Hall, William McLean and Donna Smith of HPPS took the stand on what they encountered at the Elmhurst scene that day. Melinda Jackson of the Michigan State Police discussed the forensic evidence collected. Dobson took the stand again, too. Dr. Kalil Jiraki, who performed Debbie's autopsy, talked about the process of strangulation, that a person passes out after one or two minutes then dies after about five minutes. Debbie's time of death could not be determined, Jiraki said. As Sergeant Daniel Bateman of MSP, a latent print examiner, testified, Edison wrote in his legal pad, "print can last for year."

The next day, Bertha Mason's boyfriend William testified about the last time his children saw her, about her footprints disappearing so sadly in the snow outside their house, the children telling him, "Mama went out." He filed a missing person's report near the end of December, he said, then identified Bertha's body at New Year's. Bertha's sister Yvette testified to when she last saw her. Several of those at the Mason scene testified: Sam, who found her, Sergeant James Bivens, Officer Benjamin Hoyton and evidence techs Paul Kulesa and Ron Gotowicki. Gotowicki discussed the seminal stain found on the dark coat at the scene, sent for testing, and other evidence. Dr. Laning Davidson of the Wayne County Medical Examiner noted that Bertha was several months pregnant. Bertha had smoked crack just before she died, the M.E. said. Reynolds provided the autopsy diagrams of Bertha, too, plus several photos of 12 Alger. For his cross-examinations, Edison took swings at how the evidence was collected and processed.

The case of Patricia Cannon George was explored on February 15 and 22, with testimony from the manager of the wrecking company that discovered her body on Kenilworth, along with DPD's Avis Taylor who was on the scene, Kulesa, and medical examiner Sawait Kanluen, who testified that her legs were broken after her death, presumedly in the house's demolition. Derrick Cannon testified to the last time he saw his sister and to ID'ing her body at the medical examiner's office. Reynolds was armed with an autopsy diagram of Pat as well as photos of the scene. As things progressed, he made use of the same for Vickie Truelove. Plenty of evidence from the Monterey was on the people's exhibit list, as well: photos of Juanita Hardy, Valerie Chalk and Fifteen at the scene, the DNA comparison for the tissue paper, the palm print. And there were the requisite autopsy diagrams, scene sketches and photos for Brenda Mitchell, Vicki Beasley Brown, Joanne O'Rourke, CC Waymer.

One homicide sergeant who took the stand, Carl Frederick, discussed different approaches of interrogation, such as the "good cop/bad cop" technique. Statements taken tend to be self-explanatory, he said. You don't always need to have exact words. It's a summary. He videotaped his own interrogations but had not used audio recordings. He was not aware of the location at Brush and Mack where Atkins was taken, which by now was stated to be a crime lab for DPD. Part of Edison's strategy involved digging into that decision to question Atkins at this more-obscure location, and even the decision to question him in Detroit rather than Highland Park.

As the focus turned to Vickie Truelove's murder, her daughter Sheree took the stand. She had known of her mom's drug use, she said. A few officers responding to the Truelove scene testified, as well as the man who found her.

On February 23, Lieutenant John Whitty discussed Atkins' January 1992 arrest, how he was found sleeping on a couch and claimed he had gotten into an argument with his wife before Christmas. Whitty remembered Atkins giving his name as Calvin. Sergeant Kenneth Day, by this time retired, took the stand, noting he did not tend to record his interrogations. He was not familiar with the kind of closed-circuit setup used in Atkins' interrogation. The man who made the discovery of the first body at the Monterey took the stand, as well as responding officer Sheila Herring. And Dobson was back in the hot seat that day and the next day to discuss the scene, as well. Valerie Chalk's mother Jessie testified, as did Valerie's sister Ruth. Also on the stand were Juanita Hardy's foster mother Carrie, sergeants Larry Beller and Walt Chapman, and Detective Morris Cotton, who had actually recognized Valerie as a friend. Davidson took the stand again and discussed how each of the three Monterey victims died. Edison discussed with Davidson the rate of decomposition of semen samples and how this depends on the environment. If the semen was air-dried, that would affect the rate of decomposition, Davidson said. It was difficult to pinpoint the age of the seminal fluid that was tested, Edison worked to establish.

Lieutenant Christopher Flo of the MSP, who processed the Monterey scene, described the area as littered with debris. Dirty, filthy. The trial was now at the end of February, and a DNA expert from Cellmark Diagnostics in Maryland offered explanations of DNA testing procedure and accuracy. She also discussed the examination of the condom and the match of the seminal fluid from the tissue at the scene. An MSP serology expert, David Woodford, backed up the testimony with details of his own chain-of-custody procedure with the samples sent to Cellmark. Edison took lots of notes during the DNA discussion, like the idea that there are limitations – quantity and quality of the DNA, for instance, and that the chemicals used can affect the process.

In the first week of March, the next few witnesses discussed the palm print. "Detect latent prints that are left on surfaces less than ideal," Edison jotted on his legal pad. The print had not been readily visible on the shower stall; the surface had to be powdered to bring it to light. There was no way to determine how long the print had been there, he established with one of the law enforcement witnesses. Several items taken from the three Monterey scenes were one by one discussed in the context of searching for usable prints and examining for other evidence such as semen or blood. Also part of the discussion was the unusual process for pulling prints from these three decomposed bodies – the removal of their hands for processing at the MSP crime lab.

Davidson set the record straight about Brenda Mitchell's cause of death. Brenda had three different death certificates, he explained, for lack of consultation between the examiners, but her cause of death was strangulation, not overdose. Brenda's family members Maggie, Frankie and Dianne all testified, along with the two women who found her. A few HPPS officers testified about the scene, and yes,

Dobson was back on the stand. Woodford returned to the stand, as well, to talk about finding semen on the rectal swab though not on the vaginal swab. "Cannot say conclusively that Atkins left substance," Edison noted. "Cannot separate semen from deceased body fluids."

Clarence and Gloria Beasley took the stand on March 7 to talk about their daughter Vicki. Officer Craig Pulvirenti discussed responding to the scene at 121 Highland, along with Cadwell and Dobson again, and a few others. Dr. Yung Chung of the medical examiner's office took a turn. Vicki's friend Emma, who lived in the neighborhood, had also seen Atkins around and knew him as Tony, she told the court. He had manners, was always neat and clean, and always by himself, she said. She found nothing threatening about him, Edison established in his cross.

Pulvirenti also testified about responding to the Joanne O'Rourke scene at 12223 Woodward, and Beller, Jackson and Flo returned to the stand.

CC Waymer's grandmother Ruby and sister Sheree testified. Several of the investigators returned to give an account of CC's discovery informed by Atkins' interrogation. Her body was skeletonized, the M.E. noted. "Cause of death speculation," Edison noted on his pad. He probed the officers' accounts of just how Atkins gave up the information – what he said, how he said it, what he was asked by police before he said it. Morris Cotton also knew CC, her family and her arrest record. Atkins got injured in the incident with CC, Reynolds was well-aware, so he had the records from Detroit Receiving Hospital, and Donald Smith, M.D., testified about treating Atkins on June 1, 1992. Dr. Smith said he gave him five stitches for a one-inch cut on his right knee. He had contact with Atkins for only about ten minutes, but he remembered him as alert and oriented. The doctor's understanding was that Atkins had gotten into a fight and was cut on some glass.

Edison continued probing on interrogation methods as a few more officers took the stand on March 9. Had they ever questioned suspects at this unusual crime lab location near Brush Street? No, for the most part.

On March 14, Detective Sergeant Royce Alston told the story of the night he and Darlene spotted "Tony." In Alston, Edison perhaps found a kindred spirit, because Alston said he always wrote exact words for suspect statements. He wanted the exact words, not summaries, so there would be no question. He was not present when Atkins made his statements, but Alston was familiar with the crime lab location.

Sergeant Lee Caudill, by this point retired after fourteen years in Homicide most recently, talked about conducting the interrogation with Ron Sanders. Atkins did not appear to be mentally ill to him, he said. Caudill was there at the beginning when it was Bill Rice doing the questioning and the topics were about general life, not the crimes. When Sanders arrived, the topics changed to not only the crimes but also Atkins' homosexuality, his time in foster homes, his alleged multiple personalities. Atkins denied the crimes, and Sanders said yes, you did do them, and he played on the salvation/redemption idea to coax Atkins into admission. Rice stayed with the interrogation and kept time and some notes. Sanders was getting writer's cramp, said Caudill, who filled in with the transcription and affirmed that yes, these statements were Atkins' own words.

Caudill read aloud from the statements. The words chilled the courtroom, *The Detroit News* reported, as Caudill read Atkins' explanation of placing both thumbs over the front of the woman's neck, interlocking his fingers behind her neck. "The method was always the same," Caudill quoted Atkins. Then came checking for a pulse, a heartbeat. Pushing any remaining air out of her stomach. The trial was in its tenth week, and the prosecution was winding down its case with those powerful statements.

Edison asked lots of probing questions during his cross-examination with Caudill, zeroing in on the process for interrogation, who was there, how Atkins seemed to him, how Sanders was selected to question the suspect, who else participated in what decisions and why. Maybe Caudill could not *really* say for sure the statements were Atkins' exact words, Edison pried out of him. He was not there one hundred percent of the time. He was there whenever Atkins signed the sheet, but Stewart of DPD was there for the duration of the questioning, he recalled.

And it was Stewart who was next, once Caudill finally got leave of the hot seat. Stewart had twenty years in Homicide at that point and had known Paul Lindsay since the 1970s. He got a call from Lindsay the day after Atkins' arrest, August 20, about bringing the suspect to the crime lab location, where the earlier "Tony" suspect had been interviewed, as well. Stewart said the location was used because of the closed-circuit TV setup – it was good for the other officers to be able to observe, to help inform their own interrogations. There was no facility in the Homicide Section set up for that, he said. The fact that this location was away from headquarters was an advantage, too. Stewart affirmed he was there from the beginning to the end of the questioning, watching on the monitor, though he didn't take notes. This video setup was not used for taping, Stewart said. It wasn't their policy to record statements. There had been a facility in a garage in the '70s that had a setup to record but it didn't exist anymore. Stewart had instructed Rice to take notes to protect against any challenges to the statements. He agreed that before Sanders arrived, the conversation in the room was small talk with Rice and Caudill, but that with Sanders, the discussion went to the idea of multiple personalities, which Atkins denied, though he did talk about seeing the women at the foot of his bed.

Lieutenant Tommy Alston – no relation to Royce – took the stand to discuss his presence at part of the questioning, as well. It was the first time he had seen an interrogation at the crime lab location. Neither he nor the next witness, Lieutenant William Presley, were part of any discussion of the reward money. Then Gloria Reynolds of the crime lab backed up the idea that there was no recording of the questioning. There was no recording device in the system, and the camera lens didn't cover the full room, she said.

Lindsay, "retired" from the FBI amid the publication of his telling first novel, took the stand on March 20 and 21. He explained how Atkins had given up CC Waymer's body. In his cross, Edison drew from the glossy *Vanity Fair* magazine story that had lauded the work of Lindsay and Sanders the year before, referring to Lindsay's term of a "Dragon of Vengeance," someone who takes the law into his own hands. Edison asked Lindsay if his "Dragon" included bribing Darlene with reward money. Lindsay denied it. He could not say for sure whether the statements were Atkins' exact words or summaries, though he insisted the integrity of the process was maintained. Lindsay said he had never taped a statement in twenty years. Afterward he told the media that Atkins had told law enforcement he had been planning a twelfth killing for his birthday in later August.

The next day, Bill Rice took the stand. He also never videotaped or audiotaped statements. He spoke to Atkins for about a half-hour at first, and he found nothing about the suspect to indicate mental illness. He was present when Atkins admitted the killings, he said.

Near the end of March, the prosecution rested, and Dr. Michael Abramsky testified for the defense, saying that yes, Atkins had a mental illness, but he did not say the defendant was actually insane. Abramsky discussed Atkins' upbringing, the time spent in foster homes and the home for boys, where Abramsky said Atkins had a forced relationship with a male staff member. The defendant was in conflict, even self-hatred, over his sexuality, the doctor said. The voices inside Atkins were constantly struggling.

This was not a case of multiple personalities, but "splitting." This splitting affected his recall, sometimes with an extreme repression of events. "The rage would come to the surface," Abramsky was quoted by Corey Williams of *The Detroit News*. "He began striking out at women drug addicts. He was striking out at his mother and striking out at himself in an expression of self-hate." He had fused sex and aggression together in his failure to develop normally.

In Edison's attempt to refute the idea of premeditation, Abramsky said Atkins was not planning or rehearsing these incidents; he didn't bring a "rape kit" with him, for instance. Edison laid it out plainly for *The News*' story: The defense's ultimate position was that Atkins was not guilty of the crimes, but if the juries were to believe he was, then he was not criminally responsible.

The defense rested its case, then the prosecution presented rebuttal testimony, first with Dr. Dexter Fields taking the stand. He discussed his own time with Atkins, touching on what he believed was the defendant's malingering during testing. He agreed with the idea of self-hatred, as well as Atkins' conflicts with female relationships and his hatred for women.

On April 11, Dr. Charles Clark gave another side of the psychiatric story as he testified for the prosecution. He described the various individual personas – the "voices" – Atkins had discussed with him, even an imaginary dog named Pete. Atkins derived sexual pleasure from the strangulations but was not crazy, Clark said. He did not agree on the self-hatred thing. This was sexual sadism, he said. A lack of morality, ethics and guilt. With the procedures this killer followed each time, "this is not a pattern of uncontrolled homicide," Clark said, also bringing up the malingering during testing. Again, *The News* reported that Atkins was rocking rhythmically in his chair during the testimony.

Closing statements followed on April 12. "He lured the women with promises of drugs," Reynolds told the court.

"He selected vacant, abandoned buildings. He bound and gagged most of them. He raped them and he strangled them. Doctors tell us it took five minutes for each woman to die, ample time for a killer to change his mind.

"These were crimes done by cunning, by stealth and by guile. He eluded a task force for months. And yet this man wants you to believe he was crazy."

For his turn, Edison told jurors to listen carefully when Judge Kerwin read the legal definition of insanity. "The essence of the defense of Mr. Atkins rests right within the law," Edison said. "You must decide if the prosecutor has met his burden of proof." At that time, the prosecutor had the duty of proving the defendant was legally sane during the crimes. Shortly afterward, the burden shifted to the defense being required to prove insanity.

Atkins took great exception to something Reynolds discussed during his final arguments, so much so that he hand-wrote a letter to Judge Kerwin about it. Reynolds had brought up the counselors who worked with Atkins at the home for boys. "What he spoke of was indeed true," Atkins wrote the judge, "but the women counselors he spoke of were my Psychotherapist Counselor *[sic]* rather than the Group Counselors that were in charge of my reporting to breakfast, school and etc. He failed to mention that the PsyCounselor was not in my everyday schedule, and I only visited them twice a month." There was a big difference between the two, he wrote, and the fact that the prosecuting attorney did not make this distinction was detrimental to his case. He told the judge that Reynolds no doubt would have realized from his investigation of the home's records that what Atkins claimed about his time there (read: the abuse from a staff member) was true. "I was in fact surrounded by men as well as women," Atkins wrote. (We'll dig into Atkins' time at the home in a later chapter, including this idea of male vs. female staffers.)

The two juries began deliberating on April 14 (actually late that day, which was a Thursday, but really the following Monday morning), each focused on just its own cases, Detroit or Highland Park. Judge Kerwin gave them the necessary instruction for the deliberations, including the laws regarding insanity, but the juries requested additional information a few days later. Can you instruct us further on the differences between mental illness and legal insanity, they asked.

After two and a half court days, the Wayne County jury was the first to reach a verdict. The announcement was delayed until the Recorder's Court jury had its own decision, then announced on April 21, ending a trial that had lasted forty-eight court days, by Edison's records. On, Friday, April 22, the announcement took up a small portion of the lower right corner of *The Detroit News*' front page, which was otherwise dominated by a decision in a Kevorkian case as well as a state House of Representatives vote on union political funding. "Atkins convicted of killing 11 women; faces life term," the two-column story read with just a few inches of copy before jumping inside. Accompanying it was a photo of Atkins bent over with his head against his left hand as the verdicts were read. He had carried a Bible with him into the courtroom that day, the story said.

The *Free Press* described Atkins as showing no reaction to the verdicts. "His only concern was getting a cigarette," a deputy sheriff told the paper. Both papers noted that Atkins was being called the fastest serial killer in U.S. history.

In all, Atkins was convicted of eleven counts of first-degree premeditated murder, eleven counts of first-degree felony murder, and the rape of Darlene (first-degree criminal sexual conduct). He was found not guilty of the assault and attempted murder of Darlene. It took ten minutes to read the verdicts, the *Freep* reported, a "slow roll call of death." The courtroom was nearly empty, though a few victim family members were there. None of Atkins' own family members were there, the media reported.

Vicki Beasley's mother Gloria hugged Reynolds. "This was blood, sweat and tears!" she exclaimed.

Jurors told the media that the physical evidence — the palm print and seminal sample – was strong, but the statements Atkins made were the most compelling. "We never thought he was insane," a jury foreman said. "But we had questions about mental illness until we laid it all out on a chalkboard."

The last juror holdout for convicting Atkins said, "I just hope there's a message in this. ... Society cannot be blamed for these deaths, but he should have gotten help."

"The contrast between this case and the one in Gainesville, Florida, is very interesting," the *Freep* quoted Judge Kerwin after the verdicts. "I can't help but conclude that the fact that these were poor, African-American women, addicted to crack cocaine with histories of prostitution, made them different to people than five Caucasian college students. ... It's inescapable to me, that disparity."

Kerwin pronounced the mandatory life sentences on Wednesday, May 11. *The News*, running a photo of Valerie Chalk's mother Jessie and sister Ruth, quoted Atkins denying the charges amid curses rising up from the back of the courtroom. "I'm sorry for the relatives, for what they've been through," Atkins said in a seeming reply to the sounds of outrage, "but it can never compare to what I've been through."

As the judge relayed the life sentences for each of the eleven murders, then an additional life sentence for Darlene's rape, the survivor shouted, "Thank-you, Jesus!" The judge called her a "woman of courage and valor" for coming forward to identify Atkins.

The *Free Press*, which in its own coverage ran a photo of Darlene hugging her sister Patricia, noted that relatives of Atkins were present in court that day but left before the judge gave the sentences.

In early May, Reynolds sent Edison a letter complimenting him on the "hell of a good job" representing Atkins, calling him a worthy opponent "who is also a gentleman and a genuinely decent person."

Reynolds went into civil practice after the Atkins trial (though he would return to the prosecutor's office years later). Kerwin headed north to Oakland County, still presiding over a lot of drug and murder cases, actually. For Kerwin, leaving Detroit and its Recorder's Court was a move that surprised even him, he said when reached via phone in 2023 for this book, since he was "a Detroiter through and through." Former Detroit Mayor Coleman Young even told him at the time, "I never thought you'd be the one to cross Eight Mile." Kerwin was one of the few white members of a Black lawyer's association and had been a strong supporter of the Black community. Kerwin replied to Young something to the effect of yeah, if you had only seen her legs. "I knew it had to be a bitch," Young returned in his trademark fashion.

Jim Dobson retired from HPPS the year of the trial. He recalled decades later: "It was really strange. Right after the case, within a matter of months, the judge retired, the prosecutor retired, I retired. Mike went into private practice, and then he came back to the prosecutor's office."

And FBI agent Paul Lindsay had already seen his own job situation change. On the day William Sessions issued him a commendation and a six-hundred-dollar bonus for his work on the case, Lindsay also received a notice that he was under investigation for insubordination due to his first novel, *Witness to the Truth*.

For Dobson and others in law enforcement, Atkins' conviction was the gratifying end of a long, frustrating road – long despite the fact that this was "America's fastest serial killer." He had eluded a five-agency task force for months.

"John Mattox wanted to celebrate the victory, so he had a party, and he invited everybody that was involved," Dobson said. "This was well after. John and I always got along. John and I would do things together. We'd go to the bookstore at the old Packard plant and stuff like that. Well, John, he gave me two medals. I've got two great big medals. Officer of the year, and all this. And I'm kind of proud of my medals."

But don't get the wrong idea about Dobson, who passed away in November 2023 after a year-and-a-half fight with pancreatic cancer. "You know what?" he told this author in 2022. "I look at it this way. I don't think there are any heroes in this story. The thing is, we put a stop to it. I mean, solving it is one thing. I always look at it, solving is one thing, but we put a stop to it."

It was a significant enough case for Dobson to mention it in his 1994 retirement letter. Indeed, as a packed house gathered for Dobson's memorial service on a blizzardy day in January 2024, I mentioned this to Dobson's brother-in-arms Larry Beller, who unfortunately would also pass later that year. Yes, Beller told me, the Atkins case was the biggest case he and Dobson worked on. The most high-profile case. And the rapport Dobson had established with Atkins was pretty strong – he even visited him in prison later, Jim's brother mentioned at the memorial.

HE MEETS HIS END

During Benjamin Atkins' sentencing, Judge David Kerwin said that if he could, he would have the Department of Corrections inscribe the names of each one of the victims on his cell wall, "so that every day when you woke up, you saw their names and that each one of them was a person whose life you took."

Atkins would not have had very long to look at them. Only about three years.

Atkins died in September 1997 at Duane L. Waters Hospital in Jackson, a Michigan Department of Corrections facility. He had been serving his time at the Charles E. Egeler Reception and Guidance Center also in Jackson. Cause of death was noted as HIV infection.

Atkins was appealing his conviction until the moment he died, and there's a painful irony to that, when you consider the loss of law enforcement's files on the case, which we'll get into later. The basis of his appeal, according to paperwork from July 1997: "Defendant asserts that the trial court erred in granting the prosecutor's motion to join these twelve separate files for a single trial before two separate juries." His defense attorney for the appeals, Peter Jon Van Hoek, felt that the law was pretty strong that this decision, made over Jeffrey Edison's objection, was erroneous. Under Michigan's court rule on joinder and severance, his client had the right to separate trials for the offenses, he said. He cited other Michigan cases. He tried to argue that the twelve incidents were not connected, not part of a single scheme or plan. Van Hoek was not contesting the fact that even if the cases had been tried separately, evidence from the other cases could be used in each separate case as similar acts evidence. The State of Michigan Court of Appeals affirmed the convictions, however.

Jeffrey Edison thinks about Ben from time to time. Does the case haunt him, this author asked.

"'Haunt' is — I would never use that. Because to me 'haunt' means sometimes like fear or something, a bad experience. At no time from day one to the end, did Ben project any type of aggression or fear or whatever. I mean, in spite of what occurred, my whole experience with him gave an opportunity to tap into his humanity. Right. I mean, really."

This was a case that received some national attention, put him on the phone with CNN just a day or two after he was appointed, but Edison has taken on other high-profiles cases. Did he consider Ben's case his biggest one? "I certainly would say that it probably was, in terms of what it represented, you know, and the amount of — the degree of tragedy."

EXAMINING HIS BEGINNINGS

Single, twenty-three years old, no job much of the time, no children, no family he was supporting, no family who were supporting him, for the most part. Alone. Homeless.

That's how law enforcement characterized Benjamin "Tony" Atkins at the time of his arrest.

But this ball of yarn had to unravel somehow. There had to be something in back of all this. There had to be a place where it all started. But where? And how? Have you been interested to know, as our case has unfolded, just what was this upbringing our perp kept alluding to? Kept giving hints to?

In their investigation into the killer's background, interesting aspects emerged in every direction police looked. Things that might make them shake their heads and say, "Yeah, there it is." But it's quite subjective. Some details of his life could be clues; some could be meaningless. It's at least partly based on the viewer's – and the reader's – *own* background.

A lot of people have shaken their heads at the background of Benjamin Atkins. In fact, his is a story that can evoke quite a conflicted response. Like the last juror holdout in his case who was quoted in the media that "he should have gotten help." Or his own defense attorney, who was characterized by at least one newspaper as citing society for all of this and was quoted as saying, "Nobody is born to kill. ... There's other Atkinses walking around here, and people just refuse to see it." Or perhaps like *Detroit News* columnist Betty DeRamus, who said, "Benjamin Atkins is not the only person to have been battered or sexually assaulted. The world is full of rape and assault victims who don't wind up in courtrooms facing multiple murder charges."

Listen to a podcast about the other Detroit serial killer operating a few years later, also killing prostitutes, John Eric Armstrong, for instance, and you'll hear and see angry responses among the hosts and in the posted comments. There's nothing very sympathetic about his story. Listen to a podcast about Benjamin Atkins, and you're likely to hear a more mixed response. A confused response. Do I hate this killer? Or do I have sympathy for him, for the way he was raised? For the way society failed him?

"This is the first criminal that I actually feel a little sorry for," said one commenter on YouTube. "I dont know if its because he is a Virgo like myself or what but honestly, I truely believe if he had gotten some therapy and had someone in his life that genuinely cared about him, he would have not committed the crimes that he committed. So sad. None the less, I am glad justice was served."

Another commenter on that same video about the case: "Although he was dead wrong for his crimes as all of them are ... I can't help but think bad parenting/ society makes serial killers or killers in general."

Still another YouTuber weighed in, on a different video: "Indeed a sad story, r.i.p. for the victims but we should take into account that the killer was a victim of society as well. He was abandoned, abused, raped and given a shitty card to play the game of life. The system is to blame. Poverty is to blame, capitalism is to blame. If his father and mother had opportunitties in life, education, jobs and other "privileges", things would be different. let alone that these should be granded and not being privileges."

"Turmoil ruled suspect's childhood" read one newspaper headline shortly after Atkins' arrest, as some details were being revealed. Yeah. That about sums it up. But let's dig in a bit, shall we?

***

When Benjamin Atkins was telling Dr. Charles R. Clark in 1993 about the voices he would hear, the various other "people" who were living within him who would goad him on, torture him or comfort him, he was referencing his own grandmother in one of the names he gave. Maybe this was a conscious decision, maybe not. Whatever the case, she was the one he said would comfort him. Mayolla. The name of his grandmother on his mother's side.

Atkins' mother Judy did not live with this comforting Mayolla in her earliest years, however. Judy lived with her own grandparents, Mayolla's parents, and she did so happily by her account, until she was ten years old. At that point, which would have been 1948, she went to live with her mother in Detroit. Mayolla had separated from Judy's father. Judy's life was evidently troubled at a young age. She got pregnant at age fourteen, something less-heard-of and quite forbidden in the 1950s. She put the baby – reportedly a girl – up for adoption, and in her later adolescence she admittedly supported herself through prostitution. When she was eighteen, she started living with a man named Lonnie in Toledo, Ohio. (Not to be confused with the suspect Lonnie in this case.) Judy and Lonnie lived together for eight years, and Lonnie – allegedly, by one account – fathered Benjamin and his older brother. Ben was born in August 1968.

Ben was reported to have as many as five siblings – reports unsubstantiated by any more-official sources. He told one psychiatrist, for instance, that he had two half-sisters who were "trick babies," and that he had two full brothers by his father Lonnie. He would also mention a sister to his victims as he was luring them to an abandoned building, saying they could not go to his "sister's place," but he likely meant his brother's girlfriend. There is also the "Janice" that Darlene Saunders knew as Atkins' apparent sister. It's unclear if this was another name for his brother's girlfriend, or someone else entirely, maybe an actual sister. But there was only one sibling Atkins remained close to throughout his life. That was the brother who was one year older, living in the same house with Judy and Lonnie, a brother with whom Ben lived continually, actually – in and out of whatever foster situation as the years passed – until adulthood, when he lived with him off and on then, too. His brother is still around Detroit as of this writing, and attempts were made to contact him for this book. He is respectfully nameless here, as so much of Ben's background is his own history, too. This brother's girlfriend, also such a key figure in Ben's life, died in 2018.

When Ben was about two years old, Judy separated from Lonnie – who had been staying with her and the boys only intermittently – and came back to Michigan with her two sons. She became involved with a man named William. It was then that she got addicted to heroin. She continued in prostitution and sometimes took her sons along on her tricks, as mentioned earlier. She got in trouble with the law: possession of stolen mail, felonious assault. She served time in 1970-71. In December 1971, Judy left Ben and his brother with a woman she knew, then took off. The following year, she forged checks, earning her two years of probation in a halfway house. She got a job at a manufacturing company while at the home. Authorities discovered that the two boys had been left without their mother, and on May 25, 1972, they were made wards of Wayne County Juvenile Court with placement in the Children's Aid Agency, under the supervision of the county Department of Social Services.

Weeks later, on June 18, they were placed in a foster home. They stayed in that home for the next few years.

When Judy was discharged from her two years of probation, she went from the halfway house to live with a man named Frank for two and a half years. Then she returned to William, and the two got married. William died of apparent heart failure in January 1976, an event that by one account hit Judy very hard. She would later report that she spent the following month high on pot and alcohol and even considered suicide. Also the following month, her mother Mayolla had a stroke. Mayolla was living in the city of Jackson, and Judy went there to take care of her, then bringing her back to Detroit to live with her.

In her dealings with drugs and fraud, Judy went by various names. She used the last name of Atkins sometimes, which was Ben's legal last name. She also used the names Denise Brown and Denise Evans. In the midst of all of this, as her two sons were in foster care in their early years, she had not worked out any way to take care of them. "The boys have been repeatedly disappointed by their mother's promises to plan for them," read one report in the foster care records. "Their current behavior problems, truanting from the foster home and school, is causing problems within their foster home placements." The report said the boys were acting out in the hopes of being reunited with their mother, that they had a strong emotional attachment to her. Judy would "occasionally" visit her sons, "when it is to her convenience," the foster care worker noted, but was not attempting to find a larger apartment to take them back in, or showing real interest in taking them back in. She was living with her mother at a small apartment on Holcomb Street, east side, not far from the Detroit River, and evidently working in the laundry room of the then-quite-new Renaissance Center complex. This was 1977, and the boys were at a foster home on Carter Street in Detroit, a couple miles west of Woodward. They were attending

Macculloch Elementary School nearby, then Jamieson Elementary School. Ben was nine years old and described as a friendly child, though slower in school, whereas his brother got good grades. Notably, their mother told officials that Ben had started two fires in the home years earlier, and one of his foster parents had noticed burnt matches in their home. (In his study of Atkins' background, Dr. Michael Abramsky reported that Ben and his brother had lived in four different foster homes, two of which Ben said treated them well. Abramsky's background details were based on conversations with Atkins, his mother and his brother, as well as the conversations Atkins had with law enforcement and others.)

In August 1977, the boys were moved from the home on Carter to one on Buena Vista not too far away. That month, their new foster parents called police when they went missing. The boys were found late that night wandering the neighborhood streets. Ben skipped school seven days in September, his foster parents apparently unaware.

Also in September, Judy had a drug test at the Drug Detention Center at the Frank Murphy Hall of Justice downtown. She passed the drug test, but the county wanted a permanent solution for her two sons, and it still did not seem to be forthcoming from this troubled mom. Next stop for them: a home for boys. It would have profound effects on young Benjamin.

The St. Francis Home for Boys, operated by the Catholic Archdiocese of Detroit, was actually at one time located on Woodward Avenue in Highland Park, ironically enough, before Ford Motor Co. bought the property for an expansion, in particular to train workers and support production of its new Model T. With the property purchase, Ford provided a parcel for a new location for the orphanage to the west, on the corner of Fenkell and Linwood in Detroit. The new five-story building was designed by revered architect Albert Kahn, who left his fingerprints all over the city of Detroit, on industrial plants, mansions and office buildings. The new home was dedicated in 1917 as a place for boys whose families were unable or unwilling to care for them. The book *Archdiocese of Detroit* by Roman Godzak says that it was one of the biggest and best-known child-care facilities in Detroit, built to hold up to five hundred boys under the care of the Sisters of St. Joseph.

From 1942 to 1969, the home became a military school, but then switched back. By the time Ben and his brother lived there, the home had seen thousands of boys come through its doors. A lot of the young charges were sent there by the state and had developmental or disciplinary issues. By the late 1980s, regulators were investigating alleged physical abuse by staff members, as well as sexual assaults between residents, according to a history of the facility on DetroitUrbex.com. The state shut down the home in 1992. Then Detroit Public Schools took over, utilizing the building for a special program targeting African-American youth called Paul Robeson Academy. In May 2011, fire ravaged the building. The damage proved to be too much, and the building was demolished the following year.

There have been some Facebook posts and blog posts about St. Francis where commenters have shared stories of abuse (see the selected bibliography), which would seem to independently echo Atkins' own allegation of abuse at the facility. One particular comment on a Facebook post listed out five staff members of the home by name. "All abusers," the commenter wrote below the names. To be fair, though, there is little that can be found on record about the abuse allegations. For instance, a search of the extensive databases at Bishop-Accountability.org, cataloging clergy abuse charges, witness reports and media coverage across the country and many parts of the globe, produced no specific charges for anyone serving at St. Francis Home for Boys in Detroit. The Archdiocese of Detroit has web pages devoted to the issue of abuse, plainly listing out clergy who have been accused "credibly," with cases both closed and in process. Nothing on St. Francis comes up. The Archdiocese was contacted for comment for this book; this is the response from their longtime spokesperson, Ned McGrath, who has been widely quoted in the Detroit media:

"Any allegation of abuse at the hands of Catholic clergy and/or a Catholic institution is sad and sobering. And, one too many. It is the practice of the Archdiocese of Detroit to take all such complaints, regardless how old, seriously.

"In the case you are asking about, no complaint to the Detroit archdiocese was found from Benjamin Brown/Atkins. There is no information regarding a Mr. Winfield serving at the home in the 1970s. The Sisters of St. Joseph were administrating and staffing the StFH during that time period.

"There are no allegations on our Protect–Prevent-Heal website involving cases at StFH or individuals who worked there."

The Sisters of St. Joseph organization was also contacted, resulting in some dialogue through email but not specifically addressing the allegations or Atkins' time at the home.

On October 12, 1977, the Wayne County Department of Social Services reached out to the St. Francis Home for Boys for assistance with two young charges referred by the Children's Aid Agency. The two brothers had been in a foster home, but the home was asking "that the boys be removed in a short time." The Children's Aid worker brought them to St. Francis for a tour, and the report of their visit said the two boys were anxious, asked a lot of questions, and wanted to stay at the home right then and there.

Paperwork said Judy was working at the Detroit Plaza Hotel when she applied for her sons' admission to the home. Ben was to receive not only food, shelter and other basic needs but also social work services, special education, psychological and psychiatric services, tutoring and family counseling, all at a cost of about twenty-five dollars a day, paid by the Michigan Department of Social Services.

At the time of Atkins' trial, one of the Detroit papers reported that the executive director of St. Francis denied that Atkins was once a resident there. "We have quadruple-checked our records," *The Detroit News* quoted him, "and show no indication that Benjamin Atkins was ever a resident." That same executive director had already communicated with Michael Reynolds, however, acknowledging and discussing Atkins' records (which this author has copies of). *Detroit Free Press* staff snagged a look at some of Atkins' records themselves at the time and realized the wayward contradiction. Atkins was known by the last name Brown at the home, as indicated in a fax the executive director sent to Reynolds. He was also known as Benjamin Brown on Department of Social Services paperwork from early 1977.

Reynolds did try to find the "Mr. Winfield" Atkins had named as his abuser during his psychological evaluations, and the executive director faxed back that no one worked at St. Francis by that name during the time Atkins was there, and further, he could find no records of sexual complaints at the home by Atkins/Brown – matching, essentially, what the spokesperson told this author decades later. (The Facebook commenter mentioned above did not include a Mr. Winfield in his own abuser list, by the way, and records in this author's possession do not mention anyone by that name. The records tend not to mention other day-to-day staffers by name, anyway, only the nuns who were completing the reports, and that's an important distinction we'll get into.)

Benjamin "Brown" began living at the home in October 1977, first given a physical exam – four-foot-five and a half and sixty-six pounds at age nine with all features normal. He had all of his immunizations in the 1970s while in foster care, by this account. No allergies. No hospitalizations or accidents. He was assigned to Group 4, Dorm 6 at the home, fourth grade, then later to Group 3, Dorm 5. Certain goals were set at the intake for Ben: Improving academic functioning, improving behavior so he and his brother could return to family living, assisting Judy ("to help the mother become adequate if she wishes to take them into her home"), and "to find out if the boys can adjust to the mother." The report said the boys had a strong attachment to their mother but had been away from her for five years.

Judy visited the boys a couple times in the first month they were at St. Francis, and she continued to visit. At one point early on, Ben reported to staff that the next time she was visiting, Judy was going to give him some money. The caseworker asked what he would use it for, and he said he might save it for his mom so she could buy a house. Right after that, Judy was supposed to visit and did not, and the caseworker noted that Ben was very sullen.

Judy would pick up the brothers for some time out on a fairly regular basis, and for Ben it was weekly in late 1978 through early 1979, sometimes for a night or two. It was common practice for the boys at the home to see parents on the weekend. A sign-out sheet showed she stopped picking Ben up in January; then it was simply Ben signing out weekly for a couple days with bus fare, saying he was visiting his mom. This continued through August 1979, at which point he was soon "leaving for good," the sign-out sheet said.

A goal assessment accountability record from the home dated October 1, 1978, listed for Benjamin Brown the goals of increasing academic functioning and increasing verbalization of feelings. For Judy, goals were to find a new apartment, increase level of self-esteem, and increase her visits with the boys and improve her relationship with them. A year later, on November 1, 1979, there were listed three items for Ben: (again) increase academic functioning, increase independence, improve self-esteem. A goal was set for Judy to provide a stable and secure environment for her sons. In August 1979, Ben's testing showed an IQ of 93-

95. He tested in the average age equivalent in most areas: fund of general knowledge, conceptualization and abstract, arithmetical reasoning, common sense and judgment, and the like. His behavior during testing was reported to be polite and pleasant, though apprehensive. "He worked cooperatively and quietly; he smiled easily," the psychologist nun noted in her report. Part of the testing indicated a "rather passive-aggressive youngster" who was benefiting from being in the home, and who was unsure about returning to his mother, yet very much wanted to be with her. "He just feels very inadequate and wonders – actually, worries about whether or not he can make it satisfactorily, not only with her, but will he be able to find new friends in what he views as an extremely hostile environment." Another test indicated "he seems to need further clarification of his role as a male child. He seems to be pretty much withdrawn and absorbed in his own difficulties." Improving male identification was listed as a goal, utilizing the services of a male teacher or counselor. There is no indication of any follow-up from that in the files, however.

Ben was avoiding fights with his peers at the home, and in conflicts with his brother he was physically passive, not the aggressor. He didn't back down easily when it came to defending himself, however. "Benjamin's chief defense is to deny feelings," one report read. This related to his disagreements with his brother as well as his disappointment at not being with his mother. The impression of staff at the time was that Ben was largely the follower and his brother was the leader, particularly in the behavior at the foster home that led up to their admission to St. Francis. He was strongly attached to his brother as he was to his mother, and the two would sometimes team up for a common cause. They also were observed to engage in friendly competition. But when they fought, as brothers do, it was Ben who made the overtures to reconcile. The two were later put in separate units at St. Francis, and staffers felt this was good for Ben.

In an August 1978 personality report, Ben was noted to never bully or tease others, seldom cry or daydream, seldom lie or instigate situations, seldom steal or talk back or have a temper tantrum. He was noted to be an easily influenced follower. He was noted to be very friendly and sometimes happy and lighthearted. He was not a leader, the checklist indicated, only sometimes listened to reason, and usually made his own decisions. Another report called him respectful and accepting of authority, well-liked by staff. The following February, the same checklist now noted some changes, like that Ben sometimes teased and bullied, often daydreamed, and was never an easily influenced follower. Along the way, in various reports from St. Francis staff, Ben was noted to have dreams about monsters, perhaps fairly common for a young boy, but also was drawing pictures of "good" and "bad" monsters in conflict and the innocent people stuck between them, "at their mercy," one report put it. "In drawings and fantasies he develops with toys," another report read, "he displays aggression that he cannot allow himself to show openly."

By December 1977, Judy had a fiancé named Linwood. They planned to marry in January and spoke to a caseworker about gaining custody of Ben and his brother. Linwood had a decent job making a thousand dollars a month net, and they had rented two bedrooms of a home on Belvidere. Linwood was interested in adopting the boys, and Judy struck the caseworker as sincere in wanting to provide a good home for them. "She said she decided that all her 'tomfoolery' was hurting herself and her kids and decided to change," the caseworker noted in her report. The worker wrote to the Department of Social Services to recommend the custody of the boys be transferred in June with the end of the school year. As 1978 moved along, though, those plans fell apart. The new home did not work out, Linwood was out of his job, and Judy and Linwood broke up. Judy claimed Linwood had become violent and was using drugs. She moved back in with her mother, who continued to have health problems. Judy put a deposit on a three-bedroom duplex that needed some work, and the landlord was going about that work quite slowly, but Judy gave the caseworker the impression that she genuinely wanted to provide a home for the boys. "She seems to be fearful of close relationships," the report said, "and has a need to be independent, which is hindered by self-doubt." Without the adequate housing, the petition for her to regain custody of her sons was dead in the water. To further muddy those waters, in later 1978, Judy told St. Francis staff that she had been robbed, had been beaten, and had been in a car accident that put her in the hospital for a week. Then in early 1979, Judy had a new boyfriend.

In this period, Ben would years later tell Dr. Abramsky, on their weekend visits with their mother, the boys were left to their own devices. Judy and her boyfriend were drinking heavily, he said, and were absent. Ben began to "hustle homosexually," which his brother said was an adaptation to life on the street. "You do what you have to do," his brother told Abramsky.

By July 1979, Mayolla had died, and this hit Ben pretty hard. Still, the areas that Ben needed to focus on were showing improvement, reports indicated. Judy continued to visit and was apparently continuing to work on some sort of stable place for the family to live. Then, on August 10, the boys left St. Francis to live with their mother on Brush Street in Detroit. Ben had made progress at the home in areas of adult and peer relationships, staff noted, but a firm hand and limits would be needed to assure he did not take advantage of adults. Judy was working, the two boys were enrolled in a local school, and St. Francis continued some follow-up in the ensuing months. In 1980, Ben was fully discharged and his case at the home was closed. That year he was twelve years old.

Nowhere in the many, very-detailed notes made by the St. Francis nuns, from frequent talks with Ben about day-today life and relationships with others at the home, was there any mention of a friendship or any sort of association with any male staff member, even after the nuns recommended that such a relationship would benefit him. In the coverage of his trial it was stated he was raped by a male social worker while living at St. Francis, and another account used the term "caseworker," but records clearly show that his caseworkers were nuns or other female staff members. The only male anywhere in the picture was a Department of Social Services worker assigned to Judy's case. Abramsky's report called the male with whom Ben claimed to have a relationship a "care worker" – a crucial difference. At the same time, Atkins told Dr. Charles Clark that the "Mr. Winfield" he was involved with was a "dormitory director," and their relationship was abuse, not consensual. And he told his defense attorney in one of their first jailhouse visits, just days after his arrest, that his St. Francis abuser was a "staff counselor." "I never knew why he chose me," Atkins told his lawyer. It's evident that the details surrounding his allegations of abuse at St. Francis concerned him greatly, given his letter to Judge Kerwin. So what to believe? Well, we will have a bit more discussion to come on that aspect of the home's male vs. female staff members.

Beyond the two years at St. Francis, there's not quite as much detail about Benjamin Atkins' life. No week-to-week chronicle as the nuns at St. Francis were obligated to do. No official reports to rely on. Besides a few folks interviewed here and there, we have only what Atkins chose to reveal once in custody, details that often cannot be corroborated.

Returned to their mother's care, the boys dealt with the drinking of their mom and the man Ben called his stepfather, Ernest. In fact, he told Abramsky this stepfather was verbally abusive, taunting the boys that they would never amount to anything, comparing them to his own sons, whom he claimed were successful. Ben even told Dr. Dexter Fields that his stepfather – presumedly meaning Ernest – had choked him one time until he passed out. Ben had a difficult adjustment in school, getting into fights over issues of competitiveness and envy, his brother told the psychiatrist. Ben described himself as unruly. "Often he would skip school to go hustling," Abramsky wrote, "standing on Woodward Avenue and waiting for men to pick him up."

Ben and his brother were put on probation in February 1983 after they trespassed into a business (termed "entering without breaking" to commit larceny on one report) on West Grand Boulevard in Detroit on Christmas Day 1982. Two officers spotted the teens running from the building and tracked them to where they were living with Judy and Ernest at the time, on Vinewood Street only about a block away. The kids had items from the building in their pockets: some hard candy and a drill bit, oddly enough. It looked to the officers like they had ransacked the building and sprayed fire extinguishers all over the place. A year later Ben violated that probation with school truancy. In February 1984, Judy reported that Ben had stolen some food stamps from her and tried to sell them. In June 1985, he was found guilty of home truancy in juvenile court; a count of school truancy was dismissed for insufficient evidence. He had disappeared from his mother's home for three weeks, the report said. He continued on probation. Somewhere in there, in July 1983 according to one source and in 1985 according to another, he was also arrested by Wayne State University police for a purse snatching. The charges were dismissed the next day, but Ben had to wait for his mom at the Wayne County Youth Home because she was evidently recovering from a stab wound.

Wayne County Juvenile Court records say the two boys violated their probation by skipping school and disobeying their mother. Both brothers were terminated from probation at age seventeen. One report said the brothers were sent to live with an eighty-two-year-old aunt named Willie Mae on Vinewood in Detroit, but it can't be confirmed if that was before or after their probation. Ben told Dr. Clark that the brothers and their mom were put out after a fight with Ernest when Ben was sixteen, then they lived at the Salvation Army, then were taken in by a friend of their mother. It was reported that Ben was enrolled in a guidance program for troubled youth that gave him cooking classes, which helped him land jobs later.

Mixed into all this was a relationship with Judy's friend Carl, unbeknownst to Judy, Ben said, then liaisons with Carl's friend Dobie. Carl and Dobie paid Ben for the sex. At the time Ben also would sometimes "go with" girls, though not sexually, and he found himself shy with them. He then became involved with a drug dealer named George, with whom he and his brother were later staying. This George was reportedly a friend of Judy's, as well. Ben's relationship with him lasted five years, he told Clark. Ben dropped out of Southeastern High School in the tenth grade (or ninth grade, according to his statements to police).

Ben also began smoking pot and taking psychedelics during these teen years, Abramsky reported. At age seventeen, he started using cocaine. In fact, it was on his seventeenth birthday that coke was introduced to him, when a friend described as a female impersonator brought him a woman to perform sexual favors as a birthday gift. This was his first heterosexual experience, he told the psychiatrist.

Ben graduated to crack cocaine, but his late teens and earliest twenties were marked by attempts to get clean – to not only get off the drugs, but get away from the prostitution, as well. He claimed to be clean for two years. He took up jobs at local restaurants, the aforementioned pizza place in Westland plus a couple other eateries that evidently included a different pizza place on Woodward. He had a part-time job handing out fliers for the Westland pizza place before he worked as a cook. By this point, his brother was living with his girlfriend, and Ben stayed with them sometimes. With the three of them living together, in some ways, Ben told Dr. Abramsky, he had found the family he had never had before.

The house / apartment building, abandoned in more recent years, where Benjamin Atkins once stayed with his brother and his brother's girlfriend. Photo by the author.

Ben had a number of relationships in these years – some with men and some with women – as the drugs kept drawing him back in. He was more attracted to men, felt they were more understanding, that he could be more honest with them. As far as women, there was Margaret, a woman in her forties who shot him multiple times in the arms, chest and one leg when he said he was leaving her. His brother then beat up Margaret "real bad," Ben told Clark, but no charges were pressed on either side in the whole thing. (Incidentally, there is a charge on his brother's record for an assault with intent to murder. The charge was dismissed because the "complaining or key witness would not prosecute." The timeframe is later than Ben indicated, however – September 1991, and he had said he was eighteen or nineteen – but he was often inaccurate on dates. The complainant in the case was male, however.)

When he was not living with George or with his brother, he lived with a couple friends, including the one he called a female impersonator, ironically named Anthony or Tony but using the name Chris. He lived with a girlfriend named Katie in the late 1980s. She was a few years younger than him. (Katie spoke with Jeffrey Edison via phone a couple times soon after Edison was appointed to represent Atkins. She died of COVID-19 in 2022.) The last girlfriend Ben had was a woman named Denise. These relationships with females were not satisfying, he told Clark. "It was all right. I just did it. It curbed the urge, but I got tired of it." With men, he said, "after I started using drugs, it was just a financial thing."

By Christmas 1990, his brother had enough of Ben's drug use, having struggled to get off drugs himself. He kicked Ben out of his home. It was then that Ben encountered Margie Osborn, likely his very first female assault victim on Woodward Ave. And here we pick up our story. Atkins was now twenty-two years old and on the streets full-time, working prostitution with men to get cash to buy crack. Picking up women. Wandering from one abandoned building to another. Getting a handout here and there. And so on. The following fall, he would escalate to taking a life.

"At one point you could feel pity for that guy," said former Detroit cop Melvin Toney. He's just one of many who have expressed such sentiments. One of many with mixed feelings about Benjamin Atkins. One of many who are conflicted.

Years after Judy had to watch her youngest child tried for multiple murders, years after his incarceration and death, she also passed away, in 2006.

ABANDONED BUILDINGS AS KILLING FIELD

In June 1992, just a couple months before Benjamin Atkins' arrest, *The Detroit News* reported that there were three hundred and twenty-two abandoned properties in the city of Highland Park. Around that same time, the *Free Press* said the number of abandoned buildings in the city was about three hundred. The mayor was trying to form a task force to monitor the empty buildings and parcels, reportedly begging federal and state officials and even private entities to help tear down some of these places because the destitute city could not afford to. Joanne O'Rourke had just been discovered.

"How many bodies have to be found before somebody realizes we need a million dollars to get rid of these buildings?" the *Freep* quoted the mayor. When the Atlanta child murders were happening a decade earlier, President Ronald Reagan sent one and a half million dollars in aid to Atlanta. But that kind of gift wasn't coming to this Michigan city of twenty thousand people.

Everyone – the mayor, the police, the citizens – felt like they were punched in the gut once again with the O'Rourke discovery. The city had been trying to eliminate the empty buildings, *The News* said, and beef up its police, even form a strong neighborhood watch presence. Too many transients, one resident said. People used to go for walks; now they were too scared. In March 1992 alone, Highland Park police received three hundred and ten complaints pertaining to abandoned houses. Yes, the city had struggled for years to deal with the abandoned buildings, but this case kicked it into another gear.

The media reported that HPPS had ninety-five officers that summer, having just let go of ten in budget cutbacks. Former HPPS Director John Mattox remembered it more like ninety-two. Whatever the case, the detective division had nine investigators and one juvenile officer. Even though several other law enforcement agencies were helping in the investigation into this serial killer, their efforts were described in one paper as "superficial," with HPPS carrying the brunt of it. The investigation had cost the city eighty thousand dollars in police overtime in the months since the Monterey Motel discovery.

The perception had already been out there that this tiny precinct didn't have the manpower to handle a lot of homicide action. Criminals knew it, as former HPPS officer Craig Pulvirenti noted. The small city became more and more a dumping ground for bodies, which were then so often discovered by the occasional scrapper or scavenger coming in to grab a thing or two, as happened multiple times in this case. Be careful what you wish for – and what you look for.

The fact that local residents often used these empty buildings as trash dumps only added insult to injury, as the summertime months sent a painful reminder into the air. It was assumed before Joanne was found that this odor was another pile of trash heating up in the rising temperatures because the city had not been collecting residential garbage.

"DOES NO ONE CARE?" blared a huge all-caps headline in the December 31, 1992, edition of the *Freep*. Months after the perp was arrested, the sense of desperation lingered. The empty buildings were still there, and with them, a large enough measure of the fear. What other killers could be lurking out there? Or rapists, or simply thieves, using these buildings as playgrounds?

Of the three hundred and twenty-two empty properties city officials identified, one hundred and twenty-two were owned by the city and the other two hundred owned by the state. Inspectors planned to go through them, then the city would start accepting bids in July, with "bargain basement" prices in mind. Maybe a little of something came of that, because the structures where Atkins' victims were found are now gone, and many have other buildings in their place. But Highland Park as a city is definitely still struggling.

The 2013 movie *Highland Park* explored some of the desperation of the financially strapped city. In the film, Billy Burke is a high school principal forced to cut some of his staff because of lack of budget. Driving him on is the money-grubbing, superficial mayor played by Parker Posey. She also wants to tear down the ninety-year-old library building (a heritage locale, much like the McGregory Public Library in real life) to make room for a strip mall or whatever. The principal, meanwhile, has a longstanding lottery pool with some colleagues and friends, playing the same numbers in the Mega Millions jackpot for ten years. At last, their numbers hit, and life changes. The principal sets about doing some community fix-up projects, particularly that historic library building. No need to spoil the rest of it, but the cast also includes Danny Glover, Michelle Forbes and even Bo Derek as a waitress at a Chinese restaurant. The film was actually shot in Highland Park and Detroit, with many key images around town of Woodward Ave and other places – even the street where Atkins once lived and where Debbie Friday was found, Elmhurst. The colors are muted, the atmospherics downtrodden and desolate, certainly conveying the sense of desperation felt by the characters of the film.

But it wasn't always that way. "Highland Park once was the place to be," Jim Dobson said in 2022. "I was born and raised there. Born in the Highland Park General Hospital and stayed there until I retired, and I live out here in Sterling [Heights] now."

So you've seen a lot of changes in HP, I said. "They had paved alleys before Detroit did," he replied. "They had streetlights in the alleys. They had one of the best school systems in the country. Everything. And it just …"

Yeah, it just.

In 1930, when Henry Ford was in town making that beautiful new Model T, and Chrysler was headquartered there, the population of Highland Park surged past fifty thousand. But it has fallen every decade since then. The population was 8,977 at the 2020 census. That would certainly mean some empty buildings. And you can see them, as you drive through the neighborhoods, in and out of Woodward Ave, as I did recently to check out a few of the locations from this case. The most recently reported median housing value on the city's official website as of this writing was $49,800 (from the 2020 census), with 7,249 housing units, 1,050 of them vacant. The 1999 per-capita income figure was $12,121, with median household Income of $17,737, the fourth lowest in Michigan. Census data show HP's median household income in 2021 was $25,189, while Michigan's median income was $63,498.

The more recent state of the Highland Park police force is pretty dismal, as well, Dobson said. It's a force that really serves as a steppingstone for those looking to get some experience in law enforcement and move on. "They're the lowest-paid police officers in the state of Michigan. Them and the fire department, a lot of them have to furnish their own equipment. Yes. But they do it to try to break in; they want to transfer."

In January 1994, just as Atkins' trial was starting, the HP city council voted unanimously to demolish the Monterey Motel. There was a plan at the time to build a new city hall on the site, but the large lot sits empty as of this writing. At least one victim family member at the time of the trial said she would never set foot inside that city hall, should it be built on the site.

"Usually if you go back to some of these where they had these real horrendous crimes," John Mattox said, "the city wants to get rid of it right off the bat, because it brings so much negative recognition to it, whether it was the house where Dahmer was in Milwaukee, or the one in Cleveland, the one there in Seattle, Washington. They tore them down, you know, tore 'em down, because people when they come there and kind of use it like a temple or something."

In January 2018, the local Fox TV affiliate, Channel 2, reported that Highland Park planned to redevelop a whopping one thousand abandoned properties. The city was working with the Michigan Land Bank and the Wayne County Land Bank. All of the properties were city owned and the funding for this project would come from developers. Hope springs eternal, and we'll just leave it at that.

And yeah, we haven't even discussed the abandoned buildings in the behemoth that surrounds Highland Park, the setting for three of Atkins' murders. It kinda feels like we don't have to. Just do this web search: "Devil's Night."

THE CASE OF THE MISSING FILES

The issue of abandoned buildings touched this case in another way. As I was preparing to research this case, I completed Freedom of Information Act (FOIA) requests for the homicide case files from both the Detroit and Highland Park police departments. I received the Detroit file without issue, but here's what I was told by a detective at the modern-day Highland Park PD via email:

"I have been given your FOIA request regarding Benjamin Atkins. I have been with this department since July 2007 when it was restarted. In the late 90's, a tornado struck this city and hit city hall, where records were kept.

Many were destroyed or never found. I have personally looked for cold cases and information in the old building. We do not have that case here. At the time Mr. Atkins was involved in his crime spree, I was a Detroit Police Officer assigned to the Homicide Section. One of my colleagues actually worked on it and obtained Atkins' confession. That was a very big case. My suggestion is that you check with Detroit Homicide and see if that file was archived."

Well, rats, I thought. No Highland Park files. Though Highland Park's investigation covered nine out of the twelve known victims, I figured I would just have to make do with the Detroit Police files and other docs for the case, like court transcripts. Then, when I began my web searches on the case, an interesting item popped up. It was a news story about two French photographers named Yves Marchand and Romain Meffre, who came to Detroit to photograph abandoned buildings and various "ruins" for a book project. The article came up because Benjamin Atkins' name was in this story of the photographers – one of the buildings they photographed was at one time the location of Highland Park Public Safety. And what they photographed when they visited the old police station in 2007 were the files of the Benjamin Atkins case. Those elusive files I would seek with my FOIA request years later. In this old empty building, Marchand and Meffre found "a scattering of stiff, rotting cardboard files each bearing a woman's name," the story said. And it wasn't just the files bearing the victim names. It was also vials – blood samples, other samples with DNA. Evidence in a huge criminal case, lying around an abandoned building. Showing the name of Benjamin Atkins.

"A photograph simply entitled Criminal Investigation Report, Highland Park Police Station is one of the many startling images in an extraordinary book, *The Ruins of Detroit*, that Marchand and Meffre have made from their seven week-long visits to Detroit between 2005 and 2009," the story in The Guardian said.

Above and below, two photos snapped by Yves Marchand and Romain Meffre while they visited Detroit to capture its "ruins." These were taken in the basement of the now-demolished building that used to house the police department. Below, what the photographers called "the investigation panels from Atkins' victims." The place was indeed full of scattered files from various cases when they took these photos in 2007, they told this author. Photos courtesy of Yves Marchand and Romain Meffre.

Files and evidence from a criminal case, lying on the floor of an abandoned building? So really, what on earth happened? Well, the Highland Park Police Department was once located at 25 Gerald Street. It opened there in 1917 and operated for decades. In 1984 the police and fire departments were merged into a Public Safety Department located in that building. That building was then vacated in 1999, a few years after the Atkins case. The police force moved across the street into the old Municipal Building at 28-30 Gerald. Gerald Street, right there at Woodward, is a short cul-de-sac that had just a few municipal buildings on it at the time: these two buildings plus an old fire station. This Municipal Building was vacated in 2001 with all functions moving to the Robert Blackwell Municipal Building, which is located right on Woodward Ave but about a dozen blocks south. In December 2001 (2000, by some accounts), the police/public safety unit was formally disbanded, at which time the Wayne County Sheriff Department/State of Michigan took over policing the city. The Highland Park Police Department was re-established in July 2007.

So that left both buildings on Gerald Street where police were once located empty as of 2001. There was evidently a plan to reopen them after Highland Park got its police department back in 2007. In the years after the buildings were abandoned, though, they had been broken into and looted. So then one of them, the building where the police were originally located at 25 Gerald Street (where they were at the time of this case), was demolished in 2012. A new fire department building was erected in its place with a FEMA grant made available by the American Recovery and Reinvestment Act. The other abandoned building, the Municipal Building across the street, still stands as of this writing. The original building at 25 Gerald Street was where Marchand and Meffre snapped the photos of the Atkins case files, they confirmed for this book. Bottom line is ... where those files went is unclear. The photographers said they believed the files likely were in the building when it was demolished.

In all of this, however, there doesn't seem to be any tornado (!).

Thankfully, one of the folks interviewed for this book quite frankly saved the project with his own extensive files from the case.

The Detroit photos of Marchand and Meffre, which you can get a taste of in the Guardian and Huffington Post stories (see the bibliography), are breathtaking and spooky. Just as spooky as the other building, still standing, remains to this day.

In addition to the HPPS case files being lost, a FOIA request made to the Wayne County Medical Examiner for victim records turned up empty. Those files are evidently gone (though the autopsy records were located – again, thankfully – elsewhere). The medical examiner's offices did move since the case happened, so perhaps stuff got lost in the shuffle. We'll go with that. And then, would you believe, the trial transcripts are also gone? Several persistent phone calls to the Frank Murphy Hall of Justice (bless you, exceedingly patient staff person) finally landed on the fact that because the perp is dead, and there is no chance for appeal, the records were destroyed after a certain number of years per protocol. *Weeeeellll, OK ...*

Jim Dobson was aware that the HP case files were lost. He was familiar with the French photographers' *Ruins of Detroit* project when we spoke for this book. "I'll never forget, I was at home one day," he said, "and I got a call. It was from the prosecutor's office. And we always thought that someday Atkins would find a liberal judge that would give him a new trial or whatever. And they called to say he passed away. And I said, thank God, because all that evidence was lost."

As far as the morgue files, Dobson conceded, "Record-keeping was not very good in Wayne County. Even today, it's not a very efficient operation."

SO WHY DID HE DO IT?

Though cut short by an arrest at such a young age of twenty-three, it was an interesting, lonely life Benjamin Thomas Atkins led wandering Woodward Avenue.

Holding down a job now and then. Showing up for work, then not showing up for weeks at a time. Staying with his brother sometimes, but then disappearing for days or weeks at a time. Sleeping in abandoned buildings. Drinking in bars. Prostituting himself, then hitting the crack house to try to forget, to dull the sense of guilt he felt after being with men. Then walking off the crack on the street. Picking up women, and all the thought patterns that went along with that, resulting in the deaths of eleven and the violent assault of at least two others.

It always started off the same way, he told one psychiatrist. He indulged himself with a male, or was simply getting money from the male, then smoked crack to dull it, then picked up a female. The same pattern every time. Only the locations changed, the women changed.

And of course, all the stuff that "cooked" this killer long before he hit the Woodward corridor. The abuse, in various forms, over the years of his upbringing. To call it an "upbringing," though, sounds generous. It was more of a survival. A childhood of survival until he could be old enough to make his own decisions, albeit so apparently ill-equipped to do so.

So let's come to the million-dollar question of why. The question we all wonder with every true-crime TV show we watch about a serial murderer. The question we wonder any time we hear about someone taking a life, really, whether on TV or across town.

"It doesn't justify what they did, but it brings some better understanding," said Valerie Chalk's son André, on the research he was doing in his therapy, learning more about Atkins' background. It sums up why we study the background of a killer like Benjamin Atkins.

There are many clues about Benjamin Atkins' personality and character that can be gleaned from those who spoke with him, those who knew him. The things he revealed. Or didn't. Even the things that could have been lies, like the multiple voices he heard, on which the jury's still out, so to speak.

One person who came to know him pretty well, his defense attorney, Jeffrey Edison, recalled how on the surface Atkins seemed to be a normal guy. "I'm telling you that Ben Atkins, I mean, he could be sitting right here, just talking, and you would never know that he had anything that was going on," Edison said.

However, "there was still stuff going on in his head," the attorney said. "All from childhood. All that stuff is in him. Is in him. And every now and then, in my interactions with him, there was a sense that he's not ... So say, like we're here, we're sitting down talking. And it's like, damn, Ben, you here? Come on, hey, Ben? Ben? Come on, you know. ... He was just out, you know what I'm saying? Never any kind of anything threatening or whatever, but just that he was someplace else. I don't know how to better describe those moments, other than it seemed to me that he was someplace else."

Edison recalled, and affirmed, the talk of the multiple personalities/voices. But there was something about Atkins that struck him even more and was still lingering decades later.

"One of the things that stood out with the state's psychiatrist *[Clark]*, he said that Ben Atkins did not have the capacity to love. And that just fucked me up when he said that. And I tried to emphasize that if a person doesn't have the capacity to love then where is any intent, you know? There's certainly no responsibility, legal criminal responsibility. ... If you don't have the capacity to love, then how can you distinguish between right and wrong? If you don't know what love is, if you don't have any concept of love. I almost fell out of my chair when he said that shit.

"I totally disagreed with that. I don't know how you could say a person doesn't have the capacity to love. ... I thought that was outrageous to say. I thought it was fucking outrageous. The nerve of you. And then to say that he's all right? I mean, that's the contradiction! To say he doesn't have the capacity to love, but then he's responsible."

In March 1994, as Dr. Michael Abramsky was on the stand for the defense, among the things Edison jotted down on his yellow legal pad:

- Love relationships were traumatic.
- Fused sex/aggression together.
- No positive emotional life, focus is on survival.
- Cannot experience pleasure, experience of love is blocked out ("does not have capacity to love").
- No foundation of security.
- Borderline personality disorder.

So let's dive in a little more.

POSSIBLE TRIGGERS

He's been called the fastest serial killer in American history.

At least twelve attacks in about nine months, possibly more like six to eight months. That's pretty quick, without many "cooling-down periods" as noted with most serials. In fact, he told one psychiatrist that there was typically a month between killings for him, but between the third and fourth murder, for instance, there was only about a week, and the next two followed closely behind. Sometimes the timeframe of when he would strike again would be influenced by whether or not his previous victim had been found. He was watching. Paying attention to the news, to the word on the street, he said in his questionings. And if he felt like he could, then he would strike again.

So backing up to the time before the killings, around fall 1991, wouldn't it stand to reason there was *some* trigger going on with him? An event that set this whole thing off? Or did the certain harmful elements and characteristics of his life just hit a critical mass, and there had to be release? An explosion of sorts? The idea that after twenty-three years he had just had enough, and had to act out in some way?

One trigger possibility that was raised was Atkins being thrown out of his brother's home over the drug issue. His brother remembered this occurring at Christmastime 1990, so that timeline is reasonable, for the attack on Margie Osborn and for the murders to begin several months later, after he had been on the streets and in and out of abandoned buildings. Abramsky said that Atkins' brother was his only real link in life, a sort of father figure to him at just one year older, so when his brother kicked him out, Abramsky believed that was a triggering mechanism.

You also have to consider some things that happened to Atkins at the hand of his girlfriends, if what he said is to be believed. He may have jumbled the details, but he claimed to have suffered violent physical attacks by two different girlfriends, an older woman who cut him with a knife, and a woman in her forties who shot him multiple times then was, he claimed, beaten up by his brother. For the latter incident that (sort of) fits the court records for his brother, the timeframe in those records, September 1991, would certainly qualify this one as a trigger, if it is true. Atkins' incident with Darlene Saunders would have occurred immediately after this. And even if Atkins did not relay the details accurately, perhaps there was something else about this September 1991 assault charge involving his brother that served as a trigger.

There also seems to be the idea that these killings just happened for him, that he didn't really set out to kill prostitutes, but happened to do so after drugs and sex. Almost like the crimes were accidental, and there really was no trigger. That things just escalated for him, as he got deeper into his drug use. Yet Atkins read in a book how to make sure the victim was dead, push the remaining air out of them, etc. That appears quite premeditated.

For sex offenders like Atkins, it's not about sexual urges, according to Michigan State Police criminal profiler Detective Sergeant David Minzey, when he spoke to the *Detroit Free Press* in May 1992 about the other big serial killer in the news that year, Leslie Williams. These offenders are usually acting out desires for power, control and degradation, he said. So for this killer, what was at the heart of that need to overpower, control and/or degrade?

THE MOTHER FACTOR

"In our research, there is a strong correlation between domineering mothers and men who grow up to be predators," wrote former FBI profiler John Douglas, along with collaborator Mark Olshaker, in their book *The Killer Across the Table*, where Douglas chronicled several different killers and his own interviews with them. "Though the vast majority of those with such mothers do not grow up to be offenders, of those who do, the domineering mother constitutes a significant influencing factor."

Douglas said, "Over my many years of observing and interacting with serial killers, I've found that a large percentage of them are abnormally fixated on their mothers — usually negatively."

When visiting convicted killer Gary Michael Heidnik in prison for an interview, the moment Douglas asked him about his mother, Heidnik lost it, got up from his chair as if he was going to rip off his microphone and leave. "Our research suggested that most serial predators like him had had either a severe conflict with their mothers or some tragedy where they had lost them," Douglas said.

It's well-established in the case of Benjamin Atkins that his mother was not around much when he was growing up, was not loving and supportive. Defense attorney Jeffrey Edison remembers her being there at Atkins' trial, and showing motherly concern, but this appears to be the exception and not the rule.

"It's not that I hate women; it's something relating to prostitutes. Female prostitutes." Those were Atkins' words after he had confessed to the murder of Valerie Chalk. That was his first confession on record, at one o'clock in the afternoon that day. So he set quite a tone with that.

"The prostitutes represented his mother," Edison said, echoing the words of several others involved with this case. Edison recalled in Benjamin a strong hatred for his mother. "And all this is complicated with his crack addiction. And so all of the deaths occurred during the process of getting high with the prostitutes. ... And so it was, and they were strangled, and either they were in the act of sexual acts or in preparation of sexual acts or certainly getting high. And it was his transposing his mother onto these women and choking them out."

After conferring with Dr. Dexter Fields in December 1993, Edison listed in his notes several key factors in Atkins' background: his sense of rejection at the foster homes and the home for boys, his feeling of being unwanted in that his mother could have gotten him back but did not, and his feeling no one cared in that he was kicked out of his brother's home. All very influential, in the development of a killer. Edison also noted, again evidently coming from his talk with Fields, Judy saying something to the effect of, do you really hate me that much that you killed all these women? Atkins seemed unaware of any connection between his feelings toward his mother and these killings. So much of human behavior influences at a subconscious level, and both mother and son could have been largely unaware of the effects of their actions.

"Prostitutes are hostile to men – very hostile," forensic psychiatrist Dr. Emanuel Tanay was quoted in the *Detroit Free Press* at the time of Atkins' arrest. "And that hostility can be directed toward a male child. Even if the child is not physically abused, exposing a child to acts of prostitution is in itself a hostile act."

In his analysis of Atkins, Dr. Abramsky cited FBI profiler Robert K. Ressler and his book *Whoever Fights Monsters: My Twenty Years Tracking Serial Killers for the FBI*, which had just come out in 1992. Edison checked out the book himself in the midst of his consultations with Abramsky and his prep for trial, and he noted, "When you have a situation with a distant mother, an absent or abusive father or siblings, a non-intervening school system, an ineffective social services system, and an inability of the person to relate sexually in a normal way to others, you have the formula for producing a deviant personality." A child learns what love is from birth to age six or seven, when the most important person in his or her world is the mother, Edison noted.

There's another interesting element here, the idea of the social justice killer, which ties in with the mother factor. There are some widely accepted categories of motives for serials, such as visionary, mission-oriented, hedonistic, and power/control. Atkins could be said to have a mix of these, and Dr. Dexter Fields placed him in the power/control category, but the mission-oriented category warrants some attention.

"He said he does not see himself as a killer but as a person who has rid the streets of hookers," one unnamed investigator told *The Detroit News* of Atkins at the time of his arrest. Atkins told police he hated women (though he also said he didn't). He told police he hated his victims for being women. And with his admitted hatred of prostitutes, we could assume he was a mission-oriented killer, but to take it a step further: Since many of his victims had children, is it possible he was trying in some way to save these children from their prostitute mothers, having been the child of a prostitute himself?

THE HIV/AIDS FACTOR

HIV.

Three letters that spelled a death sentence back then.

HIV was much discussed, very much feared. Quite highly publicized. In fact, if you look through the newspapers from the time of this case, as this author did at the local library, you'll see headline after headline about HIV and AIDS. It was foremost in people's minds back then, having only come to light in the 1980s.

In the years since, of course, there have been advancements in treatments that prolong life. Basketball star Earvin "Magic" Johnson was one of the very first high-profile HIV patients to demonstrate that. As of this writing, he's been doing great, since testing positive back in 1991. He became the poster child for new HIV therapies, and he has lived a long life because of them.

But the fact that Benjamin Atkins had HIV when he died in 1997 raises a few questions. Did he know he had HIV as he was killing these women? Could it have been a motivator or trigger? We know that back then, before advanced treatments, a person would live about ten years with HIV. So it's likely he became infected before the murders.

Onetime Highland Park Public Safety Director John Mattox considered the HIV angle when he heard Atkins had died in prison. He remembered how much HIV was discussed at the time of this case. What a stigma it was.

"Everybody was afraid of it. You didn't want to deal with anybody who said they had HIV," Mattox recalled. "That was, 'Oh, you're going to die.'"

And where this case was concerned, there were condoms involved. A particular condom found at one of the crime scenes, a condom that ended up linking Atkins to the crime. Possibly condoms used with other victims. So why would this killer be wearing a condom? Just so he would not leave evidence behind? (But he left a condom behind!)

"Now, was it because he had HIV then, or did he have HIV because he contracted it with having sex with some of these ladies?" Mattox said. "I thought about that. I said, well, if in fact he had HIV, we know that he had it at his death. I don't know if that was the biggest factor of his death, but that was upon his death. Now, did he ever go to any county or city of Detroit – Highland Park, we would have – it would've probably come forth of being tested for or treated for HIV. There's a record somewhere. There's a record somewhere, because if you come up positive, they've got to notify you."

And so looking at this from the killer's perspective, this author had to wonder if he contracted HIV perhaps from a prostitute, or maybe sharing needles with someone, a method we know as commonly transmissible. Perhaps he contracted it from a male client while working prostitution himself. Maybe he was infected in the 1980s and then got a test and he realized it in 1991, and that sort of set him off, because he figured he got it from a prostitute. So he began to kill prostitutes, and perhaps because his mom was a prostitute, too, and he was traumatized by that, he was working out his anger. But maybe he wore condoms because he figured, OK, I got HIV, I don't want to get anything else, you know? I don't want to get syphilis or whatever else is out there. This author had to wonder. Is that crazy?

"That's a good point," Mattox said when I relayed these thoughts, "and I'm of the same thinking. That he was going to retaliate because he contracted it through that way."

Still, Mattox only learned that Atkins had HIV when he heard about his death. It never came up during the case, that he recalled. He never heard it mentioned during Atkins' questioning by Ron Sanders as Mattox watched from the next room via closed-circuit TV, or at any other time during the case. Larry Beller and Jim Dobson also did not recall, when interviewed for this book, any mention of the HIV during the case, only learning about it upon Atkins' death. Same with Sanders. He was sure the HIV did not come up in the interrogation.

It is possible, as Mattox alluded to, that Atkins did contract HIV later, in prison, and it was simply present at the time of his death but not necessarily what killed him, since he wouldn't have had it very long. Perhaps it's possible he contracted it in prison, and it killed him in a shorter timeframe than what was common at the time.

"I don't know too much about the facility where he was at," Mattox said, "but knowing prisoners, traditionally prisoners don't think very much of rapists and pedophiles. They usually get assaulted very quickly. So I don't know. I'm sure that they probably kept them kind of quarantined a little bit for a while. And until they could maneuver him in some kind of population where he wouldn't be a problem. But at a local level, at the county, I know they had to segregate these guys. They do that automatically. You don't even have to tell them that, because they know that these guys have a sister or a cousin or somebody that's come from their neighborhood where they would take them out."

Jeffrey Edison, however, does recall learning about the HIV at the time he was representing Atkins. He is sure that he and Ben both knew about it back then. Still, by all accounts, it never came up during the investigation and trial. At least not publicly.

Dr. Clark in his psychological evaluation noted that even though Atkins engaged in prostitution and drug use on the street, he still was capable of taking care of himself (assuming he meant that among other things he used condoms to not catch anything, which would *appear* to indicate Clark was unaware of his HIV).

As wild as it now seems, one newspaper actually posed the HIV theory before the killer was identified. In a June 1992 story dubbing him the "Crack City Strangler," the Saturday Sun in Canada said, "One police theory is that the killer was infected with the HIV virus or another disease by a prostitute and is now out for revenge." Ironically, the story went on to say, "There are other theories such as the typical pattern that the killer is seeking revenge for the way he was treated by his mother."

The records for Atkins obtained during the lead-up to trial included a few different medical visits before and during the crimes:

- A March 14, 1990, visit to Detroit Osteopathic Hospital for difficulty breathing, diagnosed as pleurisy. Bloodwork was performed as part of this visit.
- A July 5, 1991, visit to the Detroit Receiving Hospital ER/walk-in, when bloodwork was done, testing for Hepatitis A and B. Atkins showed negative for A, positive for B. "My main man has hepatitis," the doctor noted on one report. Atkins told the doctor he had a close friend he had been "smoking behind and drinking behind" who had hepatitis. A TB skin test was requested during this visit.
- An August 6, 1991, visit to Detroit Receiving Hospital for rectal pain and the inability to pass urine or have bowel movements. Abscesses in his anal and

rectal regions were observed, and he was diagnosed with viral warts. He underwent an incision and drainage procedure for a large perirectal abscess, staying overnight. Atkins told the doctors he had no history of homosexual activity, though they noted him as bisexual on the paperwork. As part of this visit, bloodwork and urinalysis were done. His white blood cell count was slightly high, but otherwise there was nothing unusual found. Staff noted the skin graft on his arm from a prior gunshot wound.

- April 23, May 8 and May 15, 1992, visits to the social hygiene clinic at Herman Kiefer Hospital in Detroit. He told Dr. Charles Clark that he did blood tests there twice a month while active in prostitution.
- A June 1, 1992, visit, at three-fifteen a.m., to Detroit Receiving Hospital ER for stitches following the attack on CC Waymer.

It is possible bloodwork done at the July or August 1991 visits turned up an HIV diagnosis, but that record may have been kept separate and private, per protocol at the time. The timing would be right for a trigger into the crimes. It's also possible Atkins got a separate HIV test on his own at some point, perhaps anonymously. One report did say Atkins was tested for AIDS prior to his arrest, but no results were noted. Again, they likely were kept separate for protocol. At the time you actually could obtain a free anonymous HIV test without ever giving your name to anyone, just being assigned a number.

When asked if his HIV status could have been a trigger, Ron Sanders said he didn't believe so, based on what he discussed with Atkins. Jeffrey Edison also dismissed the idea that it could have led to a certain state of mind in Atkins. "Your reference to it that way is like an emotional reference, and I'm saying this to kind of give you a more critical legal understanding of state of mind, because in order for there to be any type of challenge in this context to the state of mind, our position was that Ben traditionally was insane."

THE MENTAL HEALTH QUESTION

While staring at the cold, sterile cell walls of a Wayne County Jail cell between his August 1992 arrest and January 1994 trial, and in the midst of evaluations and reports by four different psychiatrists as well as various jail staff, Benjamin Atkins wrote letters to his brother's girlfriend.

> *Dear Red-Bone*
>
> *Hey Baby girl I'm writing you this letter so you can explain to Moma what I'm feeling. Every day now I've been very depressed to the point of Death I just don't know what or how to go about see a better Day I really hope you understand what I'm saying and hope that you can get everyone else to understand I've got to find peace some how some way there's got to be another way cause I can't bring myself to think that God let me be spared from death twice (Being shot, or truck accident) just to Die this way so please pray that God take my life for I comit my spirit to Jesus. There has to be peace some where I love you [full name] with all my heart – thank you for what you've done these many years.*
>
> *Benjamin Atkins*

The letters are just a bit astonishing, perhaps a little more chilling, and they raise more questions than they answer. Just what was going through Atkins' mind? Was he laying bare his soul, or playing for the authorities he knew were no doubt reading his mail? Was he weak, or posturing? And just what was the nature of his relationship to his brother's girlfriend? It's been established that his brother was his closest family member, perhaps the person closest to him overall in his life, through the years. But it's evident in these letters, and even in other facts of the case such as in January 1992 when he lied to police that "his wife" had thrown him out, that his brother's girlfriend held a special place in his life. She struck a particular chord with him, even with his sometimes-admitted hatred for women. And if he was injecting these letters with lies, there was still something in his brother's girlfriend that he leaned on. Relied on. As illustrated further in this letter:

Dear Red

Hey BoDy Beautiful it's your loving Brother and I've got something to tell you I would tell [brother] or even Moma but I know they won't understand and I've confided in you before so I'm sure you would know what to do. I've been hideing from him every night now It's been twenty one day sence I first saw him and every night after I'm locked down he comes into the ward calling my name and saying don't worry he know what to do. The first two weeks he would come at nite and try to make me do things he try to get me to do awful things to myself he tells me to drink shampoo and eat my own bowl movements. how could he after all I've done for him he said do it to that boy and I did it he told me to hurt people and I did he said that he was the only family I'll ever need and that he'll protect me and now he's gone. I've done everything for him and after he left me I got in trouble now he's back he's calling me nite after nite saying do it do it it won't hurt I've been sick and he won't let me tell the nurse. ToDay was the first Day he came in the day time and he came with a woman she kind of looks like my MoMa she says don't worry she won't hurt me all she wants is to take me far far away I'm scared I love you all but I think she wants to kill me she keep saying I've got the answer only I can end It only I can set you free let me take you far far away. I'm so confussed what do I do today she told me to hang myself and I tryed I tyed a sheet to my neck and to the water pipe above my cell and hung there for two minutes and the knot came lose. I'm sorry to say every nite they come to my cell looking for me but I hide in the corner under my bed I know It's just a matter of time before they find me and next time I just might go far far away I guess that's what I really want so my question is do I go with her do what she said. Every time I ask for help something or someone changes my Question I've written everyone a letter during the time he was coming to my cell I'm sending them cause I really think I'm going to do as they say I don't know when but I'm sure that thier going to come to me one day and say It's time and I'm not going to turn them Down so I'm telling you now so you won't be surprised to her I'm not here any more I love you all very much.

Love Ben.

Some folks could read that letter and just dismiss it as a bunch of hogwash. Others could read it and be genuinely concerned, maybe horrified. But that's not all. After Atkins printed the text above on the yellow ruled paper, he wrote in contrasting cursive this paragraph right below it:

Hi my Name is Tony and Don't worry he'll be alright Me and Mary Jane is having a child and we need someone to watch over him when he comes this is the first time we even told anyone who we are so Don't tell anyon not even your Brother Benjamin or he'll pay severly.

Love Anthony Jerome Steward

The last name of "Tony" had evidently changed from what Atkins told Edison right after his arrest and what he told Dr. Clark. More interesting, though, and disturbing, is this third letter to his brother's girlfriend, just one page from a yellow ruled legal pad containing text alternating between pencil and black ink:

(Written in pencil:)
Dear Red I have someone who wants to talk to you.
(Written in black ink with words printed backward:)
I know who you are and all Bitches and whores will die I'll see to that. You will pay for what you've done to me and vengeance is mine!
(Then in pencil again:)
I asked for help and no ones answers help me [first name] *please he told me to tell you a verey evil person is encharge. I try to kill myself hoping It will end his presence If I die he might Die he comes to me at night telling me you never cared and that to kill myself is not the answer then we sit down and eat wastes from my body he says I did good by letting him use my body to do his bidding I don't remember what I done help me please.*
(Then in black ink with words printed backward:)
muRDeR to you all Satan comans it. He is the true evil to Obey paridise is with the Devil who Rules us all.
(Then in pencil again:)
Help me [first name] *I can't live this way I need to be set free and as I hide under my bed at night looking for someone to help me I can't sleep I eat shit and drink piss am I mad why won't they send me to get help I'ved hung myself. I've drunk Bleach and soap power what's next I ask you see to it I get help please.*

The black ink "devil" words of the letter – which this author is calling the "Redrum" letter – are actually superimposed onto penciled words. Atkins clearly had to write the letters out backward in pencil then trace over them in the black ink. It was perhaps a tad more effort than a "demon" would have made to write those lines. Still, though, you the reader can decide, as far as what you believe about these letters. I can't quite pinpoint where I land on all this, even as someone who has a firm relationship with the Lord. It's unnerving, I know that. In researching this case, I would often crawl into bed at night with the paper copies of a lot of these case files, examining them while I was calm and relaxed at the end of the day, absorbing what I could absorb in the first run-through to get some general impressions before digging in further in front of my keyboard the next day. With the quiet of the night around me, when I held these letters in my hand, knowing this killer had also once held those sheets of paper in his hand, I could not help but be unsettled, wondering just how much evil was present here. It was a bit surreal.

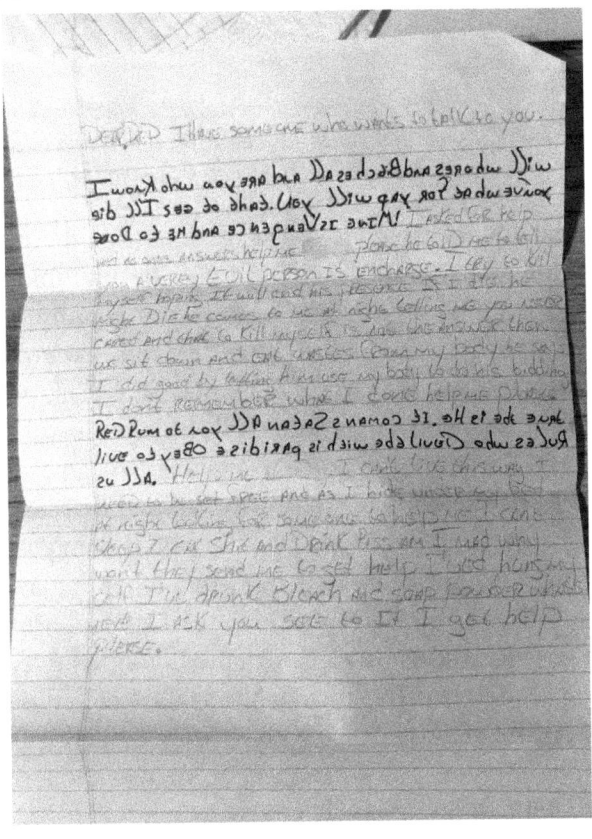

The "Redrum" letter: Atkins alternated pencil and black ink in this correspondence to his brother's girlfriend to indicate what could be perceived as multiple personalities. But was it? Also, can you see the word "redrum" and not think about the movie "The Shining," released a few years before this?

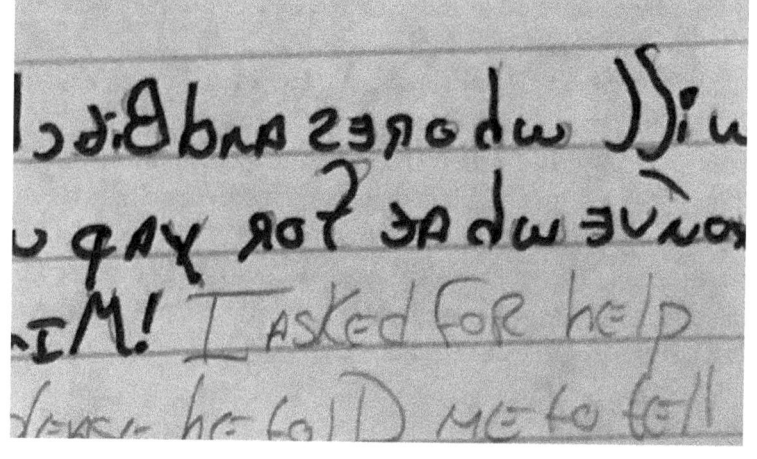

Traces of pencil can be seen all through the black-ink text in the "Redrum" letter – the backward text was carefully written in pencil first then written over in ink.

Atkins did attempt suicide, as the letters said. So that is true. He evidently tried to commit suicide multiple times, actually, including an incident of trying to hang himself in jail with a sheet at the end of July 1993. Jail records from that same time say that Atkins claimed he cut his wrist in 1991 and attempted an overdose of sleeping pills in 1992. In August 1993, a jail staffer noted in a report, "At times he says he feels as if suicide is his only way out and that he cannot tolerate being treated the way he claims he is being treated." Atkins was claiming harassment from other inmates and from staff due to his high-profile case. The staffer's report also described Atkins as alert, oriented, cooperative, well-groomed, coherent. His suicidal thoughts were situational, he was telling staff, because of how trapped and frustrated he felt at his security level in the jail; he was requesting to be placed at a different level.

Another aspect of the letters that's intriguing: Atkins' mention of doing something to "that boy." A boy is not part of this case; there is no boy mentioned in the criminal case files or in any media reports. So what did he mean by that? What boy?

During my research on the St. Francis Home for Boys, I came across the aforementioned online comments on blog posts and whatnot by former residents of the home, comments that allege various abuses at the facility. I contacted a couple of the commenters. One of them is named Michael, and we chatted over DM in 2023. He said that he knew Atkins at the facility, having lived there in the same years in the 1970s. His memories of Atkins, whom he knew by the name Benji, are anything but pleasant: Atkins assaulted him a number of times. Michael, who was a couple years younger, recalled a few different times when Benji forced him to perform oral sex on him in the stairwell that ran up one side of the building. Grabbed him by the neck and threatened to throw him down the stairs. These incidents happened at night when no one else was around.

"He would just come from nowhere and be there, you know?" Michael said. Each boy was assigned to a certain numbered group and numbered dorm, as we know with Atkins, who was in Group 4, Dorm 6, at first, then Group 3, Dorm 5. These two boys were not in the same group or dorm at the home, but Michael would certainly see Benji around the facility, like when they were all in the cafeteria or the chapel. And he would avoid Benji as much as he could.

Michael's own life has followed an interesting path, a path that has thankfully gone in a much better direction for him in more recent years. On the day when we did a follow-up interview via phone, he had just marked, the day before, twenty-three years out of incarceration, after an equal number of years *in* incarceration. You see, Michael's father and stepmother had him committed to the Hawthorn psychiatric facility in the western suburb of Northville when he was just seven years old, after his parents had gotten divorced and his dad had remarried, and, as he put it, he challenged his stepmom's authority. "She convinced my dad that I had psychological problems. And anger issues. Because I was angry about the divorce of my parents and stuff like that and the way she was treating me and my sister. And so she shipped me off there, to Hawthorn Center. And I still remember to the day, my sister, my stepmom and my dad walking out of the building. Because I could see them from the second floor of where they dropped me off at. I was looking through the window, banging on the window."

At that point, for this little boy, not quite understanding what was going on, why he had to be abandoned at some strange place, "it was game on. I was just a total wreck."

So began a long string of stays in different facilities for Michael all around the state of Michigan, from various homes to various prisons and trouble with the law when he was eighteen, to finally a release when he was thirty. And much better roads since then. A much straighter path. But back then, his next step after Hawthorn was St. Francis, when he was just eight years old. And it was every bit another incarceration for him, like Hawthorn had been, and like every place after that.

Michael wasn't at St. Francis for very long, maybe seven or eight months, he estimated. He was so young, and it was traumatic, therefore not a whole lot of details linger at the top of his head. He remembers a couple names of staff members there (but not a Mr. Winfield specifically). He remembers what the huge dormitories looked like on the fourth floor, how beautiful the chapel was, how beautiful the building overall was (he actually revisited the abandoned St. Francis building in 2001 after being released from prison, walked around a bit). He remembers the rather-grand staircase going up the first-floor entryway. The schoolrooms. What he called the chow hall, the mess hall, on the first floor. But he remembers the darker stuff, too. Like how sketchy some parts of the basement could be, where the group activity areas were located. And he vividly remembers the *other* incident with Benji. That was the time he almost lost his hand.

In this incident, Benji and another kid (he did not know this other kid's name, but thought he was a little older than Benji) were trying to drag Michael to the pool locker room. In his young mind, Michael knew it was for no good reason. "I was fighting them. That's when I swung and put my hand through a window. It was right in the hallway to the gymnasium."

He remembered Benji as a lot taller than him. A bigger kid. That's why his hand went through the window, because the window was above him, where he was reaching up and swinging to try to hit Benji's face. "As soon as the glass broke, they knew that the noise would bring people running. They took off. I took off in the opposite direction, and I ran into another locker room and grabbed a dirty towel, and I wrapped it around my wrist. And I left. I got out of the building. I was actually out of the building and out on Five Mile when they found me."

Five Mile is also known as Fenkell, one of the crossroads where St. Francis was located. "I was walking down the road," Michael went on. "And I can't remember the staff member's name, but they tracked me down by following the blood trail. And I guess, according to the nun who was from the infirmary, she said that there was a giant piece of meat hanging on the window, from my hand. I almost lost my arm, from the dirty towel."

This would have been in 1978 or 1979, he said. He was taken to the hospital. Then he was moved to a different facility. "Right after that incident with my hand, and I told the doctors or whoever was involved what had happened, or what was going on with me, they moved me from St. Francis to Sarah Fisher." The St. Vincent and Sarah Fisher Center, in the western suburb of Farmington Hills, still operates as of this writing and is a home for both boys and girls. It was not as horrifying an experience for Michael, but it still meant being locked up. At that time he was made a ward of the state.

"I believe I was one of his first victims," Michael said, describing Benji as a "very dark kid." He added, "My time at St. Francis was what definitely made me an angry person for many years and violent. ... I was an angry kid when I got placed there, but after what happened to me made me ten times worse for many years." Ironically, one of the prisons where he would later stay was the Egeler facility, and that was from 1990 to 1992, just as Atkins was being arrested but a couple years before the serial would be placed there. Michael remembers hearing about the Woodward Corridor Killer while at Egeler, but he didn't follow the case closely and did not see a photo of Atkins to actually make a connection.

So whether Michael could be the "boy" mentioned in Atkins' letter, or whether it was some other kid at St. Francis or somewhere else– maybe even someone he encountered from his time on the street – remains a mystery.

"After what happened to me at St. Francis," Michael said, "I kinda just – because I had to block everything out, obviously. But I was such an angry, angry kid, from the time I was that age until after I was in prison, and I started using my head instead of my emotions."

Another former resident of St. Francis who was reached for this book is named Scott, and he also lived there in the late 1970s, arriving when he was about eight years old. He did not recall encountering Atkins specifically, but he did explain what things were like for him at the home. What he described feels like a Stephen King movie, and it factors in to the discussion of Atkins' mental health, as well. Whereas Michael's bad experiences at the home centered around Atkins and he did not suffer any abuse at the hands of staff members, Scott offers a totally different – but just as terrifying – perspective. Being taken down to the basement and forced to fight another boy while others watched. Getting slapped across the face harder than you've ever been slapped in your life while in the dentist's chair at the infirmary because you wouldn't sit still. Having to shower while staff members watched you with demeaning comments about washing your ass. And the other abuse. The more overt abuse that happened when the lights went out and most kids were in bed.

Scott did not have a Mr. Winfield – though, as Michael said, the name sounded a bit familiar to him, but without being able to see a picture, he could not tell you if Mr. Winfield existed. But Scott had another Mr. W – a male staff member with a last name that also started with that letter but which we'll just refer to with the "W." And this guy was just as bad or worse.

"Mr. W—- was the most terrifying person I had ever come across," Scott said. "Almost think of like a drill sergeant, kind of in a way. And he was known for, if he thought you were making some kind of mistake, whatever it was, he would walk up behind you and hit you on the back of your head with his middle knuckle. And a kid my age, getting hit like that, it came to the point where I literally used to fear that man like nobody else. Yeah, Mr. W—- was just a very, very – I guess I can't go so far as being sadistic, but he sure didn't care about hurting kids. That's for sure."

Mr. W was a sort of authority figure on the staff, at least in the evening hours. He called the shots in the dorm where Scott slept. And he was, Scott said, "the man that started my abuse."

There were detailed logbooks, Scott remembered, and Michael remembered them, as well. Binders – picture the red sort that sit all the way open, Scott said – where staff members would note things like "five o'clock, walked the kids to dinner." Staff would take turns doing the logging. Sometimes it would be Mr. W, sometimes it would be a Miss B or Miss H (again, we'll abbreviate). Scott remembers their names to this day only because that's how he had to address them, with the courtesy titles and their last names. A lot of stuff going on around him – names of other staff, for instance – he tuned out back then. But he was definitely aware that what was happening to him was happening to other boys at the home. And he knew how his own day was going to go based on whether Mr. W, Miss B or Miss H were on shift. As the adults made notes in the logs of when the kids were taken here and there, given breakfast or taken outside to the playground or put to bed or whatever, there were certain things that were left off the record.

"Mr. W—- would be in charge of making sure all the kids were down and sleeping, not getting up. So Miss B——— would be logging. At night, one of the things was, once the lights went out, and I went to bed, Mr. W—- would walk by and say, 'Let's go, boy. You know where to go. Come on. Let's go, go, go.' That's exactly how it went." Then, "Mr. W—- actually … gave me to Miss B———, and then basically gave me to Miss H———-," Scott explained slowly. Uneasily. "Mr. W—-, he started my abuse, and then he actually – one night, Miss B——— was doing the log, and he said, 'You're going with Miss B——— tonight. And I don't want to hear anything out of you.' And it was like he would walk me to the end of the thing, and B——— would be like, 'I've got him.' That's the way it was."

Scott said he would be led away from the dorm room – which he recalled as a large room where about twenty kids slept, beds and lockers alternating in a row on each of two sides of the room – to a different area where there were desks set up, the old-fashioned kind of school desks with chairs attached. His abuse involved Miss B making him sit with her in one of the desks.

"That's at night when all the kids were put down for sleep," he said. "So think of this castle-looking dormitory that was pitch-black except this desk at the end of the row, way, you know, away, where there was a light on. Where there was a desk light."

Then there was Frank the Candyman, remembered pretty well by various online commenters who lived at the home back then, including Michael and Scott.

"Everybody kind of knew what his deal was," Scott said, "where he lived in the back of the facility, and his deal was if you went there, he would throw you down like 'Now-or-Later's. And one of the things was, yeah, throw them down, you're good, but don't ever let him call you up there. You could go to the back of the building and yell, 'Frank! Frank!' And then he would throw you down packs of candy. But the thing is, all the kids knew never to go upstairs. Because it wasn't safe to go upstairs."

And then there was the arranged fighting. Scott remembered that experience vividly, and it was one he often shared with another kid at the home named Donald. "It was at the group," Scott explained, elaborating a bit on something Michael had mentioned: "So down in the basement, every group kind of had their area where they were – think of it like a clubhouse. Well, it *was* a clubhouse. It was like an area that maybe had a puzzle table, maybe had a pool table, and a desk where the staff would sit, and couches. Well, they used to have me and Donald – and other people, too, but – they used to have this carpeted floor, a cement floor that had a thin carpet over it. And if maybe two kids were having issues with each other, or if it was just two kids that staff wanted to see fight, they would literally put them on the – they called it 'calling you to the carpet.' And they would have the two kids beat each other. A lot of times it was wrestling, and duck holds, and they used to have kids do that. And me and Donald were two that always got pitted against."

So physical fighting, and even if one of the kids got seriously hurt, that was no big issue? They just wanted to watch it? "They hooted and hollered it," Scott affirmed. "They even bet on it between the staff members, you know?

So yeah." He added, "You know, in the '70s, I am sure there was probably no accountability."

Scott was a fish out of water, to say the least. A young boy already experiencing a scary adjustment just being at the home in the first place, coming from a very different part of Metro Detroit. A downriver community that was, and still is, quite the polar opposite, culturally.

"I was born and raised near Taylor. 'Taylortucky.' And for me to wake up one day going to St. Francis Home for Boys in the middle – in Detroit, it was the biggest world-shaker of any world-shaker."

He was young, not equipped to deal, not equipped to relate. No tools on how to interact with people, as he put it. He did not form any friendships with the other boys – it was too difficult. "I did not, because it wasn't my world. I mean, it became my world, like literally, but it wasn't my world. Because me, from Taylor, and Detroit are two different things, you know? Almost all the kids there were from Detroit. I was the biggest target in the world when I got there, because I was a white kid that was chunky. I mean, that was open season."

To picture the atmosphere at St. Francis, Scott recommended the 1996 movie *Sleepers*, starring Kevin Bacon, Robert DeNiro and Brad Pitt, where Bacon plays the sadistic guard at a juvie hall (called a home for boys) where four young kids are sent. "Basically the staff could pretty much do what they want," he said. Like whack a kid upside the head if he wasn't sitting still in the dentist's chair, because there was no parent in the waiting room to be accountable to. Any parent or family member was far, far away from these encounters with dentists or other staff members. A kid's brief respite was a weekend away with family, if he could swing it. "Friday, you would hear over the speakers," Scott said, "you would start hearing, 'John Smith to the office. John Smith. ... Terrence Johnson to the office.' By hearing that, you knew who had people that loved them enough to come get them. That was almost like a badge of honor for a lot of people. You know, 'Hey, I'm going home.'"

If you're wondering where the nuns were in all of this, at this home run by the Archdiocese ... from how Scott described it, the nuns were only seen during the school time and when the kids attended church on the weekend. So the sisters were responsible for schooling, primarily, and that's where Scott felt the safest – at school. The nuns were stern, he said, but not at all abusive, a view that Michael echoed. It was the other staff – the non-clergy staff – those adults whom Scott termed the "minders," who ushered the kids here and there, watched them shower, took them to breakfast, put them to bed, which were responsible for his abuse, he said. The caretakers. Not the professional staff. This could explain why, as noted earlier, if you look online for any sign of St. Francis staff being charged with abuse, you're unlikely to find anything. The Archdiocese website, as an example, only lists *clergy* who have been credibly charged. Therein lies the distinction. And it relates to the distinction of male vs. female staff members Atkins discussed in his letter to the judge. The female nuns drawing up his detailed progress reports for the official record, only seeing one part of the picture, vs. the other staff members monitoring and overseeing the day-to-day life of the boys. You could hear that the place was run by nuns and assume they were the only staff. Yes, the Sisters of St. Joseph were the administrators of the facility, if you will, but there was a whole other staff running the place.

Scott is convinced that even though Mr. W was fired, and though allegations about the home came to light in the 1980s, and it was then closed in 1992, that there was a large cover-up. He has to wonder where those logbooks went, for one thing. He has also tried to get his own personal records from the home. He contacted the Sisters of St. Joseph. He was directed to an individual who responded that yes, he could get the records. They would find them. Then Scott was ghosted, he said. He tried calling back several times. No reply. No records. He believes it was because of what they found in his records, the fact that he was the one who essentially got Mr. W fired. By speaking up.

"My stepfather, my sister's father, one night I was able to tell him what was going on. And he was pissed. And he went down there and just let it be known that he was going to shoot Mr. W——. And they fired Mr. W——."

That was not the last time he saw his former caretaker at the home, however.

"I was out on the playground one day, and one of the kids in my dorm said, 'Hey, c'mere, man. I want to show you something.' And he walked me to the gate. And on the other side of the fence ... So think of it as how the urban area is, where you could walk *[from the surrounding neighborhood]* and see the kids on the other side of the fence playing. So there was Mr. W——. He had been fired. And he has a bottle of liquor in his hand, saying if I run my mouth again, he'd have me killed. And he yelled at me. Kept on saying, 'Come here! Come here now!' And I wouldn't go close to him, but he goes, 'If you keep running your fat-ass mouth, I'm going to get you, boy.' And I'm like, 'Uh, oh!' I started walking away. He goes, 'Don't think I can't have your ass killed.'"

It was shortly after that when Scott was taken out of the home. He estimates that was 1980. He has no idea if any other kids came forward to report what Mr. W or other staff members were doing, but he remains convinced that there is documentation of all this somewhere. He may never lay eyes on his St. Francis records.

"Years and years ago," Scott said as we talked via phone in 2023, "I had a hard time dealing with this. I really did." His young, confused brain had not quite computed what he was seeing around him – did not quite understand just how abnormal or unhealthy this behavior was. "And I actually ... I actually went to prison for robbing a bank. In my addiction problem, I actually ended up robbing a bank and I ended up going to prison myself. And through group therapy I always – you know, a lot of this has been because I've never dealt with this trauma that I lived. I went for a while trying to find Donald, because I knew he was the one with me that kind of – he was also part of that, from Mr. W—- to Miss B——— to Miss H————-. Years ago, I found him on OTIS *[Michigan's Department of Corrections online offender search]*. And he had been to prison. And I was trying to find a way to reach out to him because I knew he knew me. Because they used to have us fight each other and stuff like that. So he and I knew each other real well. He was another person that got abused."

He did not reach Donald, who had been incarcerated for armed robbery, but he still wants to speak to others who went through similar experiences at St. Francis. Like Michael.

All of this would seem to paint a picture of this home for boys as a pressure cooker for criminals. Scott said as much: "Going to St. Francis was almost like a training school to go to prison at some point."

Scott did not really follow the case of Benjamin Atkins when it happened. Had heard it on the news, but not really followed it. And he had not been aware that Atkins lived at St. Francis at the same time he did. "Well, I can tell you that what he did was the most reprehensible thing. It sounds like what he got convicted of, what he did, is horrible. It's just the worse. But society's got to look and say, you know, you put that in a Petri dish. If what happened to him is true, which I'm going to say it is. I'm surprised that more people from St. Francis don't have blowups in society, you know what I mean?"

Scott's mom had been told at the time it was a good place. "On paper, St. Francis sounded like a good thing. You put the kids in what's supposed to be a trustworthy facility, maybe introduce some religion into their lives, give them some education, and boom. Well, unfortunately, it was also a feeding farm for abuse. That's what it was."

Clearly the story of St. Francis is a separate book entirely. Hopefully someone will write it.

In the meantime, if you want a peek inside a run-down St. Francis before the building was demolished and when it had more recently been the Paul Robeson Academy, check out the album by user DetroitUrbex.com in Flickr.

***

The FBI's *Crime Classification Manual: A Standard System for Investigating and Classifying Violent Crimes*, authored by former FBI profiler John Douglas along with fellow noted profiler Robert K. Ressler and Ann W. Burgess and Allen G. Burgess, and ironically first published the same year Atkins was arrested, cites various classifications of sexual homicide: organized, disorganized, mixed, sadistic. The FBI profiling of Atkins said he was a disorganized killer, the classification marked by lack of criminal sophistication, use of drugs and alcohol, or mental deficiency. "The victim is often from his own geographical area because this offender acts impulsively under stress and also because he derives confidence from familiar surroundings to bolster his feelings of social inadequacy," the authors wrote. "The disorganized offender is often socially inept and has strong feelings of inadequacy. These feelings of deficiency will compel him to assault the victim in an ambush, blitz style, that will immediately incapacitate her or him." Dr. Michael F. Abramsky, however, in his own examination of Atkins, determined him to be an organized killer, displaying planning and methodical steps in each one of the murders. Before Atkins was arrested, Dr. Bruce Danto also believed he was an organized killer.

When Jeffrey Edison filed notice that he intended to pursue a defense of insanity and/or diminished capacity, Michael Reynolds queued up some rebuttal for the prosecution. Among his rebuttal witnesses was the director at St. Francis whom he had communicated with for Atkins' records, interestingly. There were also a couple women who purchased at the same crack house as Atkins on Burlingame Street. One asserted in her conversations with Reynolds that Atkins was not crazy, there was nothing wrong with him. He was polite, well-kempt, when she saw him, which was essentially every day for a stretch of months while she was still feeding her habit. She had seen crazy people before, she told the attorney, and this was not one of them. The other woman interviewed saw Atkins almost as often and again never noticed anything strange about him. Nothing violent about him, either. She knew all of the victims by face, a couple of them by name. Reynolds also lined up a local pastor who served as a jail chaplain to Atkins. He had met one-on-one with the inmate a handful of times, during which there was never any mention of hearing voices or any sort of demonic possession. Atkins struck the pastor as well-oriented and sane. Other riders on the he's-actually-sane-train included two coworkers from the Westland pizza place, a Southeastern High School teacher, two female neighbors of Atkins' brother, and a couple other women who smoked crack with Atkins and never found themselves in any situation where they felt in danger. (At least one of the four former crack users interviewed was a prostitute.) Common themes emerged from these witness statements: Atkins seemed to be a loner, was polite, neat, kept to himself, did not appear strange or mentally ill, did not mention any hatred for prostitutes, and definitely never talked about any voices. His nickname at the pizza joint, the female coworker said, was "Loc," as in rapper Tone Loc.

Whether Atkins was totally sane, really messed up or something in-between, the several psychiatrists/

psychologists who evaluated him prior to trial made their own varied professional observations. Incidentally, Edison listed all four of them as potential witnesses in support of his insanity/diminished capacity defense.

THE ROSEN REPORT FOR COMPETENCY TO STAND TRIAL

"If I don't tell a lie a day, I don't feel right."

That's a quote from Benjamin Atkins, evidently, as revealed by his family members during a meeting at Jeffrey Edison's office in the month following Atkins' arrest. Ben was known as a habitual liar, his defense attorney learned.

The case files reinforce this idea about Atkins. He lied about his name when he was arrested, he lied about his brother's girlfriend being his wife, he lied about various other things. And it was the opinion of Todd Rosen, staff psychiatrist at the Recorder's Court Psychiatric Clinic, that Atkins was lying during the psychological testing he administered to him.

Rosen's report said, "Mr. Atkins indicated that he is extremely distressed by 1) the idea that someone else can control his thoughts; 2) hearing voices that other people do not hear; 3) believing others are aware of his private thoughts; 4) having thoughts that are not his own; and 5) believing that something is wrong with his mind." Rosen also found Atkins to be bothered by feelings of paranoia, that others could not be trusted and were watching him and talking about him. But in his report, these findings were in the context of Rosen's belief that Atkins was malingering, reporting more symptoms than were probable in his psychological testing. Atkins said he was afraid of traveling on buses or trains, was uneasy in crowds. He was distressed by urges to beat or injure others, or to smash or break things. He was nervous, shaky, often afraid that something bad was going to happen to him. He was depressed, had a loss of sexual interest or pleasure, feelings of worthlessness. Others were unfriendly or disliked him. He felt inferior to them. He was even distressed by worries of carelessness and sloppiness.

So were all of these symptoms real, or was Atkins just checking off boxes on the tests? Atkins also noted headaches, faintness, dizziness, muscle soreness, a lump in his throat, and other symptoms, which Rosen noted as "somatization," emotional symptoms expressed as physical phenomena.

Conclusions from Rosen's September 1992 evaluation:

- No chronic medical illness
- Social commonsense judgment low
- Controls significantly impaired; subject overridden by his impulses
- IQ within low-average range
- Speech logical, coherent, goal-directed
- Denied suicidal or homicidal ideations
- Claimed to have not made the confessions to police, and to have not committed the crimes
- Claimed auditory hallucinations
- Correctly oriented to person, time and place
- Malingering in psychological testing
- Understood judicial process; fit to stand trial

THE FIELDS REPORT FOR RECORDER'S COURT

"He was upset that he saw himself in her – a soft, sensitive side of himself, a self-consciousness, a sense of pride," wrote Dr. Dexter Fields of the Recorder's Court Psychiatric Clinic in his evaluation of Atkins for criminal responsibility and diminished capacity. "Had he been a girl, he 'would not have gone to St. Francis and been raped ... [his] mother would not have left.'"

We have no way of knowing if that is true, but Atkins' expression of those thoughts to Dr. Fields provides just a bit more interesting and disturbing insight as we peel back the layers of the mind of a killer. It was thrown in there amid a flurry of details about the crimes – details that matched fairly well with the statements Atkins gave police. He talked with Fields about each crime, and the particular detail above came from the offense he considered second. The second one he described to the doctor, anyway.

As part of his examination, Fields administered two Minnesota Multiphasic Personality Inventories (MMPI). The MMPI, first used in 1940 then revised in 1989, is widely used to this day. It's a 567-item, true/false, self-report measure of a person's psychological state, according to the journal Occupational Medicine. It has nine validity scales assessing for lying, defensiveness, faking good and faking bad among others. In his testing, Atkins endorsed so many attributes that it led Fields to believe he was malingering.

Conclusions from Fields' spring 1993 evaluation:

- Coherent, no signs of a psychotic process
- Mentioned "Tony" but could not give examples of his influence
- Testing showed difficulty relating to females and difficulty with interpersonal relationships overall
- Testing indicated an attempt to appear more ill than he was
- Methodical, purposeful and reality-oriented in his decisions
- Able to form the intent to commit the crimes (and the cocaine was not a factor/did not impair that intent)
- No symptoms of psychotic or mood disorder
- Did not appear to fit the law's definitions of diminished capacity (mental retardation, mental illness, intoxication) during the crimes

THE CLARK REPORT FOR THE PROSECUTION

"Sometimes I be afraid to go to sleep – dreams, nightmares," Atkins told Dr. Charles Clark in an evaluation for the prosecution. "Sometimes I see visions sometimes, and I stay woke to see if they come back."

Atkins was haunted by his crimes, it had become clear by the time Clark examined him, and one interesting takeaway from the hours Clark spent talking with him is Atkins' claim that the murders stopped when he stopped using drugs, and that to stop using drugs he simply made the decision one day to not do them anymore. That would seem contrary to the nature of addiction, any addict will tell you – this whole "cold turkey" notion. Nevertheless, the murders did stop for a couple months before his arrest, as far as we know.

Several of the things Atkins said to Clark also matched the letters he sent to his brother's girlfriend. He likely wrote the letters around the same time Clark was evaluating him.

As part of his examination, Clark administered the MMPI and the good old-fashioned Rorschach test.

Conclusions from Clark's summer and fall 1993 evaluation:

- Polite, cooperative, patient, responsive during examination
- Well-oriented to time, place and person
- Functioning in low-average range of intelligence
- Judgment assessed as poor
- Speech coherent, goal-directed and relevant
- Indicated memory for all of the offenses
- Attributing his crimes to "Tony" differed from what he had told police and Dr. Fields
- Crack use appeared to be incidental, not key to his intent to kill

- Statements of those who knew him did not indicate any obviously disordered behavior other than substance abuse
- Reports of his drug and alcohol use not consistent
- Testing indicated he was trying to present a false picture of extreme mental disturbance
- No good reason to conclude he was mentally ill or legally insane
- Understood that what he was doing was wrong and illegal
- Actions showed control
- Did not have diminished capacity simply because of his hatred for prostitutes, history of abuse, or any other elements of his background

THE ABRAMSKY REPORT FOR THE DEFENSE

As part of his testing of Atkins, Dr. Michael Abramsky administered the MMPI as Clark and Fields had done, plus the second incarnation of the Millon Clinical Multiaxial Inventory (MCMI). The MCMI, named for Theodore Millon, is an objective computerized test measuring general characterological traits and acute pathology. The MCMI was intended to improve upon the long-established MMPI, according to the 1998 book *Comprehensive Clinical Psychology*. The MCMI has fewer items, is based on an elaborate theory of personality and psychopathology, and explicitly focuses on diagnostic links to criteria from the *Diagnostic and Statistical Manual of Mental Disorders*. Abramsky also administered a couple projective psychological test instruments: the Thematic Apperception Test and the Rorschach test. Combined, these latter two tests measure conscious and unconscious themes of a person's character, psychopathy and general concerns. Abramsky's testing showed Atkins had a good sense of reality, was not psychotic, and knew the difference between right and wrong.

The primary identification for a child is a mother, Abramsky noted, and for a boy, a father breaks this bond and plants the seeds of masculinity. Benjamin was torn away from his mother while his identification with her was still prominent in his childhood, Abramsky said. Seeds of feminine identification were planted. Because his homosexuality was (allegedly) traumatically induced at the home for boys, it was accompanied by self-hate. And because of the early trauma, the normal separation between sexual and aggressive feelings never developed. Therefore, his sexuality and aggression fused, reflected in his sadism. A lack of love in his life and a lack of viable sexual role models only furthered this. He also learned from his mother that sexuality earned money and gained favors. And, he told Abramsky, some of his encounters in prostitution involved abuse, so the fusion of homosexuality and self-hate deepened.

Abramsky believed Atkins suffered from a condition called anhedonia, the inability to experience pleasurable effects. He could seem to have joy on the surface, but no sense of pleasure in a deeper emotional way. Not quite what Jeffrey Edison will always remember Dr. Clark testifying, that Atkins "does not have capacity to love," but perhaps related.

In the superego aspect of personality that Freud popularized, also called the conscience, Atkins was lacking, since a father figure typically provides that. Thus his development of conscience was immature; he saw things as bad "only if you get caught," Abramsky said.

As with the other psychiatric examiners, Abramsky found poor judgment in Atkins. And as with Dr. Fields, Atkins showed Dr. Abramsky a sort of envy for women: "He told me that if he were a woman, his life would be different. 'Parents treasure little girls,' that little girls are the image of a mother and loved by a father. He felt the women had opportunities, that they could essentially do what they want and would be taken care of. They had opportunities he never had. 'If I were a cute little girl, my foster parents would have loved me, my mother would have never deserted me and right now I would have a baby and be taken care of by a man."

Conclusions from Abramsky's November and December 1993 evaluation:

- Women seen as unreliable and objects of scorn
- Pathological envy for people who have loving family relationships
- Foster homes nurtured feelings of aggression and of being "second place"
- Sexuality and aggression fused
- Poor judgment; difficulty anticipating consequences of actions
- Difficulty delaying impulses
- Depersonalization – sense of one's reality lost or changed
- Relationships transient or superficial, only existing to fill certain needs
- Illness not acute like depression or schizophrenia, but a failure of development
- Borderline personality disorganization with psychopathic trends
- Borderline mental state so deep and atypical as to constitute a mental illness under Michigan statute, but not rising to the level of legal insanity

TONY

Tony, whoever he is or whatever he means, comes up a lot in the case of Benjamin Atkins.

Tony was a nickname Atkins used, a sort of alias for his life on the street.

Tony, or Anthony, was also the name of the lover Atkins said he had, a real person. Atkins' coworkers at the pizza place in Westland remembered seeing this Tony come in to visit, and Atkins mentioned this other Tony to Jeffrey Edison, saying he was very happy being with him. He is the one Atkins described as a female impersonator, who would also use the name Chris. He lived over in the Cass Corridor.

Heck, even the rapper who inspired Atkins' nickname at the pizza joint, Tone Loc, has a real name of Anthony.

But beyond each of those Tonys, Tony was also a person Atkins claimed he saw or heard whenever he was distressed, happy or lonely, someone who told him to do things, even told him what to do in a fight, how to survive. Tony seemed to be an alternate personality – or was he?

Really, who on earth was Tony?

The movie *Three Faces of Eve* depicts the real-life 1950s case of a woman, played by Joanne Woodward, who would transform into three distinct personalities: the meek housewife Eve White, the racy temptress Eve Black, and a third woman who at first doesn't even know her name but is given the name Jane. Throughout the film, a couple psychiatrists attempt to treat her and discover which of the three is the "real" her. At first, it's shown as the housewife, who is the one that seeks treatment and is not aware of the others. In this story, the patient actually becomes each of the other personalities at times, with hardly a moment's notice. She switches in and out of these personalities quickly and seemingly at random.

Though the movie gets mentioned in the case files of Benjamin Atkins – woven into the questioning Ron Sanders did upon the arrest, for instance – there are some marked differences between this case of multiple personalities and what Atkins claimed. One big one is that Atkins did not "become" another personality and then have amnesia for what that personality did while inhabiting his body. He claimed his three alternate "people" – Tony, Mary and Mayolla – were real people who interacted with him essentially inside his head, not present to the rest of people around him. So they were voices, influences, he claimed, who would visit him and taunt him, but they did not interact with others using his physical body.

He did tell Dr. Fields, however, of Tony, "I don't know if he became me, or I became him." Of course, that could simply speak to the grave influence he claimed Tony had over him.

Multiple personality disorder, referred to in more recent years as dissociative identity disorder, is one of a few different dissociative disorders, according to the American Psychiatric Association. These disorders involve problems with memory, identity, emotion, perception, behavior and sense of self. Examples of dissociative symptoms include the experience of detachment or feeling as if one is outside one's body, and loss of memory or amnesia. Dissociative disorders are frequently associated with previous experiences of trauma, and dissociative identity disorder in particular is associated with overwhelming experiences, traumatic events and/or abuse that occurred in childhood. Symptoms include the existence of two or more distinct identities (or "personality states"), which are accompanied by changes in behavior, memory and thinking. This may be observed by others or reported by the individual. There are also ongoing gaps in memory about everyday events, personal information and/or past traumatic events. Those with abuse in their past are at increased risk for dissociative identity disorder, and suicide attempts are common among people with the disorder.

Dr. Abramsky explored what he called Atkins' "splitting," the side-by-side existence of complete psychological attitudes in depth. Splitting has also been identified as an aspect of borderline personality disorder, based on alternating between extremes of idealization or devaluation, all or nothing, and good or bad. According to *Psychology Today*, in people with BPD, splitting behavior relates to fears of rejection or abandonment to prevent feeling hurt. It's a self-protecting primitive defense mechanism that helps them feel "safe" when they're feeling threatened, scared, judged, or misunderstood.

In his own assessment, Abramsky said splitting gives rise to disassociation and, at a deeper level, multiple personalities. He did not see Atkins as that far advanced, noting that Atkins did not switch to other personalities that had amnesia for each other's actions. But, "there is definitely some disassociation having to do with contradictory working parts of his personality." He saw Atkins' various voices like Tony as his internal contradictory dialogue. Still, Abramsky said, it appeared that even in the commission of the murders, these warring personalities within Atkins stepped in at varying times, each aware of what the others had done but not necessarily able to comprehend the actions.

In the book *Killer Across the Table*, John Douglas said that he sees this sort of claim quite a bit in his study of serials. "Many of us had imaginary friends as young children," he wrote. "But I have come across a fair number of serial predators who had something similar as adults, or at least claimed they did. These 'friends' took several forms. The ones with which prosecutors are most familiar are those supposedly caused by multiple personality disorder."

MPD/dissociative identity disorder is rare and generally shows up in young children who have been severely abused and "escape" into other personalities that are stronger and/or detached from the actual personality, Douglas said. There are some very real cases, but so often the claim of MPD comes *after* a perp's arrest. As in the case of Atkins, Douglas said, "Though the suspect/defendant may never have given any indication to those around him that he has more than one personality, if the evidence against him is strong and there is no other way to explain his action, he or his attorney will put forth a multiple personality disorder defense." Douglas told the story of interviewing South Carolina killer Larry Gene Bell and playing "the MPD card," which then had Bell conceding that though the "good" version of him would never do such a thing, maybe the "bad" one did. And other killers have claimed multiple personalities, some personalities or voices popping up anew as questioning progressed. "I have seen this trait of setting up an avatar to take the rap with some frequency in my career," Douglas said.

At its heart it's a control issue – the perp is not in control of his actions, this other personality is. It's similar to the question of nature vs. nurture, genetics vs. upbringing, which Douglas also addressed: "Many killers would have it that their murderous actions were not their own choice at all, that killing was a fixed, nonnegotiable action for them. Yet nothing I have seen in all my years of criminal investigation leads me to accept that premise, except in the most extreme cases of mental illness."

Atkins claimed to have not only the infamous Tony, Mary and Mayolla, but he also claimed an imaginary friend that was a dog named Pete. At least, at times the dog was named Pete, like when he spoke to Dr. Clark. Sometimes it was named Ralph, like when he spoke to Dr. Fields. (Atkins told Clark that Fields had just gotten the name wrong – it was really Pete.) With Dr. Clark, the dog came up during the Rorschach test, when Atkins was describing what he saw in one of the shapes. There are no other attributes of the imaginary dog in the case files, however – no indication if the dog tried to influence Atkins' actions a la the Son of Sam killer, David Berkowitz, and his neighbor's dog.

Atkins said he could actually physically feel the touch of Mayolla, the one he named for his grandmother. He could feel her holding him at times, trying to comfort him. Mayolla had her hands on his shoulder while he was talking to Ron Sanders after his arrest, and she encouraged him to confess, even though Tony was telling him not to. Tony was sometimes in the office during his psychiatric exams, but Atkins said he did not tell the examiner that, for fear he would not be believed.

These three different people each had a physical appearance he could describe. Somewhat. Tony didn't really have a look, he said, maybe Asian. Maybe black all over. No emotion. He did not wear clothes. He did not have a sex organ. He was just a figure, Atkins told Clark. But he did have a height – about six foot. "I'm five-nine, he's much taller. … Oh, I would say he weigh one seventy, one eighty; he's wide."

Mary had long hair, all black. "She hasn't got a color. She doesn't wear clothes, but she doesn't have sex organs either … got a loving face – her eyes are black, no white, no pupil, but she always have comforting words – (it) helps a lot."

And for Mayolla: "She has an older image. Her hair is gray, long. So I take it she wear clothes, but no form, body, no facial (features)." Her clothes, he said, were patterned with flowers all over. That was in an initial meeting with Clark. In a subsequent interview, Mayolla was light-skinned with gray hair, wearing a flowing outfit with a shawl. And Mary had "caramel skin, black hair, normally wears a dress."

"Mary and Tony, they're friends," Atkins told Clark, "always together. Tony is foul, disgusting. Ask me to do things that disgust me. One time he had me roll around in my own bowel. I tried to commit suicide several times … try hanging. Mayolla would only comfort me. Mary would just talk to me. Mayolla is more like a mother. All Mary do, she protect me from Tony, tell him to stop." Still, Mary was negative like Tony, while Mayolla was a positive voice. "Mayolla was the love I was seeking from my own mother," Atkins said. And though he had seen (or heard) all three since before his arrest, he did not tell his family about them. (By the same token, though, he said he had never told anyone close to him about his homosexuality.)

Whomever was talking to him at whatever time, Tony remained the dominant force. And the description of Tony grew richer as time went on, same as the descriptions of all the voices progressed over time, from denial with Sanders at the arrest, to three full-blown people and a dog with Clark. Tony was the one who egged him on, who demeaned him for his homosexual behavior, who dared him to "be a man" and pick up a woman, who told him to kill, who told him to rape a woman after she had passed out or died, who told him to hide the body, who even picked out the woman for him in the first place. Afterward, Mary would tell him he did a bad thing, then later Mayolla would rock him to sleep. Tell him not to worry, it will be all right. Sometimes, however, Mary would comfort him, too, and Mary would assist in hiding the body. Mary also encouraged him to go to police like Mayolla did, Atkins told Clark. The lines were blurry among the roles of these three.

Atkins told Fields that Tony had been with him since age seventeen. He told jail staff it was age thirteen. He told Clark it was age ten. Fields found Atkins' demeanor different when speaking of Tony – evasive, but frequently smiling.

"Tony hates me," he told Clark. "I used to think that's because I hated my own life and what I done. Some people have an imaginary friend, they hate part of their lives. (Tony) called me all kinds of names – bitches and whores." (Exactly what Atkins called his victims.) "He used to always down me. He had nothing positive to say. Since I got into religion, he sees me very seldom. He down-talks religion, tells me I'm nothing. I've been so far as to drink bleach, soap powder, let food sit up and get spoiled. Tony say just do as I say. I cut myself with a razor. When Tony comes, Mary comes with a reason to not do it (so) I don't cut myself too deep."

Why do you pay attention to Tony, Clark asked. "I don't know. He looks so – he's deceiving. I would just jump up and become violent. He says I deserve it, everything he asks me to do, which I try. It's somewhat like with the offenses, when a woman would ask why is this happening to me, I can't explain. If not for Mary, I would probably be dead by now."

Explaining when the murders stopped in the summer of 1992, Atkins told Clark, "I wasn't bothered (by Tony) ... because when I stopped crack, I basically stopped going out on the street. Everything was in peace, because I was doing what made him (happy)." As to Mary and Mayolla: "They would come and they would tell me – remember I was depressed? – and now that I was doing good, they'd say you're doing good."

A Wayne County Jail Health Services report from August 1993 said, "Descriptions of the voices he claims to hear occasionally not very convincing in terms of representing a true psychotic process." A week later, Atkins told a different evaluator he had been hearing the voices since he was a kid but lately they had gotten worse. This staff member drew much the same conclusion as the first: "Presentation frankly not convincing for any acute psychotic process." A week after that, a report noted there was "no evidence whatsoever of any acute mental illness." Atkins' treatment while in the jail included medications, though it's unclear exactly what kind. He complained of shortness of breath from whatever they were giving him, but he also asked for something for depression.

Dr. Fields wrote, "It should be noted that the defendant's friend, Tony, seems unrelated to mental illness. To begin, were the defendant as psychotic and hallucinated as he would like to suggest, he would undoubtedly have presented many details and personal thoughts concerning the offenses. In situations where defendants have been found insane at the time of the offense and diminished in their capacity, the defendant has little need to cover information or choose what information he will reveal and what information he will keep to himself." Atkins was very imprecise in talking about Tony, Fields said, and sometimes he didn't listen to Tony, proving he was using his own will. It just wasn't adding up for Fields. Plus, when he first asked Atkins about the name Tony, Atkins said he just used a different name so people on the street wouldn't associate him with his family.

So what to make of all of this? What do you think? Was Atkins malingering? Or was he actually hearing Tony and the others?

The first time the idea of multiple personalities or voices was mentioned for Atkins was during his interrogation with Ron Sanders, and from all that can be gleaned from the files, Sanders was the one who brought up the idea. He was evidently jumping off from the fact that Atkins went by the name Tony on the street and appeared to have this sort of "alter ego," at the very least, and from Atkins' claims of seeing the women standing at the foot of his bed at night. Sanders had just watched the movie *Raising Cain* the day before. Atkins denied any kind of alternate personalities or voices at the time. Said he was sane. Didn't have that problem. So just to play devil's advocate, in itself a rather bad pun ... was it that interrogation that planted the idea in Atkins' mind? An idea he would later adopt and develop further, especially given the fact that Atkins told Clark he would rather go to a hospital than a prison?

Well, you could look at it that way. Defense attorney Jeffrey Edison still thinks about it all to this day. If you are malingering, there is still something "off" about you. You're messed up in some way. Well-adjusted people don't need to malinger.

KILLER COMPARISONS

Some described him as unassuming, his confessions unemotional. Police said he was well-spoken with a good vocabulary. Larry Beller in particular remembered decades later never being afraid of this perp or what he might do in custody. He remembered him as rather nonthreatening. "Gentle Ben," as Beller put it. Jim Dobson remembered him that way, as well, after several talks with him. And there was never any hard edge that defense attorney Jeffrey Edison saw – the only thing that stood out to him was the way his client would sometimes stare into space, go somewhere else entirely.

Just thinking about the term "serial killer" can conjure up images of the chilly and analytical Jeffrey Dahmer as he described his crimes, the smooth and so-handsome Ted Bundy as he tried to deny his, or maybe the darker Richard Ramirez being led into court, his eyes making contact with the camera, evil seeming to emanate from every pore. So how does Benjamin Atkins compare to other serial killers we've known?

A killer whose mother was a prostitute, who prostituted himself with men and killed women who were prostitutes. A drug addict who was homeless. A man who claimed to have other people living inside him, dictating his moves. There haven't been many serials like him. Add in the race factor – bucking the stereotype of the white male in his mid to late twenties – and you've got a true one-of-a-kind.

Serials have targeted prostitutes for a very long time – a fact so famously brought to light by the Jack the Ripper case – and they have targeted them for a variety of reasons. Prostitutes are easy to access; they will go with a stranger for a promise of money, or drugs in this case. If a prostitute is deep into an addiction, her judgment is impaired, making her even easier prey. Prostitutes are marginalized. The perception is that they won't be missed by friends or family, though from this case we know that's not true. They are "the missing missing," as an episode of ID's *Very Scary People* put it – missing from their families before they go missing anywhere else. But always missed. And another perception: that prostitutes are not of any value. This author would certainly hope that we as a culture know that's not true, either.

But misguided ideas about prostitutes linger (see the companion book *The 'Baby Doll' Serial Killer: The Homicides of John Eric Armstrong* for an extended discussion on that). Influenced by these ideas and perceptions, many notable serials have chosen to target those of the world's oldest profession:

- **Gary Ridgway**, known as the Green River Killer, had forty-nine confirmed kills but many others unconfirmed in the Pacific Northwest from 1982 to 1998. Like Atkins, he strangled his victims, and he often had sex with them after they were dead. Ridgway had issues with prostitutes and could perhaps be categorized as a mission-oriented or social justice serial, but he also patronized prostitutes without killing them, reportedly having an insatiable sexual appetite.

- **John Eric Armstrong** was known to have attacked ten in Detroit, five of whom survived, and was believed to have killed as many as ten others around the globe while in the U.S. Navy. He was also a strangler. He had a more stable upbringing than Atkins, however. He targeted women but picked up a couple transgender prostitutes, as well.

- **DeAngelo Martin**, another Detroit serial arrested in more recent years, 2019, preyed on older female prostitutes, most in their fifties, and like Atkins left them in the city's abandoned buildings. He was convicted of murdering four and raping two and was sentenced to life in prison in 2022.

- **Samuel Little**, called the Choke-and-Stroke Killer or Mr. Sam, confessed to murdering ninety-three women between 1970 and 2005. The FBI has confirmed at least sixty of those murders. For these stats, he's known as the most prolific serial in the U.S. He killed in many different states across the country as he traveled, and like Atkins was a strangler.

- **Robert Hansen**, nicknamed the Butcher Baker, murdered between seventeen and twenty-one women near Anchorage, Alaska, between 1971 and 1983. Like Atkins, he once played with fire, arrested for burning down a garage. He used a gun to subdue his victims, however, and he was an avid hunter who took victims to remote locations to "hunt" them.

- **Joel Rifkin**, sometimes called Joel the Ripper, was convicted for nine murders in New York and New Jersey between 1989 and 1993 but was believed to have seventeen victims. Like Atkins, Rifkin strangled his victims, who were women. He also performed poorly in school due to learning disabilities, and his lack of social skills caused him to be unpopular in school.

- **Lorenzo Gilyard Jr.**, aka the Kansas City Strangler, was believed to have raped and murdered at least thirteen women and girls from 1977 to 1993. He was convicted for six. Most of Gilyard's victims were prostitutes that he strangled with items like nylon stockings and wire. His sister was also a prostitute, and his father was convicted of rape. Gilyard strongly denied his crimes in interviews such as one with British journalist Piers Morgan.

- **Charles Albright**, called the Dallas Ripper, the Dallas Slasher or the Eyeball Killer, was convicted of killing one female prostitute but suspected of killing three others in 1990-1991. He shot his victims, however, and he surgically removed their eyes; he had at one time pursued a career in medicine. He was thought to target prostitutes as a personal mission.

- **Steve Wright**, of England, dubbed the Suffolk Strangler and the Ipswich Ripper, was convicted of killing five women in 2006 and, like Ridgway, was a frequent patron of prostitutes he did not kill. He was suspected in a few other unsolved murders of sex workers.

- Another English serial, **Peter Sutcliffe**, known as the Yorkshire Ripper, killed thirteen women and attempted to kill seven others between 1975 and 1980. He claimed God sent him on a mission to kill prostitutes, though not all of his victims were prostitutes.

- **Robert Pickton** of Canada, called the Pig Farmer Killer or the Butcher, confessed to killing forty-nine women, many of them prostitutes and drug addicts, but was convicted of killing six, beginning in the 1980s through 2002. He was raised on a pig farm, where his victims were believed to have been killed.

- **Lonnie David Franklin Jr.**, called the Grim Sleeper because of the fourteen-year break in his crimes, was believed to have killed several female prostitutes in California in the 1980s, then in the 2000s. He was convicted for ten murders but suspected to have up to twenty-five victims, including one male. His crimes were known as the "Strawberry Murders," "strawberry" being slang for a woman who exchanges sex for drugs, another similarity with the Atkins case.

- **Maury Travis**, called the Street Walker Strangler and the Videotape Killer for recording his crimes, was convicted in Missouri of killing two women but suspected of killing as many as twenty in 2000-2002.

- **Robert Lee Yates**, the Grocery Bag Killer, known to have murdered at least eleven women in Spokane, Washington, between 1975 and 1998, did drugs with his victims. He was sentenced to death but as of this writing is serving out life sentences since the Washington Supreme Court ruled capital punishment unconstitutional.

- **Terry Blair,** convicted for killing seven women in Missouri in 1982–2004 but believed to have killed more, had several family members also charged with murder. One of Blair's victims was the mother of his children; he was angry that she had been working as a prostitute.

- **Richard Cottingham,** the Times Square Killer or the New York Ripper, killed at least eighteen women and girls in New York and New Jersey from 1967 to 1980. Not all of them were prostitutes. He claimed to have killed at least eighty women across the U.S.

- **Andre Crawford**, aka the Southside Strangler, killed eleven women in the 1990s in Chicago, many of them prostitutes and drug addicts. He also had sex with their corpses.

- **Bobby Joe Long,** the "Classified Ad Rapist" and killer, targeted sex workers but also other females in Florida in 1984. Like Atkins, he moved fast, murdering at least eight women – and maybe ten or more – over an eight-month period.

- Cousins **Kenneth Bianchi** and **Angelo Buono Jr.**, who worked together as the Hillside Stranglers, claiming women and girls in California in the 1970s, were known to pick up prostitutes for their horrific, torturous crimes, though not only prostitutes. These two, like Bobby Joe Long, could rival Atkins' claim to infamy for being the fastest-moving serial in the U.S., except that they worked as a pair, not solo. They had ten confirmed victims, but Bianchi is believed to have at least a couple more.

- **William Suff**, the Riverside Prostitute Killer, operated in Riverside, California, in the late 1980s/early 1990s, mainly, though he was convicted of killing his baby daughter in the 1970s. Suff reportedly hated prostitutes and had some "rigid ideas about women," as one TV doc put it. He was known to have killed thirteen women and girls, but several other murders have been attributed to him.

- **Robert Ben Rhoades**, the long-haul trucker nicknamed the Truck Stop Killer, was suspected of torturing, raping, and killing more than fifty women between 1975 and 1990. He preyed on what some have so distastefully termed "lot lizards," women who roam the truck stop lots to cater to truckers.

- **Daniel Lee Siebert,** a convicted killer in Alabama, targeted a variety of victims including sex workers, and was believed to have worked prostitution himself at one time.

- The hefty six-foot-two, two-hundred-fifty-pound **Chester Turner** attacked prostitutes as he operated in Los Angeles in the 1990s and early 2000s, though he killed non-prostitutes, as well. He was convicted of assaulting and killing fourteen women and an unborn baby. Like Atkins, he had a single mom, and he was said to sometimes explode into a rage, though his background was not as troubled as Atkins'. He strangled his victims, who, like Atkins, he would lure into secluded spaces with the promise of crack. He was in and out of prison for years but then finally sentenced to death in California for the murders.

- The Canadian-born **Keith Jesperson,** nicknamed the "Happy Face Killer" because of the smiley-face notes he sent to law enforcement and media, targeted prostitutes as he worked as a truck driver on the U.S. West Coast. He had eight confirmed female victims, but crazy enough, confessed to as many as one hundred eighty-five.

- **Dayton Leroy Rogers** picked at least eight women off the streets in Oregon in the 1980s, earning the nickname of the "Molalla Forest Murderer." He was said to have a strange fixation on women's feet.

- **Arthur Shawcross**, known as the Genesee River Killer, targeted prostitutes among others (including children) in the 1970s and '80s in New York. He was said to be misogynist. He killed most of his fourteen victims after an early parole from a manslaughter conviction.

- **Sean Vincent Gillis**, a serial said to be geeky in his love for computers and *Star Trek*, targeted prostitutes, but not only prostitutes, as he killed eight women in Louisiana from 1994 to 2004. He even killed a female friend. Like Atkins, he engaged in necrophilia, but also dismembered his victims, sometimes cutting off their tattoos.

- **Paul Stephani,** nicknamed the "Weepy-Voiced Killer" for the frantic 911 calls he would place following his crimes, targeted one prostitute and four other women as he operated in the Minneapolis/St. Paul area in the 1980s. He killed three; two survived.

- **Walter E. Ellis**, known as the Milwaukee North Side Strangler, was convicted of killing seven female prostitutes between 1986 and 2007. Like Atkins, his background includes drugs and a juvie record.

- At least some of the women kidnapped in New Mexico by **David Parker Ray,** whose story is about as grisly as can be, were sex workers. He was called the Toy-Box Killer and was convicted of kidnapping and torture, but not of the sixty to one hundred murders he was suspected of. Authorities never found the bodies.

- **Gary Michael Heidnik**, working in Philadelphia in the 1980s, picked up prostitutes. He kidnapped, raped and tortured six women, four of which survived.

- In New Jersey, **Khalil Wheeler-Weaver** was called the Catfish Killer in his online hunt for victims, some of whom were sex workers. He was convicted of killing three women and attacking another who survived.

- The **Bigfoot Killer**, who is yet to be identified, is believed to have killed seven female prostitutes working the Cass Corridor in Detroit in 1975. His M.O. included strangulation, beating and wielding a knife. The Bigfoot Killer case came up in DPD's investigation of the Atkins case before Atkins was arrested, and the chief suspect in that case was considered.

That's not meant to be an all-inclusive list, of course, but it shows the proliferation of prostitutes as victim. Unlike Atkins, many of these killers had wives and children.

There have been other killers besides Atkins who targeted prostitutes and whose mothers were prostitutes. Joel Rifkin comes to mind. He was adopted but suspected his birth mother was a prostitute, and it shaped his decisions. He grew up a bit of a loner, often disheveled in appearance. A strangler, he sometimes dismembered his victims. As of this writing, he's serving out his sentences. In interviews, he has been very frank and has spoken of the addiction aspect of killing, the idea of not being able to stop once you have taken a life.

Samuel Little's life matches a little more closely with Atkins. He claimed that his mother was a teenage prostitute and that she had abandoned him. He was raised by his grandmother but said he began to have fantasies about strangling women even as a child. He reportedly collected true crime magazines at a young age to see female choking victims. Like Atkins, he was arrested for breaking and entering as a teen. His mother could not be found at the time. And like Atkins, he tried his hand at legit jobs in his early years. He moved around the country a lot and racked up arrests for various crimes – violent and nonviolent – wherever he went. His collection of mug shots over the decades is immense. He seems to have had a better and more accurate sense of recall, however, offering law enforcement many details of his crimes and even portraits of his victims. Little was the very definition of a career criminal and died in custody at age eighty in December 2020.

Quite coincidentally, another serial killer arrested in Detroit the same year as Atkins, Leslie Williams, who confessed to killing four teenage girls, was evidently the son of a prostitute who neglected her children. Williams, a career criminal who had been paroled in 1990, targeted younger females who were not sex workers. He hunted in the western suburbs rather than the city, though he did engage in necrophilia like Atkins, before he was arrested himself in 1992.

There are eerie similarities between the cases of Atkins and Andre Crawford, who was believed to have killed eleven women and had at least one survivor, probably more, from the talk on the streets. He also lured prostitutes and drug users into abandoned buildings with drugs. He killed later in the '90s, from 1993 to 2000, and he strangled and beat his victims, sometimes stabbing them, as well. He covered their faces and took their shoes, then returned to have sex with their lifeless bodies. As chronicled in an episode of Oxygen's *Mark of a Serial Killer*, Crawford hated his mother for often abandoning him and his sister when they were kids. He told people his mother was a drug user and prostitute. His father had left the family when he was very young, and he and his sister were placed in foster care. He also claimed to have suffered physical and sexual abuse while in foster care over the years, and to have been forced into prostitution. He became addicted to drugs and dropped out of school. He enlisted in the military, was dishonorably discharged, then returned to Chicago and lived on the streets. It was theorized that he was taking out his anger toward his mother on his victims, who were all Black females. Ultimately, it was about power, one interviewee said in the Oxygen episode. Crawford wanted to make them suffer. There's even a similarity in how Crawford described one particular incident with police, when he started strangling a woman because she just wanted the drugs and didn't want to do the sexual transaction they had agreed on. Atkins said that same thing about one of his victims.

The life of Walter E. Ellis is also similar to that of Atkins. He was a Black perp who dropped out of school and was involved with crack. He strangled Black prostitutes. Like Atkins, he got in trouble with the law before he starting killing. There's no notion that his mother worked as a prostitute, but Ellis certainly showed signs of a troubled childhood, reflecting antisocial behavior and being labeled a bully early on. He also died while incarcerated, albeit from complications of diabetes.

Convicted killer Henry Lee Lucas said in an interview that his mother had been a prostitute. "I was made to watch her," he said. She beat him when he was a child and ended up being one of his victims when he grew up.

Mommy issues have been common among serials. Henry Louis Wallace was said to have misogynist anger due to the abandonment by his mother. He had a troubled childhood, later became addicted to crack, and he even claimed a sort of split personality thing like Atkins, saying there was a "good" and "bad" Henry. Gary Ridgway told psychologists that when he was a kid, he had conflicting feelings of anger and sexual attraction toward his domineering mother, who would wash his genitals after he wet the bed. Ridgway fantasized about killing her. Bobby Joe Long was said to have a dysfunctional relationship with his mother, in whose bed he slept until he was a teenager. Ted Bundy reportedly had a lifelong resentment toward his mother and was born in a home for unwed mothers. He had the added confusion of not knowing who his real mother even was for a long time. He targeted pretty co-eds, though, not prostitutes. Like Atkins, he was into necrophilia. He also showed intense rage. A survivor of Bundy said on an episode of the UK's *World's Most Evil Killers* that he choked her until she passed out, then revived her so he could choke her again, another trait he shared with Atkins.

Charles Albright's adoptive mother was said to be very strict and overprotective of him. He had trouble with the law early on, even being arrested for assault at age thirteen. Edmund Kemper, known to have killed ten people including family members, was reportedly locked in a rat-infested basement by his verbally abusive, alcoholic mother. He said in interviews that often he would kill after an argument with his mother, and it was theorized the women he killed were surrogates for her (yes, he did later kill her). David Berkowitz, aka Son of Sam, was said to have deeply resented his birth mother, who gave him up as a baby and with whom years later he had a disappointing reunion. Dennis Rader, aka BTK (Bind-Torture-Kill), felt he was ignored by his mother growing up and reportedly resented her for it.

Rader's case raises the issue of the fusion between sexuality and aggression or violence, which Dr. Abramsky spoke of in his report on Atkins. This issue was explored in the A&E special on Rader, *BTK: Confession of a Serial Killer*, airing in 2022. Rader called it "Factor X." He said that he knew as a kid he had this Factor X, which he described as a sexual arousal when seeing others in pain, and later, when killing. On the series it was also referred to as a demon. Others have said this Factor X theory refers to certain undefined but irrepressible urges that evidently make sexual killers different from everybody else. Rader wanted forensic psychologist Dr. Katherine Ramsland to find out where this Factor X came from, but she said Rader "had a trajectory toward violence": opportunities to kill combined with unusual sexual proclivities and a desire for fame. She felt Rader was using this Factor X as an excuse. John Wayne Gacy is another killer who was said to be aroused by the act of killing. And Dahmer said in an interview that he started having fantasies as a teen about violence intermingled with sex.

A killer's M.O. can be tangled up with this arousal. "The primary way serial sexual murderers kill is by strangulation," said Louis B. Schlesinger, Ph.D., on the *Very Scary People* episode on Richard Cottingham. "The most efficient way to kill somebody is with a gun, but they don't want to kill somebody efficiently with a gun. They want to control their death and control their agony so that the victim is aware of the power and control and domination that the offender has over her. This is arousing to serial sexual murderers."

David Edward Maust is an interesting case, having a background of abuse and being shuffled between various homes like Atkins. His father left when he was only seven years old, and his mother had him placed in a psychiatric institution, claiming he had set fires in the home and tried to kill his brother. There was a question of the mother's own stability, however, and it was suspected she just didn't want him around. Maust was reportedly sexually molested as a child, then encountered abuse when he was placed in a children's home. Maust's crimes were against young boys, and he killed in the U.S. and while stationed in the military in Germany. He committed suicide in custody.

Aileen Wuornos was a female serial killer worth mentioning for her troubled upbringing, like Atkins, and for the fact that she worked prostitution, herself, beginning at a very young age.

Like Atkins, Missouri serial Maury Travis moved pretty fast, killing as many as seventeen to twenty prostitutes, though authorities linked him to twelve and convicted him of two, between 2000 and 2002. He also targeted Black females, though not much is known about his possible motivations. Police could find no signs of an abusive or troubled upbringing. He also lured his victims with drugs, and he bound them, then discarded them along area highways. His victims and possible victims showed a large age span, from nineteen to sixty-one, and he left behind several Jane Does. He made videotapes of some of his tortures and murders. Travis committed suicide just three days after his arrest. Age thirty-six, he didn't seem to have issues with his mother – in fact, he addressed her in his suicide note, calling her "the best mother a man can have." Interestingly, he explained, "I've been sick for long time (sick in the head) since I was about fourteen. I don't know why. I was just sick."

Regarding sexual orientation, there have been other homosexual or bisexual serials like Atkins, for instance Dahmer, Maust and Gacy, though unlike Atkins they chose victims of their same gender. Ottis Toole was a convicted killer whose background included a father who abandoned the family, an abusive mother, sexual abuse and incest by multiple people he knew as a child, serial arson, and a history of drifting, living in abandoned houses and working as a male prostitute. But Toole was suspected of murdering a variety of people – man, woman and child.

Law enforcement has long noted patterns in the backgrounds of many of these killers – early markers such as habitually wetting the bed and setting fires, maybe terrorizing the family pet or another pet in the neighborhood. It's called the Macdonald Triad, developed in 1961 by John Macdonald: bedwetting, fire setting, animal cruelty. How does Atkins stack up to that? He was alleged to have set a fire or two as a kid. No evidence of animal abuse, though. No note of bedwetting. What about taking mementos of his crimes, another pattern that has been cited for serials? The media quoted an unnamed cop at the time of Atkins' arrest saying he would take the women's clothing, and at least one profiler before his arrest surmised that he was keeping items, but there's nothing in the files that supports this assertion, other than perhaps the idea that sometimes at a crime scene – in particular Fifteen's scene at the Monterey – there was no clothing noted in the room that could have belonged to the victim. Another investigator said no, he did not take any souvenirs. He did return to at least one or two of his crime scenes, also a habit of serials.

THE RACIAL ASPECT

Serial killing has been known to be a largely white vocation, but there have been notable serials of color over the years like Atkins:

- Samuel Little
- Lorenzo Gilyard Jr.
- Andre Crawford
- Wayne Williams
- Lonnie David Franklin Jr.
- DeAngelo Martin
- Maury Travis
- Anthony Sowell
- Paul Durousseau
- Terry Blair
- Mark Goudeau
- Jarvis Catoe
- Carl "Coral" Watts
- Chester Turner
- Henry Louis Wallace

- Derrick Todd Lee
- Walter E. Ellis
- Khalil Wheeler-Weaver
- The Bigfoot Killer, said to be a muscular, tall, African-American man with facial hair and an afro, likely between the ages of thirty and thirty-five

You could also consider that killers Richard Ramirez and Ángel Maturino Reséndiz bucked the white serial stereotype, along with Charles Ng, born in Hong Kong and convicted of eleven murders in California in the 1980s.

Unlike many other serials, Atkins stayed within his own race for his crimes, whether it was for what several folks considered his desire to kill his mother over and over or some other reason. There are others who did this. Robert Hansen's victims appear to all have been white like him. Ted Bundy is known to have killed within his own race, and his victims were all young like him. Steve Wright killed women who were white like him. Same deal for Wright's fellow UK serial, Peter Sutcliffe. Canadian killer Robert Pickton chose, for the most part, victims who were white like him. John Wayne Gacy's victims were white males like him, as were those of Randy Kraft and William Bonin. The Gainesville Ripper, Danny Rolling, chose females who were white like him, and who were petite with brown hair like his ex-wife, actually. David Berkowitz chose mostly white victims, male and female. Aileen Wuornos chose men who were white like her. Wayne Williams certainly stayed inside his race, killing two Black men and suspected of killing many Black children in Atlanta. And Lonnie David Franklin Jr. targeted Black prostitutes, as did Maury Travis, Andre Crawford and Terry Blair. Paul Durousseau targeted young, single, Black women. Anthony Sowell chose Black victims.

William Suff chose white women for the most part, plus a Hispanic female or two, but when police called out this fact during a press conference, he immediately killed a

Black female. But is it more common for serials to choose victims across a mix of ethnicities, perhaps due in large part to opportunity? Many serials have had a mix in their victims, across ethnicities and often across genders:

- Jeffrey Dahmer
- Gary Ridgway
- Richard Ramirez
- Dennis Rader
- John Eric Armstrong
- Edmund Kemper
- Samuel Little (by sheer volume alone it was clear he was not choosy, and as with the case of Armstrong, there were even transgender victims)
- Joseph James DeAngelo, known as the Golden State Killer and East Area Rapist among other names; he tended to choose white women (and men), though if you factor in his high volume of rapes, he no doubt crossed ethnic lines for the same reason as Little
- Joel Rifkin
- Lorenzo Gilyard Jr.
- Charles Albright
- Terry Rasmussen
- Robert Lee Yates
- Andrew Urdiales
- DeAngelo Martin
- Charles Ng
- Ángel Maturino Reséndiz
- Sean Vincent Gillis
- Ronald Dominique
- Mark Goudeau
- Bobby Joe Long
- Kenneth Bianchi and Angelo Buono Jr.
- William Suff
- Chester Turner
- Derrick Todd Lee

- Paul Stephani
- Joshua Wade
- Albert Fish
- The Bigfoot Killer, who killed five Black and two white prostitutes

Atkins' choice to stick within his own race may have reflected what some have called his "killing his mother" over and over again. He chose victims who looked like his mother, were addicted to drugs like his mother and worked prostitution like his mother, though his victims had a wider spectrum where age was concerned. Perhaps this is where the idea of opportunity kicks in, along his hunting ground of Woodward Ave.

Whatever the choice of victim, whatever the motivation, Benjamin Atkins chose to take human life, and chose to do it in a savage fashion, there on the main street of the Motor City. That much we know.

"Alternating ego states, derealization, depersonalization and gross splits in his personality," Dr. Abramsky said in his analysis of this perp. Abramsky dug into the possible psychological motivations quite a bit harder than the other doctors who examined our perp. But really, what it all boils down to is … it's thorny, and it's speculation. Lots of issues, lots of factors. So many aspects of his life to consider.

Nobody really knows for sure what the answer is to that million-dollar question of why. Not even Atkins himself knew, most likely. But wouldn't it be interesting to ask him, this many years later, if he were still alive. Wouldn't it be interesting to see how he interviews, compared to the other serials above who have spoken on camera over the years, some forthcoming, some not so much. Some frank, some introspective, some cold and clinical.

I have often wondered what a serial killer thinks about as he sits in prison, year after year. I wondered that about John Eric Armstrong. I kinda got a sense for it, after my visits with him. I am disappointed that I can never ask Benjamin Atkins.

Short of that, now that you've read the facts of the case, I'll leave it to you to form your own theories. And I would love to hear them if you want to share: brbates.author@gmail.com

ACKNOWLEDGMENTS

This author admires those true-crime writers who use footnotes and endnotes to indicate their sources. That kind of transparency really serves the reader well, because I've also read a couple true-crime authors who indicated nary a source, other than directly quoting people they interviewed. Then when you read any intimate details in the story – private conversations, or individual thoughts and feelings – you have to wonder where on earth that stuff came from, or if it was a bit of poetic license.

Though I like it when footnotes are there, I also find them a bit jarring. I have tended to carry over my journalistic (newspaper!) training into my books, citing sources in the same sentence as the material, generally, throughout the text. So you'll find that approach here, in my second true-crime outing.

Plus, I'll note that a lot of the material in this book, whether noted in the text or not, comes from sources such as police records, autopsy and toxicology reports, and other official documents obtained through the Freedom of Information Act. These were used as the primary sources of the information herein, wherever possible, along with the personal interviews of many of the folks below.

For some other sources, often specifically named in the text, I am including a bibliography to indicate where you can read more, if desired. These sources were considered secondary, to fill in gaps from the more official sources above.

And with all that being said, I'd like to issue a special, heartfelt thanks to the following folks who assisted with this material, in ways small and large.

    André Chalk
    Craig Pulvirenti
    David Kerwin
    Demerio
    Derrick Cannon
    Detroit Police Department and Law Department
    Ed Yike
    Elizabeth Walker
    Everett Monroe
    Gerald Cliff, Ph.D.
    Gloria Beasley
    Grigg Espinosa
    Highland Park Police Department
    Jeffrey L. Edison
    Jim Dobson
    John Mattox
    Larry Beller
    Lisa Gass and the Michigan Department of Corrections
    Lisa Gibbon and the Sisters of St. Joseph/Congregation of St Joseph
    Livonia, Michigan, Public Library main branch staff
    Margie Osborn
    Melvin Toney
    Michael
    Michael Hodges
    Ned McGrath and the Archdiocese of Detroit
    Paul
    Rashad Green
    Renée M. Beavers
    Ron Sanders
    Royce Alston

Scott
Yves Marchand and Romain Meffre

SELECTED BIBLIOGRAPHY

BTK: Confession of a Serial Killer, A&E, 2022.

"Class of 2019 Spirit Awards: Allan J. Warnick, D.D.S. '64, forensic dentist," Forever Titans Blog, https://sites.udmercy.edu/alumni/2019/03/22/class-of-2019-spirit-awards-allan-j-warnick-d-d-s-64-forensic-dentist/

Concerned But Not Consumed, a book by Ron Sanders, formerly at http://www.concernednotconsumed.com

Crime Classification Manual: A Standard System for Investigating and Classifying Violent Crimes, by John E. Douglas, Ann W. Burgess, Allen G. Burgess, and Robert K. Ressler, John Wiley and Sons, second edition, 2006.

"Detroit - The Ruins of an Empire: A Conversation with Photographers Marchand and Meffre," by Kisa Lala, Huffington Post, January 31, 2011, https://www.huffpost.com/entry/detroit-the-ruins-of-an-e_b_810688?fbclid=IwAR2G0gGCIGMgPh-B4GpdD7K9HoCj0IEHaF1GkdehSDdCatS1c3fgBULxJLE

"Detroit in ruins: the photographs of Yves Marchand and Romain Meffre," by Sean O'Hagan, The Guardian, January 1, 2011, https://www.theguardian.com/artanddesign/2011/jan/02/detroit-ruins-marchand-meffre-photographs-ohagan

Detroit Free Press coverage of the case by Janet Wilson, Jim Schaeffer, Jeffrey Ghannam, Joe Swickard and others, 1991-1994.

Detroit News, The, coverage of the case by Ann Sweeney, Corey Williams, Francis Hopkins, Scott Bowles and others, 1991-1994.

"Detroit serial killing suspect pleads guilty," by Sarah Raza, *Detroit Free Press*, September 3, 2022, https://www.freep.com/story/news/local/michigan/detroit/2022/09/03/serial-killer-suspect-deangelo-martin-pleads-guilty/65471875007/

Federal Bureau of Investigation Crime Data Explorer/Uniform Crime Reports, for homicide stats: https://cde.ucr.cjis.gov/
https://web.archive.org/web/20200309050211/http://www.cus.wayne.edu/media/1391/leaddetroitcrime.pdf

First Blood, S1E8 episode "Henry Louis Wallace: Bad Henry," AETV, August 2022.

Highland Park city, Michigan, U.S. Census Bureau, https://data.census.gov/profile?g=1600000US2638180

Highland Park official website, https://www.highlandparkmi.gov/Community/Community-Profile.aspx

"Highland Park plans redevelopment of 1,000 abandoned properties," Fox 2 Detroit, January 8, 2018, https://www.fox2detroit.com/news/highland-park-plans-redevelopment-of-1000-abandoned-properties

Killer Across the Table, The, by John Douglas and Mark Olshaker, HarperCollins, 2019.

"Killing of transgender woman in Detroit red-light district opens dialogue," Gus Burns, mlive.com, https://www.mlive.

com/news/detroit/2015/08/detroit_police_meet_with_lgbt.html

"Lost Boys," a post about St. Francis Home for Boys, Nailhed blog, https://www.nailhed.com/2015/01/lost-boys.html

Mark of a Serial Killer, S3E4 episode, "The Englewood Killer," Oxygen, April 2021.

"Michael Reynolds, dogged prosecutor with a big heart for victims, dies at 67," Joe Swickard, special to the *Detroit Free Press*, March 5, 2022, https://www.freep.com/story/news/local/michigan/detroit/2022/03/05/michael-reynolds-prosecutor-dies-obituary/9389564002/

"Millon Clinical Multiaxial Inventory," From: Comprehensive Clinical Psychology, 1998, ScienceDirect, https://www.sciencedirect.com/topics/nursing-and-health-professions/millon-clinical-multiaxial-inventory

Paul Robeson/Malcolm X Academy/St. Francis Home for Boys, Detroit Urbex, http://detroiturbex.com/content/schoolsrobeson/?fbclid=IwAR0PjPcBypCnJjfOqcWC-UODkGjZOV7TzCPpJxI9aLdB33cDCRIaUwEGdDdI

"Serial killer trial: No film at 11," Toni Swanger, *Metro Times*, May 11-17, 1994.

"Splitting in Borderline Personality Disorder," *Psychology Today*, September 5, 2022, https://www.psychologytoday.com/us/blog/understanding-ptsd/202209/splitting-in-borderline-personality-disorder

"The map that led St. Louis police to 'The Videotape Killer,'" Fox 2 St. Louis, Nexstar Media Inc., https://fox2now.com/news/true-crime/serial-killer-maury-travis-the-street-walker-strangler/

"The Minnesota Multiphasic Personality Inventory-2 (MMPI-2)," Occupational Medicine 2009;59:135–136, doi:10.1093/occmed/kqn182

United States Census Bureau, population figures, https://www.census.gov/

Very Scary People, episode "The Times Square Killer," Investigation Discovery, 2023.

Welcome to Detroit, information on Highland Park Police Station, Fire Station, Municipal Building, https://detroitgutz.weebly.com/highland-park-police-station-fire-and-city-hall.html

"What Are Dissociative Disorders?" by American Psychiatric Association, https://www.psychiatry.org/patients-families/dissociative-disorders/what-are-dissociative-disorders

What Is 'Factor X' That BTK Blamed for His Urge to Kill?, A&E TV

Wikipedia, article on Highland Park, Michigan, https://en.wikipedia.org/wiki/Highland_Park,_Michigan

"Woman found murdered in rolled up carpet at abandoned home on east side," Fox 2 Detroit, June 13, 2019, https://www.fox2detroit.com/news/woman-found-murdered-in-rolled-up-carpet-at-abandoned-home-on-east-side

World's Most Evil Killers, produced by Woodcut Media of the UK, Sky Television, 2017-present; episodes on Danny Rolling, Peter Sutcliffe, Steve Wright, Kenneth Bianchi and Angelo Buono Jr., Ted Bundy, William Suff, Daniel Lee Siebert, Chester Turner and others.

*For More News About B.R. Bates,
Signup For Our Newsletter:*

http://wbp.bz/newsletter

Word-of-mouth is critical to an author's long-term success. If you appreciated this book please leave a review on the Amazon sales page:

https://wbp.bz/CrackCityStranglerReviews

ALSO AVAILABLE FROM B.R. BATES AND WILDBLUE PRESS

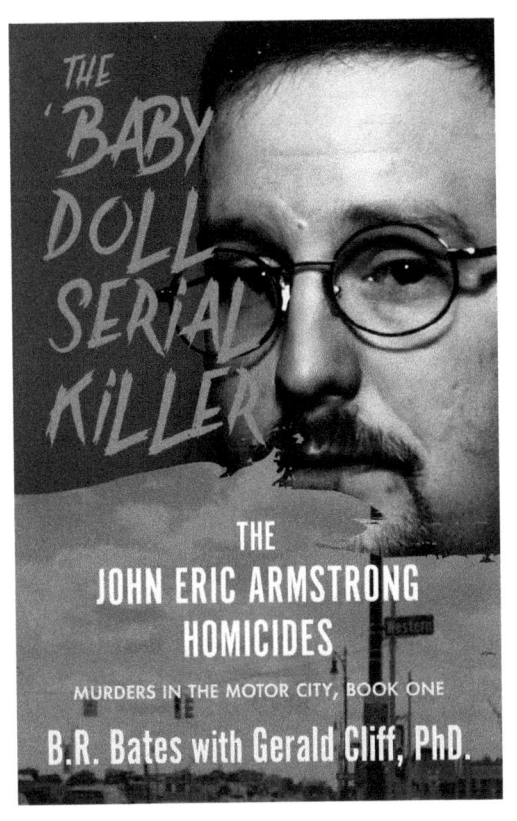

http://wbp.bz/babydoll

In THE 'BABY DOLL' SERIAL KILLER: The John Eric Armstrong Homicides, journalist B.R. Bates lays out the gripping story of this chameleon of a serial killer through his crimes – with a compassionate look at the life of each one of his victims – and the heroic efforts of law enforcement to catch him.

ALSO AVAILABLE FROM WILDBLUE PRESS

A MURDER ON CAMPUS
THE PROFESSOR, THE COP, AND NORTH CAROLINA'S MOST NOTORIOUS COLD CASE
BRIAN SANTANA
CAMERON SANTANA

http://wbp.bz/amoc

The fascinating story of how two brothers—one an English professor, the other a cop, and as different as night and day—tag team as authors to solve North Carolina's most notorious cold case ...